RACE AND REGION
A Descriptive Bibliography

RACE AND REGION

*A Descriptive Bibliography Compiled with Special
Reference to the Relations Between Whites
and Negroes in the United States*

BY

EDGAR T. THOMPSON

AND

ALMA MACY THOMPSON

Chapel Hill

THE UNIVERSITY OF NORTH CAROLINA PRESS

1949

Manufactured in the United States of America
Printing by The Seeman Printery, Inc., Durham, N. C.

To

N. C. Newbold

Introduction

IN 1935 a Division of Cooperation in Education and Race Relations was established in North Carolina through a cooperative arrangement entered into by the General Education Board, the University of North Carolina, Duke University, and the State Department of Education. The formal arrangement now is terminated, but during the decade of its existence the Division wrote an impressive chapter in the history of progress in race relations in the South.

The moving spirit in the program was the Division's Director, Dr. N. C. Newbold. In his quiet and unassuming way Dr. Newbold brought together white and Negro students and leaders from every corner of North Carolina. Patiently he helped more than one citizen of this State to see his neighbor of another color in a new and different light. Yet Dr. Newbold rarely spoke of race itself; he preferred to speak of health and education, of religion and economic opportunity. It was just that he wanted more of these things for all North Carolinians. Accordingly, he sought to create or to encourage all sorts of occasions when whites and Negroes striving together for these values might say "we."

As part of the program of the Division a generous contribution was made each year to the libraries of the University of North Carolina and Duke University to supplement their regular funds for the purchase of books and other literature dealing with the Negro and the subject of race generally. Beginning about 1938 a sum was allotted each year to the library of North Carolina College in Durham to aid the graduate and professional instruction of Negroes then getting under way at that institution. At the present time the libraries of the three institutions have more than 12,000 volumes on the subject of race and racial groups, exclusive of duplicate volumes and extensive manuscript and pamphlet material.

Except for rare books, and books in constant local demand, all material in each of the three libraries is available for inter-library loans (including high-school and public libraries) and to responsible individual citizens of North Carolina who have no local library facilities through which to borrow. The borrower is expected to pay carrying charges each way, but there are especially low postage rates in effect on books mailed for this purpose.

To promote the more general use of the race material available in the three libraries a committee was appointed to prepare a sample bibliography for publication. The present writer was named chairman of the committee. His name and the name of his wife now appear as authors of this work because many interruptions and the exigencies of war led the other members to other states and to other duties. Responsibility for its shortcomings is therefore easily assigned in spite of the fact that the authors have had the benefit of help and advice from many others, including Dr. Carl M. White, former Director of the University of North Carolina libraries, Dr. Guy B. Johnson, of the University of North Carolina, and Dean James T. Taylor, of North Carolina College. Special mention must be made of Mrs. Helen A. Whiting, who gave valuable assistance in connection with the section on children's literature, and of Dr. Clarence Schettler and Mrs. Marian Hamilton, for assistance in checking references. Thanks are due Mr. C. C. Spaulding of Durham and the late Dr. James E. Shepard, former President of North Carolina College, for financial aid incident to publication.

The bibliography follows an outline directed to the interests of the student and the general reader rather than to the interests of the specialist. It is hoped, too, that teachers of high school and college courses dealing with race relations will find it useful. The titles have been classified with the interests of teachers, students, and general readers in mind, but it goes without saying that no classification is ever completely satisfactory; the contents of books and articles simply will not fit perfectly into any logical scheme of categories. Attention is called to the fact that every title listed in this bibliography will be found in one of three libraries in the Durham-Chapel Hill area and many will be found in all three. The symbols NcD (Duke University), NcU (University of North Carolina), and NcC (North Carolina College) following each title will indicate the library possessing at least one copy of the item at the time this listing was made, though not necessarily the particular edition listed.

The experience of preparing even a very limited bibliography on the subject of race relations is, to say the least, a highly interesting one. During the period of preparation one keeps company with all manner of people; people who have, however, one thing in common, namely, the itch to write. They are the letter writers, the diary keepers, the story tellers, and those who like to recount their experiences and to report their discoveries. They are people who feel cheated of an experience or an opinion unless it is told. The literature on the Negro and other racial groups created by these writers is extraordinarily varied and fascinating, a veritable human anthology.

In recent years the number of books and articles dealing with the race problem has increased enormously. Most of this literature is controversial in character. Much of it is theological or pseudo-scientific intended to prove dogmas of long standing. Opinions are not now so dogmatic as they once were, but in the hands of popular writers the facts are capable of almost as many different interpretations as they were fifty years ago. Especially significant is the rise of a literature of counter-attack.

To the student of human nature, none of this literature is unimportant. Even the literature of misconception and downright nonsense is interesting and valuable as a record of the sentiments and attitudes which the racial struggle has called forth. The strange distortion of fact and opinion which it records is significant, not for what it tells us about the Negro or any other racial group, but for what it reveals of the intensity of the racial conflict and of the nature of the passions involved.

This bibliography contains samples of all these varieties of race literature, but the emphasis is upon the more serious studies of social scientists. Competent and systematic studies of race and the relationships of race are appearing in larger number than ever before. The definitive study of race relations, however, has not yet appeared. With such a wealth of racial and human material awaiting scientific interpretation before them, social scientists interested in this field have no need to occupy themselves with mere historical and literary trivia.

Since the manuscript was submitted, many new titles have appeared. It has been possible to insert only a few of the more important ones into the proof.

EDGAR T. THOMPSON

Duke University
July 6, 1948

Contents

xii CONTENTS

RACE AND REGION
A Descriptive Bibliography

I. Race and Race Relations

ARENDT, HANNAH. "Race-Thinking Before Racism," *The Review of Politics*, VI (January, 1944), 36-73. NcD, NcU.
"Race-thinking, with its roots deep in the 18th century, emerged during the 19th century simultaneously in all Western countries. Racism has been the powerful ideology of imperialistic policies since the turn of the century."

ARMITAGE, FRANCIS PAUL. *Diet and Race; Anthropological Essays.* London: Longmans, Green and Co., 1922. Pp. 144. NcU.
Diet as a causal factor in color, physique, and head form.

ASHLEY-MONTAGU, M. F. *Man's Most Dangerous Myth: The Fallacy of Race.* 2d ed., rev. and enl. New York: Columbia University Press, 1945. Pp. xiv, 304. NcD, NcU, NcC.
A fighting attack on racism.

BARZUN, JACQUES. *Race: A Study in Modern Superstition.* New York: Harcourt, Brace and Co., 1937. Pp. x, 353. NcD, NcU, NcC.
A vigorous attack upon "race-thinking."

BENEDICT, RUTH. *Race: Science and Politics.* Rev. ed. New York: The Viking Press, 1943. Pp. xi, 273. NcD, NcU, NcC.
An anthropologist examines race theories for the layman.

BENEDICT, RUTH, and WELTFISH, GENE. *The Races of Mankind.* New York: Public Affairs Committee, 1943. Pp. 31. NcD, NcU, NcC.
A booklet for the layman presenting facts about race in simple, clear, and concise form.

BLOOM, LEONARD. "Concerning Ethnic Research," *American Sociological Review*, XIII (April, 1948), 171-77. Discussion, pp. 177-82. NcD, NcU.
"The most orderly kind of research on ethnic groups . . . would be built upon a solid empirical base of knowledge about the characteristics of the population, their manifestations of solidarity and structural integration on the one hand, and their differentiation and inter-group relations on the other."

BOAS, FRANZ. "Race," *Encyclopaedia of the Social Sciences*, XIII, 25-36. NcD, NcU.
An excellent brief summary of race from the point of view of physical anthropology prepared by an outstanding authority.

BOAS, FRANZ. *The Mind of Primitive Man.* Rev. ed. New York: The Macmillan Co., 1938. Pp. 285. NcD, NcU, NcC.
In this classic work, Boas argues that the black man is not significantly inferior to the white man in intellectual capacity and that racial, as compared with individual differences, are small and relatively unimportant.

BOAS, FRANZ. *Race, Language and Culture.* New York: The Macmillan Co., 1940. Pp. xx, 647. NcD, NcU, NcC.
A collection of the author's writings elaborating his thesis that "knowledge of the life processes and behavior of man under conditions of life fundamentally different from our own can help us obtain a freer view of our own life and of our life problems."

BOAS, FRANZ. *Race and Democratic Society.* New York: J. J. Augustin, 1945. Pp. 219. NcD, NcU, NcC.
A collection of the writings and speeches of the famous anthropologist.

[1]

BRADLEY, JOHN HODGDON. *Patterns of Survival: An Anatomy of Life* (Chapter XI, "The Embarrassment of Being Different"). New York: The Macmillan Co., 1938. NcD.
Racial differences are special environmental adaptations.

BREARLEY, H. C. "Race as a Sociological Concept," *Sociology and Social Research*, XXIII (July, 1939), 214-18. NcD, NcU.
". . . the transformation of race from a biological to a social fact is not a function of conditions inherent in human biology. Rather it can be understood only in terms of the social situations and culture of a given society."

BRYCE, JAMES B. *The Relations of the Advanced and Backward Races of Mankind*. Oxford: Clarendon Press, 1902. Pp. 46. NcD.
At the beginning of the present century, Lord Bryce called attention to the "close and widespread contact of the advanced and backward races" as one of the most pressing problems of the modern world.

BUNCHE, RALPH J. *A World View of Race*. Bronze Booklet No. 4. Washington: The Associates in Negro Folk Education, 1936. Pp. 98. NcD, NcU, NcC.
Contends that race is an idea, and explains its operation in world economics and in world political conflicts.

DAHLBERG, GUNNAR. *Race, Reason and Rubbish*. New York: Columbia University Press, 1942. Pp. 240. NcD, NcU.
A primer of race biology. Translated from the Swedish by Lancelot Hogben.

DELOS, JOSEPH T. "The Rights of the Human Person vis-à-vis the State and Race," in Joseph M. Corrigan and G. Barry O'Toole, eds., *Race, Nation, Person: Social Aspects of the Race Problem: A Symposium*, pp. 39-68. New York: Barnes and Noble, Inc., 1944. NcD.
A worthy example of Catholic scholarly thought concerning the ethics of race relations.

DIXON, ROLAND B. *The Racial History of Man*. New York: Charles Scribner's Sons, 1923. Pp. xvi, 583. NcD, NcU, NcC.
An investigation of morphological forms based upon the assumption of the stability of the cephalic and nasal indices.

EYRE, EDWARD, et al. *European Civilization*. Vol. III. New York: Oxford University Press, 1939. NcD, NcU, NcC.
A history of relations between European and non-European peoples.

FAIRCHILD, HENRY PRATT. *Race and Nationality: As Factors in American Life*. New York: Ronald Press, 1947. Pp. vii, 216. NcD.
It is the author's thesis that the welfare of the nation as a whole, in relationship to the other nations of the world, must not be overlooked in the development of any internal program for the amelioration of the condition of minorities. Racial tensions in the United States may be intensified by laws against discrimination.

FISHBERG, MAURICE. *The Jews. A Study of Race and Environment*. New York: Charles Scribner's Sons, 1911. Pp. xix, 578. NcD, NcU, NcC.
Attempts to explain certain so-called "racial traits" as a result of imitation and suggestion.

FLEURE, H. J. "The Distribution of Types of Skin Color," *Geographical Review*, XXXV (October, 1945), 580-95. NcD, NcU, NcC.
A review of the facts relating to the diversities of skin color.

FOUILLÉE, ALFRED. "Race From the Sociological Standpoint," in G. Spiller, ed., *Papers on Inter-Racial Problems*, pp. 24-29. London: P. S. King and Son, 1911. NcD, NcU.

"In discussions of the race problem there is one factor of supreme importance which has been so far disregarded, to wit, the opinion or *idea* which a race has of itself and the influence exerted by this idea."

GILLIN, JOHN. "'Race' Relations Without Conflict: A Guatemalan Town," *The American Journal of Sociology*, LIII (March, 1948), 337-43. NcD, NcU, NcC.

The Indians and *ladinos* in the Guatemalan community have parallel cultures oriented toward different goals. In the South, on the other hand, whites and Negroes are so much alike culturally that the emphasis is placed upon real or alleged physical difference.

GLICK, CLARENCE. "Collective Behavior in Race Relations," *American Sociological Review*, XIII (June, 1948), 287-94. NcD, NcU.

Distinguishes between *racial* movements, *interracial* movements, and *non-racial* movements.

GRÉGOIRE, HENRI. *An Enquiry Concerning the Intellectual and Moral Faculties and Literature of Negroes*. Translated from the French by D. B. Warden. Brooklyn: Thomas Kirk, 1810. Pp. viii, 253. NcD.

In this early essay, written about 1800, the author protested against "ascribing Negro characteristics to inborn racial traits."

HANKINS, FRANK H. *The Racial Basis of Civilization; a Critique of the Nordic Doctrine*. New York: A. A. Knopf, 1926. Pp. xii, 384. NcD, NcU, NcC.

The first part of this book surveys and criticizes the literature purporting to find an explanation of civilization in the fact of race. The second part is a systematic examination of race viewed as a factor in the development of civilization.

HIRSCHFELD, MAGNUS. *Racism*. Translated and edited by Eden and Cedar Paul. London: Victor Gollancz, Ltd., 1938. Pp. 320. NcD, NcU, NcC.

Posthumous publication of an expatriated Jewish-German sexologist. He deals with sex irregularities, culture, heredity, etc. Explores causes of racial persecution.

HOLMES, SAMUEL JACKSON. "The Changing Effects of Race Competition," *Science*, LXXV (February 19, 1932), 201-8. NcD, NcU, NcC.

A discussion of some factors in the interracial struggle for existence.

HOOTON, E. A. "Methods of Racial Analysis," *Science*, LXIII (January 22, 1926), 75-81. NcD, NcU, NcC.

"Races are great groups and any analysis of racial elements must be primarily an analysis of groups, not of separate individuals. One must conceive of race not as the combination of features which gives to each person his individual appearance, but rather as a vague physical background, usually more or less obscured or overlaid by individual variations in single subjects, and best realized in a composite picture."

HOUSE, FLOYD N. "Viewpoints and Methods in the Study of Race Relations," *American Journal of Sociology*, XL (January, 1935), 440-52. NcD, NcU.

The methods that have been used in the study of race relations have been determined in part by prevailing theories or points of view. At least five such points of view have existed—the naïvely ethnocentric, religio-ethical, taxonomic, cultural, and sociological.

HOUSE, FLOYD N. "Some Methods of Studying Race and Culture," *Social Forces*, XV (October, 1936), 1-5. NcD, NcU, NcC.

A consideration of two concepts regarded as especially important in the definition of the field, i.e., culture and "marginal man."

HOWELLS, WILLIAM WHITE. *Mankind So Far*. Garden City, N. Y.: Doubleday, Doran and Co., 1944. Pp. xii, 319. NcD, NcU.

A book, written for popular reading, on the evolution and the varieties of mankind.

HUXLEY, JULIAN S. "The Concept of Race in the Light of Modern Genetics," *Harper's Magazine*, CLXX (May, 1935), 689-98. NcD, NcU, NcC.

"It would be highly desirable if we could banish the question-begging term 'race' from all discussions of human affairs and substitute the noncommittal phrase 'ethnic group.' "

JENNINGS, H. S. *The Biological Basis of Human Nature*. New York: W. W. Norton and Co., 1930. Pp. xviii, 384. NcD, NcU, NcC.

The first five chapters of this well-known book summarize the contributions of modern experimental biology to the problem of understanding human personality and society.

JENNINGS, H. S., et al. *Scientific Aspects of the Race Problem*. Washington: The Catholic University of America Press. New York: Longmans, Green & Co., 1941. Pp. ix, 302. NcD, NcU.

Although sponsored by the Catholic University of America, this is not a sectarian book. The six chapters in this symposium were prepared by H. S. Jennings, Charles A. Berger, Thomas Verner Moore, Aleš Hrdlička, Robert H. Lowie, and Otto Klineberg.

KAUTSKY, KARL. *Are the Jews a Race?* New York: International Publishers, 1926. Pp. 255. NcD.

After examining the characteristics of a pure race as over against a geographical race the author concludes that the Jews are not a race.

KROGMAN, WILTON M. "Is There a Physical Basis For Race Superiority?" *Scientific Monthly*, LI (November, 1940), 428-34. NcD, NcU, NcC.

"My answer must be that there are observable and measurable quantitative racial differences both as to physical and cultural development; but there are no measurable physical or social qualities which are in any given group superior or inferior."

KROGMAN, WILTON M. "What We Do Not Know About Race," *Scientific Monthly*, LVII (August, 1943), 97-104. NcD, NcU, NcC.

The author outlines six areas of scientific ignorance concerning race biologically considered.

KROGMAN, WILTON M. "The Concept of Race," in Ralph Linton, ed., *The Science of Man in the World Crisis*. New York: Columbia University Press, 1945. NcD, NcU.

"Race is biologically irrelevant."

LOCKE, ALAIN, and STERN, BERNHARD J., eds. *When Peoples Meet: A Study in Race and Culture Contacts*. Rev. ed. New York: Hinds, Hayden and Eldredge, 1946. Pp. xii, 825. NcD, NcU, NcC.

A valuable compilation of excerpts from the writings of competently selected authorities on race and race relations. Race questions are viewed in the universal context of culture contacts and conflicts.

MacIVER, ROBERT M., ed. *Group Relations and Group Antagonisms*. New York: Harper and Brothers, 1944. Pp. ix, 237. NcD.

"Only our attitudes make the problem," says the editor, "and only by changing our attitudes can we solve the problem."

McKENZIE, RODERICK D. *The Evolving World Economy.* Reports of the Albert Kahn Foundation for the Foreign Travel of American Teachers, Vol. V. New York, 1928. Pp. 71. NcD.
The author shows the extent to which the world's peoples and regions are linked in a vast network of interdependence.

McKENZIE, RODERICK D. "Industrial Expansion and the Interrelations of Peoples." Chap. II in E. B. Reuter, ed., *Race and Culture Contacts.* New York: McGraw-Hill Book Co., 1934. NcD, NcU, NcC.
The present world community pictured as a result of the expansion and competition of national groups.

MASUOKA, JITSUICHI. "Race and Culture Contacts in the Emporium," *American Journal of Sociology,* L (November, 1944), 199-204. NcD, NcU, NcC.
If the emporium—that is, the area over which the city and the market extend—rather than highly specialized aspects of the race problem be taken as the unit of study more fruitful and systematic investigations could be carried out.

MASUOKA, JITSUICHI. "Racial Symbiosis and Cultural Frontiers; A Frame of Reference," *Social Forces,* XXIV (March, 1946), 348-53. NcD, NcU, NcC.
The study of race has moved through the taxonomic and the statistical phases. We are now entering the dynamic or sociological phase of the study, not so much of race, as of race relations.

MAUNIER, RENÉ. *Sociologie coloniale.* 2 vols. Paris: Domat-Montchrestien, 1932, 1936. NcD.
The different forms of sovereignty, represented by such expressions as "protectorate," "sphere of influence," etc., are generally associated with corresponding degrees, or stages, of economic penetration, cultural assimilation, and racial amalgamation.

MILLER, HERBERT A. *Races, Nations, and Classes. The Psychology of Domination and Freedom.* Philadelphia: J. B. Lippincott Co., 1924. Pp. xvii, 196. NcD, NcC.
An outline of the sociology of politics. Among the many useful ideas elaborated upon is the concept "oppression psychosis."

PARK, ROBERT E. "A Race Relations Survey," *Journal of Applied Sociology,* VIII (March-April, 1924), 195-205. NcD, NcU.
Park proposes an answer to the question, "What is a race relations survey?"

PARK, ROBERT E. "Experience and Race Relations," *Journal of Applied Sociology,* IX (September-October, 1924), 18-24. NcD, NcU.
"In the study of race relations, we are concerned with more than the formal facts. We are concerned with experiences and with the personal reactions of individuals and races."

PARK, ROBERT E. "Methods of a Race Survey," *Journal of Applied Sociology,* X (May, 1926), 410-15. NcD, NcU.
Some comments on the procedure and objectives of the Race Relations Survey on the Pacific Coast.

PARK, ROBERT E. "Our Racial Frontiers on the Pacific," *Survey,* LVI (May, 1926), 192-96. NcD, NcU.
"The race relations cycle—contact, competition, accommodation, and eventual assimilation—is apparently progressive and irreversible."

PARK, ROBERT E. *The Problem of Cultural Differences.* New York: Institute of Pacific Relations, 1931. Pp. 16. NcD.
An introduction to the problem of analyzing the principal cultural differences between the Occident and Orient.

PARK, ROBERT E. "Race Relations and Certain Frontiers." Chap. V in E. B. Reuter, ed., *Race and Culture Contacts*. New York: McGraw-Hill Book Co., 1934. NcD, NcU, NcC.

A discussion of European expansion with particular attention to the resulting development of mixed-blood communities on certain frontiers.

PARK, ROBERT E. "The Nature of Race Relations." Chap. I in Edgar T. Thompson, ed., *Race Relations and the Race Problem*. Durham: Duke University Press, 1939. NcD, NcU, NcC.

"One speaks of race relations when there is a race problem."

PETRIE, W. M. FLINDERS. "Race and Civilization," *Annual Report of the Board of Regents of the Smithsonian Institution to July (1895)*, pp. 589-600. NcD, NcU.

"A race is a group of people whose type has become unified by their rate of assimilation which exceeds the rate of change produced by foreign elements." Religion, like geography, has been an isolating condition enabling racial types to emerge.

PITTARD, EUGENE. *Race and History: An Ethnological Introduction to History*. New York: A. A. Knopf, 1926. Pp. xxiii, 505. NcD, NcU, NcC.

A well-indexed source book. Historical development of geographical groups and methods of differentiating and recognizing various races.

RACE and Culture. By a Committee Appointed by the Royal Anthropological Institute and the Institute of Sociology in April, 1934. London: LePlay House Press, Royal Anthropological Institute, 1936. Pp. 24. NcD.

The joint committee, after careful deliberation, proposed a formal definition of race. But a minority disagreed.

RADIN, PAUL. *The Racial Myth*. New York: Whittlesey House, McGraw-Hill Book Co., 1934. Pp. ix, 141. NcD, NcU, NcC.

Traces the growth of the racial myth through the ages.

REDFIELD, ROBERT. "What We Do Know About Race," *Scientific Monthly*, LVII (September, 1943), 193-201. NcD, NcU, NcC.

It is the believed-in racial differences, and not the actual differences, that have consequences for the affairs of men.

REDFIELD, ROBERT. "The Ethnological Problem" in George B. de Huszar, ed., *New Perspectives on Peace*. Chicago: The University of Chicago Press, 1944. NcD, NcU.

An anthropologist considers peace as a problem of race relations. The Negro-white relationship in the United States "is perhaps the most immediately crucial point at which the problems of race enter into the task of making a peaceful world."

REUTER, EDWARD B. "Fifty Years of Racial Theory," *American Journal of Sociology*, L (May, 1945), 452-61. NcD, NcU, NcC.

". . . there are no present indications that the development of racial theory will be rapid: there are very few competent scholars working on racial problems, and the encouragement of scholarship and the support for theoretical research is very small."

RIPLEY, WILLIAM Z. *The Races of Europe: A Sociological Study*. New York: D. Appleton and Co., 1923. Pp. xxxii, 624. NcD, NcU, NcC.

An old but still useful book on the physical anthropology of the peoples of Europe. The original lectures upon which the book is based were delivered in 1898.

ROBACK, A. A. *A Dictionary of International Slurs.* Cambridge, Mass.: Sci-Art Publishers, 1944. Pp. 394. NcD, NcU.
A choice collection of epithets and other wounding words.

SELIGMANN, HERBERT J. *Race Against Man.* New York: G. P. Putnam's Sons, 1939. Pp. xii, 248. NcD, NcU, NcC.
An examination of the evidence in the fields of biology, anthropology, archaeology, and history on the subject of race.

SHALER, NATHANIEL. *The Neighbor: The Natural History of Human Contacts.* Boston: Houghton Mifflin Co., 1904. Pp. 342. NcD, NcC.
"At the beginning of any acquaintance the fellow-being is evidently dealt with in the categoric way."

SNYDER, LOUIS L. *Race: A History of Modern Ethnic Theories.* New York: Longmans, Green and Co. and Alliance Book Corporation, 1939. Pp. x, 342. NcD, NcU, NcC.
"The purpose of the present volume is to describe and analyze the various racial theories of the last century and a half, as well as to consider the roles played by individual theorists in constructing the race myth."

TAYLOR, EDMOND. *Richer by Asia.* Boston: Houghton Mifflin Co., 1947. Pp. 432. NcD.
How an American journalist sought to "feel himself" into the Oriental mind.

THOMAS, WILLIAM I. "The Comparative Study of Cultures," *American Journal of Sociology,* XLII (September, 1936), 177-85. NcD, NcU.
It is a frequent experience of science that the problems of a given situation are understandable only by going outside that immediate situation. There is at present a growing interest in the comparative study of cultures, especially in connection with such problems as education, race, crime, insanity, etc.

THOMPSON, EDGAR T. "Race in the Modern World," *Journal of Negro Education,* XIII (Summer, 1944), 270-79. NcD, NcU, NcC.
We are not agreed as to what race is, but we know it is something we have in reserve for which we will fight, something which can be counted upon to unite those who regard themselves as belonging to the same race.

VOEGELIN, ERICH. *Rasse und Staat.* Tuebingen: J.C.B. Mohr, 1933. Pp. 277. NcD.
A monograph on racial ethnocentrism.

VOEGELIN, ERICH. *Die Rassenidee in der Geistesgeschichte von Ray bis Carus.* Berlin: Junker und Dunnhaupt, 1933. Pp. viii, 160. NcD.
The history of the conception of race in Europe to the middle of the nineteenth century.

VOEGELIN, ERICH. "The Growth of the Race Idea," *The Review of Politics,* II (July, 1940), 283-317. NcD, NcU.
"The race idea should be distinguished from the race concept which is used in natural science. . . . [It] is not a body of knowledge organized in systematic form, but a political idea in the technical sense of the word."

WOOD, MARGARET MARY. *The Stranger.* New York: Columbia University Press, 1934. Pp. 399. NcD, NcU.
"It is the essence of race relations that they are the relations of strangers."
—Park.

II. The Geography of Race Relations

1. AREAS OF RACE CONTACT IN OTHER PARTS OF THE WORLD

ALEGRIA, CIRO. *Broad and Alien is the World.* New York: Farrar and Rinehart, 1941. Pp. 434. NcD, NcU.
A novel which deals with a group of North Andean Indians and their disintegration and destruction under outside pressure. This novel won the Latin-American Prize Novel Contest.

BARNES, LEONARD. *Caliban in Africa: An Impression of Colour-Madness.* London: V. Gollancz, Ltd., 1930. Pp. 245. NcD.
An indictment of the Dutch Boers of South Africa for their unrelenting attitude of hostility toward the natives. The author predicts an eventual explosion.

BEYNON, ERDMANN D. "The Gypsy in a Non-Gypsy Economy," *American Journal of Sociology*, XLII (November, 1936), 358-70. NcD, NcU.
Gypsies, like other pariah peoples in an economy dominated by groups other than their own, usually perform certain functions which are considered too low in status to be performed by other elements in the economy.

BRAUNSTEIN, BARUCH. *The Chuetas of Majorca.* New York: Mennonite Publishing House, 1936. Pp. xv, 227. NcD, NcU.
A revealing study of the persecutions visited upon Christian descendants removed by centuries from their Jewish ancestors.

BROWN, WILLIAM O. "White Dominance in South Africa: A Study in Social Control," *Social Forces*, XVIII (March, 1940), 406-10. NcD, NcU, NcC.
For the native masses "collective submission to the restrictive ritual of caste represents the strategy of survival rather than assimilation to a role."

COON, CARLETON S. *The Races of Europe.* New York: The Macmillan Co., 1939. Pp. xvi, 399. NcD, NcU, NcC.
Offered as a textbook in a specific branch of physical anthropology. But the thesis is maintained that physical anthropology cannot be divorced from cultural and historical associations.

CUNHA, EUCLIDES DA. *Rebellion in the Backlands.* Translated from *Os Sertões.* Chicago: The University of Chicago Press, 1943. Pp. xxxii, 526. NcD, NcU.
"Brazil's greatest book" is the story of a rebellion complicated by racial and cultural factors.

DOMINIAN, LEON. *The Frontiers of Language and Nationality in Europe.* New York: Henry Holt and Co., 1917. Pp. xviii, 375. NcD, NcU.
This linguistic atlas of Europe is also an atlas of what are often popularly regarded as races.

EVANS, MAURICE S. *Black and White in Southeast Africa. A Study in Sociology.* New York: Longmans, Green and Co., 1911. Pp. xviii, 341. NcU.
It is easy for a reader to get the impression that the situation for blacks is worse in Southeast Africa than it is in the South.

FORSTER, EDWARD MORGAN. *A Passage to India.* London: E. Arnold and Co., 1924. Pp. 325. NcD, NcU, NcC.
A novel portraying the Moslem, Hindu, and Anglo-Indian minds in the setting of India.

[8]

FRAZIER, E. FRANKLIN. "A Comparison of Negro-White Relations in Brazil and in the United States," *Transactions of the New York Academy of Sciences*, Series II, Vol. VI, No. 7 (May, 1944), pp. 251-69. NcD, NcU.
A revealing summary of similarities and differences.

FREYRE, GILBERTO. *Sobrados e Mucambos*, Sao Paulo, Brazil: Companhia editura nacional, 1936. Pp. 405. NcD, NcU.
As political and economic power in Brazil shifted from the plantations to the towns and cities, educated whites and mixed-bloods rose to positions of importance.

FREYRE, GILBERTO. *The Masters and the Slaves. A Study in the Development of Brazilian Civilization.* New York: A. A. Knopf, 1946. Pp. xxi, 537. NcD, NcU.
Samuel Putnam's translation of the author's well-known and distinguished *Casa-Grande e Senzala* (Rio de Janeiro, 1936).

GRACA ARANHA, JOSÉ PEREIRA DA. *Canaan.* Boston: The Four Seas Co., 1920. Pp. 321. NcD, NcU.
The real subject of this social novel of Brazil, says Guglielmo Ferrero in his Preface, is "the encounter of the races, the mixing of cultures, the disturbance caused in the social organization of all American countries by the masses of men arriving from overcrowded Europe."

HANDMAN, MAX. "Conflict and Equilibrium in a Border Area." Chap. VI in E. B. Reuter, ed., *Race and Culture Contacts.* New York: McGraw-Hill Book Company, 1934. NcD, NcU, NcC.
Tension, conflict, and adjustment between Germans, Roumanians, and Magyars of the Transylvanian plateau.

HERSKOVITS, MELVILLE J. and FRANCES S. *Trinidad Village.* New York: A. A. Knopf, 1947. Pp. viii, 351. NcD, NcU.
Whatever his economic status, the Trinidad Negro is proud and jealous of his rights.

THE Hispanic-American Historical Review, Vol. XXIV, No. 3 (August, 1944). NcD, NcU, NcC.
The entire number is devoted to aspects of the history of the Negro in Latin America outside Brazil and the Caribbean area. There is included an excellent bibliography of titles not listed in Work's *Bibliography.*

HUGHES, EVERETT C. *French Canada in Transition.* Chicago: The University of Chicago Press, 1943. Pp. ix, 227. NcD, NcU.
A study of the changes that have been taking place in the relations between English Canadians and French Canadians.

ICAZA, JORGE. *En Las Calles.* Buenos Aires: Publicaciones Atlas, 1936. Pp. 164. NcD, NcU.
This novel won the "America" prize in 1938. It tells the story of the migration of Indians from the Andes to the cities of Ecuador and the disintegrating effects of uprooting and unsuccessful urbanization.

KEESING, FELIX M. *The South Seas in the Modern World.* New York: The John Day Company, 1941. Pp. xv, 391. NcD, NcU, NcC.
A large amount of material has been brought together to throw light upon the peoples of the South Seas.

KEESING, FELIX M. *Native Peoples of the Pacific World.* New York: The Macmillan Co., 1945. Pp. xv, 144. NcD, NcU.
There are 100,000,000 of these brown and dark-skinned people, their island homes scattered halfway around the globe from Sumatra to Easter Island.

10 RACE AND REGION

KEITH, AGNES NEWTON. *Land Below the Wind.* Boston: Little, Brown
and Co., 1939. Pp. x, 371. NcD, NcU, NcC.
An account of the democratic association of natives, Malays, Chinese,
Japanese, Filipinos, and English in North Borneo.

KUPER, HILDA. *The Uniform of Colour: A Study of White-Black Relationships in Swaziland.* Johannesburg: Witwatersand University Press, 1947. Pp.
xii, 160. NcD, NcU.
"Economic exploitation is largely a reflection of political subordination."

LANDON, KENNETH PERRY. *The Chinese in Thailand.* New York: Oxford
University Press, 1941. Pp. xi, 310. NcD, NcC.
The Chinese in Thailand (Siam) have played a role somewhat like that of
the Jews in Europe.

LEYBURN, JAMES G. *The Haitian People.* New Haven: Yale University
Press, 1941. Pp. x, 342. NcD, NcU, NcC.
The story of a black man's country in a white man's world.

LEYS, NORMAN. *Kenya.* 2nd ed. London: L. and V. Woolf, 1925. Pp. 409.
NcD, NcC.
Relations between the English and the natives in East Africa. "This book
belongs to that extremely small and valuable class which embody in concen-
trated form the experience, the emotion and the hard thinking of a lifetime."—
Gilbert Murray.

MacCRONE, IAN D. *Race Attitudes in South Africa.* New York: Oxford University Press, 1937. Pp. xiii, 328. NcD, NcC.
Historical, experimental, and psychological studies. The thesis of this study
is "that in any total situation of racial antagonism the social and psychological
attitudes of the dominant group are of paramount importance and that no
improvement in the situation is possible until these social attitudes are understood and appreciated. The study, therefore, has much more than South
African importance."

MacLENNAN, HUGH. *Two Solitudes.* New York: Duell, Sloan and Pearce,
1945. Pp. 370. NcD.
A mature and adroit novel dealing with the Quebec state of mind.

MARSHALL, ROBERT. *Arctic Village.* New York: Smith and R. Haas, 1933.
Pp. 319. NcD, NcU, NcC.
An arctic Middletown. A study of the seventy-six whites, forty-four Eskimos,
six Indians, and one Negro, comprising the population of Wiseman, Alaska.
There is no discrimination on racial grounds.

MILLIN, SARAH GERTRUDE. *The South Africans.* New York: Boni and
Liveright, 1927. Pp. vii, 280. NcD, NcC.
There are chapters on the Boers, the English, the Jews, the Asiatics, the half-
castes and the Kaffir natives. "It is the struggles of these different racial and cultural elements . . . to become a society that dominates other political, social
and economic interests in South Africa."

MILLS, LENNOX A. *British Rule in Eastern Asia: A Study of Government
and Economic Development in British Malaya and Hongkong.* Minneapolis:
The University of Minnesota Press, 1942. Pp. viii, 581. NcD, NcU.
Special attention is given in this book to the roles played by the various
racial and cultural groups in Malaya.

MOCKFORD, JULIAN. *Here Are South Africans.* Forest Hills, New York:
Transatlantic Arts, 1944. Pp. 111. NcD.
A history of the Dutch, British, and natives in South Africa.

MOORE, WILLIAM HENRY. *The Clash: A Study in Nationalities.* 7th ed. New York: E. P. Dutton and Co., 1919. Pp. xxiii, 333. NcD, NcC.

Deals with the roots of Anglo-French rivalry in Canada and the problem of recalcitrant Quebec.

NEUMANN, ROBERT. *By the Waters of Babylon.* New York: Simon and Schuster, 1940. Pp. 356. NcD, NcU, NcC.

A strange novel showing the varied and yet similar experiences of Jewish people in many countries.

OLIVEIRA VIANNA, FRANCISCO JOSÉ DE. *Evoluçao do Povo Brasileiro.* Sao Paulo, Brazil: Companhia editora nacional, 1938. Pp. 349. NcD.

Almost alone among Brazilian writers Vianna regards both Indians and Negroes as inferior to Caucasians.

ORTIZ, FERNANDO. *Cuban Counterpoint.* New York: A. A. Knopf, 1947. Pp. xii, 312. NcD.

The Cuban mores developed from "transculturation," *i.e.,* a fusion of Iberian, African, and Indian traditions.

PIERSON, DONALD. "The Negro in Bahia, Brazil," *American Sociological Review,* IV (August, 1939), 524-33. NcD, NcU.

"Although more Africans were imported into Brazil than into any other regions of the New World, and they at one time constituted, in centers of concentration like Bahia, an overwhelming majority of the population, the Negro *as a racial unit* is throughout Brazil, gradually, but to all appearances inevitably, disappearing."

PIERSON, DONALD. *Negroes in Brazil. A Study of Race Contacts at Bahia.* Chicago: The University of Chicago Press, 1942. Pp. xxviii, 392. NcD, NcU, NcC.

In Brazil whites and Negroes are, and long have been, going into a common melting pot at a considerably faster rate than in the United States.

PONCINS, GONTRAN DE. *Kabloona.* New York: Reynal and Hitchcock, 1941. Pp. 339. NcD, NcU.

The experiences of a white man among the Eskimos of King William Land. Written in collaboration with Lewis Galantière.

RAMOS, ARTHUR. *The Negro in Brazil.* Translated from the Portuguese by Richard Pattee. Washington: Associated Publishers, 1939. Pp. xx, 203. NcD, NcU, NcC.

This manual on the Brazilian Negro contains a brief historical treatment of slavery and the slave trade, slave uprisings and the abolition movement, African survivals, the contributions of blacks and mixed-bloods to politics, art, literature, and science, and a brief survey of studies of the Brazilian Negro.

REDFIELD, ROBERT. "Race and Class in Yucatan," in *Cooperation in Research.* Carnegie Institution of Washington Publication No. 501 (1938), pp. 511-32. NcD, NcU.

In Yucatan a word for a biological hybrid, *mestizo,* has come to designate the lower of two social classes. "This coalescence of mixed-blood and Indian groups suggests the manner in which mulatto and Negro came in the United States to form a single caste-like class, but with the important difference that Yucatan, like the rest of Latin America, drew no color line, and that the badge of the Yucatecan class was a costume, not a skin color."

RISLEY, SIR HERBERT. *The People of India.* London: W. Thacker and Company, 1915. Pp. xxxii, 472. NcD, NcC.

The classic account of the castes and classes of the people of India.

RUSSELL, ALAN GLADNEY. *Colour, Race and Empire.* London: Victor
Gollancz, 1944. Pp. 278. NcD.
On the practical importance of color differentiation in the British colonial
empire.

SENART, EMILE. *Caste in India: The Facts and the System.* Translated by
Sir E. Denison Ross. London: Methuen and Co., 1930. Pp. xxiii, 220. NcD,
NcC.
One of the best and most readable interpretations of the complex subject of
caste in the country where caste is most important.

STRONG, ANNA LOUISE. *Peoples of the U.S.S.R.* New York: The Macmillan
Co., 1944. Pp. viii, 246. NcD.
A colorful review of the assorted population of the Soviet Union. For high-
school children.

WILLIAMS, ERIC. *The Negro in the Caribbean.* Washington, D. C.: Associates in Negro Folk Education, 1942. Pp. 119. NcD, NcU, NcC.
A popular account of the past and present situation, with emphasis on class
differences among Negroes and on the relations of the United States to the
West Indies.

2. THE RACE PROBLEM IN THE UNITED STATES AND POSSESSIONS

ADAMIC, LOUIS. *From Many Lands.* New York: Harper and Brothers, 1940.
Pp. vi, 350. NcD, NcU, NcC.
This book introduces us to, and makes us acquainted with, Americans born in
other lands, or born here of immigrant parentage. It is a book full of people,
and it tells, by means of life histories, what America means to them.

ADAMS, ROMANZO. "The Unorthodox Race Doctrine of Hawaii." Chap. IX
in E. B. Reuter, ed., *Race and Culture Contacts.* New York: McGraw-Hill
Book Co., 1934. NcD, NcU, NcC.
Historical circumstances have given race relations in the Hawaiian Islands a
more harmonious character than is to be found in most other interracial
societies.

ADAMS, ROMANZO. *Interracial Marriage in Hawaii: A Study of the Mutually
Conditioned Processes of Acculturation and Amalgamation.* New York: The
Macmillan Co., 1937. Pp. xvii, 353. NcD, NcU, NcC.
Racial intermarriage has long been accepted in the law and public opinion
of Hawaii although not always without criticism.

ANDERSON, ELIN L. *We Americans.* Cambridge: Harvard University Press,
1937. Pp. xii, 286. NcD, NcU.
A prize-winning study of group relationships in the city of Burlington, Vermont. The book gives us a picture of conflict between the Old Americans, the
Jews, the Irish, and the French-Canadians.

ARCHAMBAULT, ALBERIC A. *Mill Village.* Boston: Bruce Humphries, 1943.
Pp. 191. NcD.
A fictional life history of an ethnic group in New England dealing with the
acculturation of first- and second-generation French Canadians.

BAILEY, THOMAS A. *Theodore Roosevelt and the Japanese-American Crisis:
An Account of the International Complications Arising from the Race
Problem on the Pacific Coast.* Stanford University: Stanford University
Press, 1934. Pp. ix, 353. NcD, NcU, NcC.
A study of the international implications of the race question on the Pacific
coast in their beginnings.

BOGARDUS, EMORY S. *The Mexican in the United States.* University of Southern California School of Research Studies, No. 5. Los Angeles: The University of Southern California Press, 1934. Pp. 126. NcD, NcU.
The configuration of the personality of the Mexican in the United States. Discusses family life, labor, religion, child welfare, etc.

BROWN, FRANCIS J., and ROUCEK, JOSEPH S. *One America.* New York: Prentice-Hall Co., 1945. Pp. xvi, 717. NcD, NcU, NcC.
This is a revised edition of *Our Racial and National Minorities.* The editors and contributors are concerned with the diversities, divisions, and adjustments of American minority groups.

BROWN, IRVING H. *Gypsy Fires in America.* New York: Harper and Brothers, 1924. Pp. viii, 244.
To Irving Brown the members of this world-old vagrant race are men and women to be passionately envied because they do not live in houses.

COOK, S. F. *The Conflict between the California Indian and White civilization: I. The Indian versus the Spanish Mission; II. The Physical and Demographic Reaction of the Nonmission Indians in Colonial and Provincial California; III. The American Invasion, 1848-1870; IV. Trends in Marriage and Divorce since 1850.* Ibero-Americana, Nos. 21, 22, 23, 24. Berkeley: University of California Press, 1943. NcD.
A series of important monographs examining "the reaction of a primitive human population to a new and disturbing environment."

EDITORS of *Fortune. Jews in America.* New York: Random House, 1936. Pp. 104. NcD.
An account of anti-Semitism in America, the principal anti-Semitic organizations, and the degree of control exercised by Jews in various professions and occupations in America.

FOSTER, LAURENCE. *Negro-Indian Relationships in the Southeast.* Ph.D. dissertation, University of Pennsylvania, 1935. Pp. 86. NcD, NcU.
"No history of the New World can be regarded as complete without a consideration of Negro-Indian relationships."

GAMIO, MANUEL. *Mexican Immigration to the United States: A Study of Human Migration and Adjustment.* Chicago: The University of Chicago Press, 1930. Pp. xviii, 262. NcD, NcU.
The background of the Mexican immigrant and his social and economic position in the United States.

INN, HENRY. *Hawaiian Types.* New York: Hastings House, 1946. Pp. xlvii, 46. NcD.
The photographs of beautiful Island girls which make up this book include the usual "pure" ethnic stocks as well as an array of hybrid types. There are Negro-Hawaiian mixtures in the Islands but for some reason the author did not include any representatives.

JARVIS, J. ANTONIO. *The Virgin Islands and Their People.* Philadelphia: Dorrence and Co., 1944. Pp. vii, 178. NcD, NcU, NcC.
A lively and intimate description.

KENNEDY, GEORGE ALLAN. *Who Are the Americans?* Newburgh, N. Y.: The Paebar Co., 1943. Pp. 176. NcD, NcC.
A history and description of the racial groups which make up our country.

KOENIG, S. "Ethnic Groups in Connecticut Industry," *Social Forces,* XX (October, 1941), 96-105. NcD, NcU, NcC.

A study of variations in the positions occupied by Italians, Irish, British-Americans, Poles, French-Canadians, Germans, Swedes, Lithuanians, Jews, and Ukranians in Connecticut industry.

LASKER, BRUNO. *Filipino Immigration to Continental United States and to Hawaii.* Chicago: The University of Chicago Press, 1931. Pp. xxii, 445. NcD.
Facts on the economic conditions confronting the 75,000 Filipinos in Hawaii and in mainland United States. They are neither aliens nor citizens.

LIND, ANDREW W. *An Island Community.* Chicago: The University of Chicago Press, 1938. Pp. xxii, 337. NcD, NcU, NcC.
A study of racial invasion and economic succession in the Hawaiian Islands.

LIND, ANDREW W. *Hawaii's Japanese: An Experiment in Democracy.* Princeton: Princeton University Press, 1946. Pp. 272. NcD.
A report on the post-Pearl Harbor behavior of Hawaii's Americans of Japanese ancestry.

MacLEOD, WILLIAM C. *The American Indian Frontier.* New York: A. A. Knopf, 1928. Pp. xxiii, 598. NcD, NcU.
The moving and tragic story of the decimation of the Indians before the tide of white settlement. "The first attempt at an analysis of American frontier history made particularly from the viewpoint of the Indian side of the frontier development."

McWILLIAMS, CAREY. *Brothers Under the Skin.* Boston: Little, Brown and Co., 1943. Pp. 325. NcD, NcU, NcC.
A discussion of the "colored" elements of the American population—Indians, Mexicans, Chinese, Japanese, and Negroes—the relation of each to the others, the national problems involved, and the manner in which each is bound to international problems.

McWILLIAMS, CAREY. *Prejudice—Japanese-Americans: Symbol of Racial Intolerance.* Boston: Little, Brown and Co., 1944. Pp. 337. NcD, NcU.
"For nearly fifty years prior to December 7, 1941 a state of undeclared war existed between California and Japan."

MARTIN, RALPH G. *Boy From Nebraska: The Story of Ben Kuroki.* New York: Harper and Brothers, 1946. Pp. xii, 208. NcD, NcU.
An American boy of Japanese ancestry had to struggle to get into the war, then struggled to stay in.

MAYO, SELZ C. *The Foreign-Born White Population in North Carolina.* Progress Report No. RS3. North Carolina Agricultural Experiment Station, State College Station, Raleigh, June, 1944. Pp. 9. NcD, NcU.
Only three states have a smaller foreign-born white population than North Carolina.

MEARS, ELIOT G. *Resident Orientals on the American Pacific Coast: Their Legal and Economic Status.* New York: American Group Institute of Pacific Relations, 1927. Pp. xvi, 526. NcD.
The operation and effects of the laws, regulations and judicial decisions.

MILLER, HERBERT A. "The Negro and the Immigrant," in Kimball Young, ed., *Social Attitudes,* pp. 328-46. New York: Henry Holt and Co., 1931. NcD, NcU.
A comparison of the two groups.

OKUBO, MINÉ. *Citizen 13660.* New York: Columbia University Press, 1946. Pp. 209. NcD.
A documentation in drawings with text of two years spent by an American girl of Japanese ancestry at Topaz Relocation Center in the Utah desert.

ORIENTALS and Their Cultural Adjustment. Nashville: Social Science Institute, Fisk University, 1946. Pp. x, 138. NcD, NcC.
Interviews, life histories, and experiences of Chinese and Japanese of varying backgrounds and length of residence in the United States.

REDFIELD, ROBERT. "The Japanese-Americans," in W. F. Ogburn, ed., *American Society in Wartime.* Chicago: The University of Chicago Press, 1943. NcD, NcU, NcC.
The Japanese-American posed a crucial case for the testing of the fairness and justice implied in the American ideal.

SCHRIEKE, B. J. O. *Alien Americans.* New York: The Viking Press, 1936. Pp. xi, 208. NcD, NcU, NcC.
The impressions of an expert foreign observer during a visit to this country at the invitation of the trustees of the Rosenwald Fund. There are chapters on the Chinese, the Japanese, the Mexicans, and the Indians but half of the book is devoted to the Negro.

SCHULTZ, JAMES WILLARD. *My Life as an Indian: The Story of a Red Woman and a White Man in the Lodges of the Blackfeet.* New York: Doubleday, Page and Co., 1907. Pp. x, 426. NcD, NcU.
The author, a white man who married a Blackfoot woman and lived the life of the tribe while the buffalo were still plentiful, makes it possible for his readers to see the Indian as a human being.

STEINER, JESSE F. *The Japanese Invasion: A Study in the Psychology of Inter-Racial Contacts.* Chicago: A. C. McClurg and Co., 1917. Pp. xvii, 231. NcD, NcU.
A study of the race consciousness which appears to be at the heart of the American-Japanese problem.

TAYLOR, PAUL S. *An American-Mexican Frontier: Nueces County, Texas.* Chapel Hill: The University of North Carolina Press, 1934. Pp. xiii, 337. NcD, NcU, NcC.
A stratified white, Negro, and Mexican society. In a drug store it was explained, "We serve Mexicans at the fountain but not at the tables. . . . The Negroes, we serve only cones."

WARNER, W. LLOYD, and SROLE, LEO. *The Social Systems of American Ethnic Groups.* New Haven: Yale University Press, 1945. Pp. xii, 318. NcD, NcU, NcC.
"A study of the social life of the Irish, French-Canadians, Jews, Armenians, Italians, Poles, Greeks, and Russians of a New England town, characterizing them by generation, sex, age, class, with a 'time-table' showing how long after arrival immigrants in each group begin to form associations and the status of the latter in American society."

WISSLER, CLARK. *The American Indian: An Introduction to the Anthropology of the New World.* 3rd ed. New York: Oxford University Press, 1938. Pp. xvii, 466. NcD, NcU, NcC.
A general summary of anthropological research in the New World. "From that eventful day in 1492 when Columbus first laid eyes upon the Indian, down to this very hour, he has been the most studied of peoples. No other race in the world can so stir the imagination of the European."

WISSLER, CLARK. *Indians of the United States: Four Centuries of Their History and Culture.* New York: Doubleday, Doran and Co., 1940. Pp. xvi, 319. NcD, NcU, NcC.
Discusses (1) the Indian in prehistoric America, (2) the great Indian families, and (3) Indian life in general.

WOOFTER, THOMAS J., JR. *Races and Ethnic Groups in American Life.*
    Recent Social Trends Monograph. New York: McGraw-Hill Book Co.,
    1933. Pp. xii, 247. NcD, NcU, NcC.
A resumé of data presented by other authors during the past thirty years
or more.

YOUNG, DONALD R. *American Minority Peoples: A Study in Racial and
    Cultural Conflicts in the United States.* New York: Harper and Brothers,
    1932. Pp. xv, 621. NcD, NcU, NcC.
An attempt to understand comprehensively the attitudes of minority groups
toward one another and toward the dominant old-stock white group. This
book is based upon the assumption that "the problems and principles of race
relations are remarkably similar regardless of what groups are involved."

3. THE SOUTH

ADAMS, FRANKIE V. *Soulcraft.* Atlanta: Morris Brown College Press, 1944.
    Pp. 65. NcD.
Thirteen episodes mirroring race relations in America and particularly in
the South.

BERGLUND, A., STARNES, GEORGE T., and DE VYVER, FRANK T.
    Labor in the Industrial South. Charlottesville: University of Virginia, In-
    stitute for Research in the Social Sciences, 1930. Pp. xiii, 176. NcD, NcU.
An account of the relative transition from agriculture to industry in the
economic life of the South. The real wages of the Southern industrial worker,
in the industries studied, are considerably below those of the Northern worker.

BLOOM, LEONARD. "Role of the Indian in the Race Relations Complex of
    the South," *Social Forces,* XIX (December, 1940), 268-73. NcD, NcU, NcC.
The role of the Indian in the complex of race relations in the South appears
to have escaped any systematic investigation. Dr. Bloom suggests some lines
of investigation worth exploring.

CABLE, GEORGE W. *The Silent South.* New York: C. Scribner's Sons, 1885.
    Pp. vi, 213. NcD, NcU.
Cable was a Southern critic of Southern life.

CARPENTER, JESSE THOMAS. *The South as a Conscious Minority, 1789-
    1861: A Study in Political Thought.* New York: The New York University
    Press, 1930. Pp. x, 315. NcD, NcU, NcC.
The Old South as a sectional minority "consciously striving for seventy-odd
years to evolve an adequate philosophy of protection to its interests in the
American Union."

CASON, CLARENCE E. *90° in the Shade.* Chapel Hill: The University of
    North Carolina Press, 1935. Pp. xiii, 186. NcD, NcU, NcC.
A journalistic account of the characteristics of Southern people.

COHN, DAVID L. *Where I Was Born and Raised.* Boston: Houghton Mifflin
    Co., 1948. Pp. xi, 380. NcD, NcU.
The salient features of life in the Mississippi Delta. Much of the matter of
this book was originally published in the author's *God Shakes Creation,* New
York: Harper and Brothers, 1935. Pp. 299. NcD, NcU, NcC.

CONNOR, R. D. W. *Race Elements in the White Population of North Caro-
    lina.* North Carolina State Normal and Industrial College, Historical Pub-
    lications, Nos. 1-3 (1920). Pp. 115. NcD, NcU.
The English, Highland Scotch, Scotch-Irish, and German elements in North
Carolina.

COTTERILL, ROBERT SPENCER. *The Old South*. Glendale, California: The Arthur H. Clark Company, 1936. Pp. 354. NcD, NcU, NcC.

A history of the ante-bellum South: geography, economy, society, politics, culture, institutions, and nationalism.

COUCH, WILLIAM T., ed. *Culture in the South*. Chapel Hill: The University of North Carolina Press, 1934. Pp. xiv, 711. NcD, NcU, NcC.

A symposium to which thirty-one authorities contributed and in which "every phase of Southern culture is presented from farming to folk-songs, from the fine arts to murder."

COUCH, WILLIAM T., ed. *These Are Our Lives: As Told by the People and Written by Members of the Federal Writers' Project of the Works Progress Administration in North Carolina, Tennessee, and Georgia*. Chapel Hill: The University of North Carolina Press, 1939. Pp. xx, 421. NcD, NcU, NcC.

Thirty-five life histories of various types of people in the Southeast.

CRAVEN, AVERY O. "The South in American History." *The Historical Outlook*, XXI (March, 1930), 105-9. NcD, NcU.

The southerness of the South grows out of three fundamental facts: (1) it is primarily a rural-agricultural region, (2) it has maintained an old world tradition, and (3) it has a large Negro population. The South has, on occasion, been Southern enough to act and feel as a unit when stirred by resentment against other sections of the country.

CRAVEN, AVERY O. *The Repressible Conflict, 1830-1861*. University, Louisiana: Louisiana State University Press, 1939. Pp. xi, 97. NcD, NcU.

The three lectures in this little book deal with (1) Southern Nationalism, (2) The Peculiar Institution, and (3) The Repressible Conflict. The Civil War was the work of "crack-pot reformers" on the one hand and extravagant "fire-eaters" on the other.

DANIELS, JONATHAN. *A Southerner Discovers the South*. New York: The Macmillan Co., 1938. Pp. xiii, 346. NcD, NcU, NcC.

A report of a tour of exploration through the South with the conclusion that the South's salvation must come out of the South itself.

DAVIS, ALLISON, GARDNER, BURLEIGH B., and GARDNER, MARY R. *Deep South: A Social Anthropological Study of Caste and Class*. Chicago: The University of Chicago Press, 1941. Pp. xv, 558. NcD, NcU, NcC.

An intimate study of social class among both whites and Negroes in a Southern community. The emphasis is upon the rigid dominance of the "caste system" but apparently caste in the South is marked by numerous exceptions and inconsistencies.

DODD, WILLIAM E. *The Cotton Kingdom: A Chronicle of the Old South*. New Haven: Yale University Press, 1919. Pp. x, 161. NcD, NcU, NcC.

Perhaps the most interesting chapter in this book on the customs, the literature, and the politics of the lower South in 1850 is the one entitled "The Philosophy of the Cotton Planter."

ELZAS, BARNETT A. *The Jews of South Carolina From the Earliest Times to the Present Day*. Philadelphia: J. B. Lippincott, 1905. Pp. 352. NcD.

A well-documented work covering the colonial period through the nineteenth century.

EVANS, MAURICE S. *Black and White in the Southern States*. New York: Longmans, Green and Company, 1915. Pp. xii, 299. NcD, NcU, NcC.

A study of the race problem in the United States from the point of view of a South African.

FAUST, ALBERT BERNHARDT. *The German Element in the United States*:
*With Special Reference to Its Political, Moral, Social, and Educational In-
fluences*. 2 vols. Boston: Houghton Mifflin Co., 1909. NcD, NcU.
In this standard authority, reprinted in 1927 in one volume, there are chapters
on the Germans in the Southern colonies and states.

FRAZIER, E. FRANKLIN. "Role of the Negro in Race Relations in the
South," *Social Forces*, XIX (December, 1940), 252-58. NcD, NcU, NcC.
The heart of the race problem in the South is the struggle of the Negro for
status.

HAMILTON, PETER JOSEPH. "The Indian Problem in the South." Vol. IV,
pp. 423-42 in *The South in the Building of the Nation*. Richmond: The
Southern Historical Publication Society, 1909. NcD, NcU.
A summary account of various Indian tribes, and especially the Cherokees,
Muscogees, Choctaws, and Chickasaws, in relationship to the history of the
South.

HARPER, ROLAND M. "Contrasts Between Northern and Southern and Urban
and Rural Negroes in the United States," *Social Forces*, XII (May, 1934),
576-78. NcD, NcU, NcC.
In the North the Negro population is nearly all urban; in the South it is
predominantly rural.

HEBERLE, RUDOLF. *The Impact of War on Population Redistribution in the
South*. Nashville, Tennessee: Vanderbilt University Press, 1945. Pp. 64. NcD.
Wartime changes have intensified the South's population problem.

HEBERLE, RUDOLF. "A Sociological Interpretation of Social Change in the
South," *Social Forces*, XXV (October, 1946), 9-15. NcD, NcU, NcC.
Some evidence of the general shift from status to contract in the relation-
ships of Southern society.

HEER, CLARENCE. *Income and Wages in the South*. Chapel Hill: The Uni-
versity of North Carolina Press, 1930. Pp. 68. NcD, NcU.
A comparison of Southern income and wages with other sections of the United
States.

HIRSCH, ARTHUR HENRY. *The Huguenots of Colonial South Carolina*. Durham: Duke University Press, 1928. Pp. xv, 338. NcD, NcU.
This valuable study of the French Protestants in South Carolina is based
upon extensive research but unfortunately is marred by numerous minor errors.

INGRAHAM, JOSEPH HOLT. *The Southwest*, by a Yankee. 2 vols. New York:
Harper and Brothers, 1835. NcD, NcU.
A descriptive work on the old Southwest offered as fiction.

JOHNSON, CHARLES S. "The Present Status of Race Relations, with Particular Reference to the Negro," *Journal of Negro Education*, VIII (July,
1939), 323-35. NcD, NcU, NcC.
White-Negro relations, both in the North and in the South, vary significantly
between different areas within the same region. But everywhere the essence of
the race problem is change.

JOHNSON, CHARLES S. *Statistical Atlas of Southern Counties: Listing and
Analysis of Socio-Economic Indices of 1104 Southern Counties*. Chapel Hill:
The University of North Carolina Press, 1941. Pp. x, 355. NcD, NcU, NcC.
A county index of the South by crops, industries, and degrees of rurality to
serve as a guide "to conditions which vitally affect education and all the other
social relations throughout the region."

JOHNSON, CHARLES S. "Social Changes and their Effect on Race Relations in the South," *Social Forces*, XXIII (March, 1945), 343-48. NcD, NcU, NcC.
" . . . racial incidents in themselves are not conclusive; rather they are symptoms of basic social changes which, in the long run, might well prove wholesome."

JOHNSON, GUION G. *Ante-Bellum North Carolina: A Social History*. Chapel Hill: The University of North Carolina Press, 1937. Pp. xvi, 935. NcD, NcU, NcC.
"An account of the way in which a frontier community, composed of widely scattered settlements, each with a different origin and cultural tradition, slowly and painfully, out of conflict and compromise and the pressure of necessity, evolved a political tradition and a communal organization upon which the social structure of the existing state rests."

KANE, HARNETT T. *Deep Delta Country*. New York: Duell, Sloan and Pearce, 1944. Pp. xx, 283. NcD, NcU.
The region from New Orleans to the Gulf of Mexico has been a melting pot of many peoples and today exhibits a unique way of life.

KENDRICK, BENJAMIN BURKS, and ARNETT, ALEX MATHEWS. *The South Looks at its Past*. Chapel Hill: The University of North Carolina Press, 1935. Pp. viii, 196. NcD, NcU, NcC.
An interpretative study of the ante-bellum South, the social and economic causes of the Civil War, and various phases of the contemporary South.

KENNEDY, STETSON. *Palmetto Country*. New York: Duell, Sloan and Co., 1942. Pp. xii, 340. NcD, NcU, NcC.
A picture of life in the deepest South.

LANDES, RUTH. "A Northerner Views the South," *Social Forces*, XXIII (March, 1945), 375-79. NcD, NcU, NcC.
"As the war years move on, [the South] draws just such issues within our borders as we already are facing in battle overseas."

LARKINS, JOHN R. *The Negro Population of North Carolina*. Special Bulletin No. 23. Raleigh, N. C.: State Board of Charities and Public Welfare, 1944. Pp. 79. NcU.
Facts about North Carolina Negroes of special interest to social workers.

MILLING, CHAPMAN J. *Red Carolinians*. Chapel Hill: The University of North Carolina Press, 1940. Pp. xxi, 438. NcD, NcU.
An account of those Indian tribes in contact with provincial South Carolinians.

NIXON, HERMAN CLARENCE. *Possum Trot. Rural Community, South*. Norman: University of Oklahoma Press, 1941. Pp. xi, 192. NcD, NcU.
Mr. Nixon seems to see the universal in his home community of Possum Trot, Alabama.

O'BRIEN, ROBERT W. "Status of Chinese in the Mississippi Delta," *Social Forces*, XIX (March, 1941), 386-90. NcD, NcU, NcC.
An account of the 900 Chinese in the Delta who hold an intermediate social position between white and Negro.

ODUM, HOWARD W. *Southern Regions of the United States*. Chapel Hill: The University of North Carolina Press, 1936. Pp. xi, 664. NcD, NcU, NcC.
A source book and a work book on the paradoxes and problems of the South, mainly the Southeast.

OGBURN, WILLIAM F. "Southern Folkways Regarding Money," *Social Forces*, XXI (March, 1943), 297-301. NcD, NcU, NcC.

Nothing better illustrates the feudal order of the old South than its folkways regarding money.

OLMSTED, FREDERICK LAW. *A Journey in the Back Country.* New York: Mason Brothers, 1860. Pp. xvi, 492. NcD, NcU, NcC.
One of a trilogy picturing Southern society just previous to the Civil War. Olmsted was an open-minded traveler and observer with a passion for facts.

PAGE, WALTER HINES. *The Southerner, A Novel; being the Autobiography of Nicholas Worth.* New York: Doubleday, Page and Co., 1909. Pp. vi, 424. NcD, NcU.
This autobiography of a white North Carolinian, written in the form of a novel, was regarded as exceptionally liberal in the South of his day.

PARKINS, ALMON ERNEST. *The South: Its Economic-Geographic Development.* New York: John Wiley and Sons, Inc., 1938. Pp. ix, 528. NcD, NcU, NcC.
The author aims "to describe the Southern environment, . . . to describe, interpret, and explain . . . the cultural features and patterns and institutions that Europeans and their descendants have evolved." This seems to leave the Negro out.

PHILLIPS, ULRICH B. "The Central Theme of Southern History," *The American Historical Review,* XXXIV, No. 1 (October, 1928), 30-43. NcD. NcU. Reprinted in E. Merton Coulter, ed., *The Course of the South to Secession: An Interpretation by Ulrich Bonnell Phillips.* New York: D. Appleton-Century Co., 1939. NcD, NcU, NcC.
The South "is a land with a unity despite its diversity, with a people having common joys and common sorrows, and above all, as to the white folk a people with a common resolve indomitably maintained—that it shall be and remain a white man's country."

PHILLIPS, ULRICH B. *Life and Labor in the Old South.* Boston: Little, Brown and Co., 1929. Pp. xix, 375. NcD, NcU, NcC.
A rich accumulation of the facts, and as full of entertainment as it is of facts.

PHILLIPS, ULRICH B. "The Historic Civilization of the South," *Agricultural History,* XII (April, 1938), 142-50. NcD, NcU.
An address delivered in Blacksburg, Virginia, and published after the author's death.

"THE Racial Elements in the South." Vol. X, Part II, pp. 97-183 in *The South in the Building of the Nation.* Richmond: The Southern Historical Publication Society, 1909. NcD, NcU.
Part II consists of separate articles on the English, French, Spanish, Germans, Jews, Indians, and Negroes in the South.

REDDING, J. SAUNDERS. *No Day of Triumph.* New York: Harper and Brothers, 1942. Pp. 342. NcD, NcU, NcC.
A Negro discovers the South.

REUTER, EDWARD B. "Southern Scholars and Race Relations," *Phylon,* VII (Third Quarter, 1946), 221-35. NcD, NcU, NcC.
"The scholar might well replace the political buffoon in the determination of social and racial policy."

SIMKINS, FRANCES BUTLER. *The South, Old and New: A History, 1820-1947.* New York: A. A. Knopf, 1947. Pp. 527. NcD, NcU.
A social history of a "cultural province conscious of its identity."

SMITH, WILLIAM M. "Racial Strains in Florida," *Florida Historical Society Quarterly,* XI (July, 1932), 16-33. NcD.

Florida is still, in many respects, a frontier state and to it have migrated Spanish, French, English, and Negro stocks. The native Indians still inhabit lower Florida.

SYDNOR, CHARLES S. "The Southerner and the Laws," *Journal of Southern History*, VI (February, 1940), 3-23. NcD, NcU, NcC.
Another penetrating search for the unifying theme in Southern history.

TATE, ALLEN. "Regionalism and Sectionalism," *The New Republic*, LXIX (December 23, 1931), 158-61. NcD, NcU, NcC.
An analysis of "sectionalism," "regionalism," and "traditionalism."

THOMPSON, EDGAR T. "Sociology and Sociological Research in the South," *Social Forces*, XXIII (March, 1945), 356-65. NcD, NcU, NcC. ˙
"The relations between the races is the axis upon which Southern life has turned for a hundred years or more. Southern sociology began with it, developed with it, and must continue with it. . . . It is in the field of race relations, perhaps, that Southern sociologists have their finest opportunity to contribute to the science of sociology."

THOMPSON, EDGAR T. "Purpose and Tradition in Southern Rural Society: A Point of View for Research," *Social Forces*, XXV (March, 1947), 270-80. NcD, NcU, NcC.
How can education be used to alter the subtle yet powerful force of tradition as it is handed down informally in the family and in the community?

TWELVE Southerners. *I'll Take My Stand: The South and the Agrarian Tradition*. New York: Harper and Brothers, 1930. Pp. xx, 359. NcD, NcU, NcC.
A symposium on a single theme: to sustain the Southern heritage of "decent formality and tolerant social balance." An interpretation and advocacy of the Southern way of life.

UNITED STATES, National Emergency Council. *Report on Economic Conditions of the South*. Washington: U. S. Government Printing Office, 1938. Pp. 64. NcD, NcU.
It was in connection with this report that President Franklin D. Roosevelt referred to the South as "the Nation's No. 1 economic problem—the Nation's problem, not merely the South's."

VANCE, RUPERT B. *Human Factors in Cotton Culture: A Study in the Social Geography of the American South*. Chapel Hill: The University of North Carolina Press, 1929. Pp. xi, 346. NcD, NcU, NcC.
"There exists a kind of natural harmony about the cotton system," says Vance. "Its parts fit together so perfectly as to suggest a fatalism of design."

VANCE, RUPERT B. *Human Geography of the South: A Study in Regional Resources and Human Adequacy*. Chapel Hill: The University of North Carolina Press, 1932. Pp. xiv, 596. NcD, NcU, NcC.
Race relations are treated only incidentally in this study which describes the soil, topography, climate, and historical background of the South.

VANCE, RUPERT B. *All These People: The Nation's Human Resources in the South*. Chapel Hill: The University of North Carolina Press, 1945. Pp. xxxiii, 503. NcD, NcU, NcC.
What social policies should we adopt for the conservation and development of our human resources in the South?

4. MIGRATION AND RACE CONTACT

BECKWOURTH, JAMES P. *Life and Adventures of James P. Beckwourth*. Edited by T. D. Bonner. New York: A. A. Knopf, 1931. Pp. x, 405. NcD.
The facts about the life and adventures of this Negro pioneer and frontiersman are in dispute. Is Beckwourth's personal story true or, as Bernard de Voto says, mythology?

BEYNON, ERDMANN D. "The Southern White Laborer Migrates to Michigan," *American Sociological Review*, III (June, 1938), 333-43. NcD, NcU.
Where the white Southerner is treated like an immigrant from any other part of the world he discovers himself to be a Southerner.

FREY, FRED C. "Factors Conditioning the Incidence of Migration Among Louisiana Negroes," *Southwestern Social Science Quarterly*, XV (December, 1934), 210-17. NcD, NcU.
Migration among Louisiana Negroes is part of the general urbanward current organization. Migrants are somewhat better educated than non-migrants and members of the middle classes migrate less than members of the upper and lower classes. Catholics migrate more frequently than members of other faiths and family disorganization is a factor promoting migration.

JOHNSON, GUY B. "The Negro Migration and Its Consequences," *Social Forces*, II (March, 1924), 404-8. NcD, NcU, NcC.
"The Northward movement of the Negro attracts attention, not because it is a migration, but because it is a *Negro* migration."

LEWIS, EDWARD E. *The Mobility of the Negro: A Study in the American Labor Supply*. Columbia University Studies in History, Economics and Public Law, No. 342. New York: Columbia University Press, 1931. Pp. 144. NcD, NcU, NcC.
A statistical study of the economic causes of the migration of southeastern Negroes to the industrial centers of the North between 1919 and 1924. The author concludes that the push of bad agricultural conditions outweighed the pull of industrial opportunity.

MUNTZ, EARL EDWARD. *Race Contact*. New York: The Century Company, 1927. Pp. xiv, 407. NcD, NcU, NcC.
An analysis of the cultural effects resulting from the impact of Caucasian cultures on the cultures of peoples of other races.

MYRDAL, GUNNAR. *An American Dilemma*. 2 vols. (Vol. I, Chap. 8, "Migration"). New York: Harper and Brothers, 1944. NcD, NcU, NcC.
Since the Civil War, Negroes have been probably more mobile than other elements in the American population but their moves have been restricted to a few main streams.

REID, IRA DE A. *The Negro Immigrant, His Background, Characteristics and Social Adjustment, 1899-1937*. New York: Columbia University Press, 1939. Pp. 261. NcD, NcU, NcC.
A study of the background, composition and characteristics of the 100,000 foreign-born Negroes now in the United States.

REUTER, EDWARD B. "Race and Culture Contacts." Chap. I in E. B. Reuter, ed., *Race and Culture Contacts*. New York: McGraw-Hill Book Company, 1934. NcD, NcU, NcC.
"Certain universals in the contact of race and culture groups are presented in the merest outlines of their general patterns."

ROSS, FRANK A., and KENNEDY, LOUISE VENABLE. *A Bibliography of Negro Migration*. New York: Columbia University Press, 1934. Pp. 251. NcD, NcU, NcC.
Thirteen hundred titles of material published in the United States since 1865.

SCOTT, EMMETT JAY. *Negro Migration During the War*. New York: Oxford University Press, 1920. Pp. 189. NcD, NcU.
A review of the facts concerning the movement of population among Negroes during World War I.

SELL, MANFRED. "Die schwarze Völkerwanderung," *Preussische Jahrbücher,* CCXXIV (April-June, 1931), 157-81. NcD.

A discussion of the redistribution of the New World Negro population since the termination of the African slave trade.

WOODSON, CARTER G. *A Century of Negro Migration.* Washington: Association for the Study of Negro Life and History, 1918. Pp. vii, 221. NcD, NcU.

Discusses Negro migration from South to North, back to the South and to the West.

WOOFTER, THOMAS J., JR. *Negro Migration: Changes in Rural Organization and Population in the Cotton Belt.* New York: W. D. Gray, 1920. Pp. 195. NcU.

Statistical in method, this is a readable analysis of the factors involved in Negro migration within the United States. Prior to 1910 the migration was largely from one rural community to another. After 1910 industrial centers began to draw the migrants.

III. The Negro in Africa

BATES, ORIC, ed. *Harvard African Studies.* 8 vols. The African Department of the Peabody Museum of Harvard University, Cambridge, Mass., 1917-32. NcD.

The volumes in this series constitute an African anthology in the widest sense.

BLYDEN, EDWARD W. *Christianity, Islam and the Negro Race.* London: W. B. Whittingham and Co., 1887. Pp. xv, 432. NcD.

An important work by a writer of West Indian birth and African residence.

BROWN, GEORGE W. *The Economic History of Liberia.* Washington: Associated Publishers, 1941. Pp. ix, 366. NcD, NcU.

An American Negro's competent evaluation of this offshoot of American Negro colonization. It is a story of the contest between western capitalism and the African economic system.

BUELL, RAYMOND LESLIE. *The Native Problem in Africa.* 2 vols. New York: The Macmillan Co., 1928. NcD, NcU, NcC.

"The purpose of this report is to set forth the problems which have arisen out of the impact of primitive peoples with an industrial civilization, and to show how and to what extent these problems are being solved by the governments concerned."

CENDRARS, BLAISE, comp. *The African Saga.* New York: Payson and Charles Co., 1927. Pp. 378. NcD, NcU.

Tales and proverbs of the native Africans. This work is translated from "l'Anthologie nègre" by Margery Bianco.

CLINE, WALTER B. *Mining and Metallurgy in Negro Africa.* General Series in Anthropology No. 5. Menasha, Wisconsin: George Banta Publishing Co., 1937. Pp. 155. NcD.

Few Americans, white or black, realize how extensive and how skilled were Negro mining and metallurgy on the African continent.

COULTER, CHARLES W. "Problems Arising from Industrialization of Native Life in Central Africa," *American Journal of Sociology,* XL (March, 1935), 582-92. NcD, NcU.

In Central Africa problems of race relations began with the decline of resources necessary to sustain native life.

DELAFOSSE, MAURICE. *The Negroes of Africa; History and Culture.* Washington, D. C.: Associated Publishers, Inc., 1931. Pp. xxxiii, 313. NcD, NcU.

"The object of this book is to establish a sort of synthesis of what is common to all African Negro civilizations."

DOUGALL, JAMES W. C. *Christianity and the Sex Education of the African Natives.* London: Society for Promoting Christian Knowledge, 1937. Pp. vii, 128. NcD.

A description of the economic and social impact of European culture upon African native cultures. The conflict of cultures, with its attendant personal and social disorganization, resulted in radical changes in the conditions which govern the use of sexual energy.

DUBOIS, W. E. B. *Black Folk—Then and Now: An Essay in the History and Sociology of the Negro Race.* New York: Henry Holt and Co., 1939. Pp. ix, 401. NcD, NcU, NcC.
The major emphasis of this book is upon the history and present status of efforts to Europeanize and exploit black folk in Africa and in America.

DUBOIS, W. E. B. *The World and Africa.* New York: The Viking Press, 1947. Pp. 276. NcD.
Among other matters, the author gives a first-hand account of the Pan-African Congress.

FROBENIUS, LEE. "Early Negro Cultures as an Indication of Present Negro Potentialities," *Annals of the American Academy of Political and Social Science,* CXL (November, 1928), 153-66. NcD, NcU, NcC.
". . . the native peoples of Africa evidence a vastly greater degree of cultural differentiation than the peoples of Oceania or even the Americas."

FURBAY, ELIZABETH JANE. *Tophats and Tom-Toms.* Chicago: Ziff-Davis Publishing Co., 1943. Pp. 307. NcD, NcU.
An interpretation of life among the aristocratic Negroes who rule the Republic of Liberia.

HAILEY, WILLIAM MALCOLM. *An African Survey: A Study of Problems Arising in Africa South of the Sahara.* London: Oxford University Press, 1938. Pp. xxviii, 1837. NcD, NcU.
A survey including a review of the extent to which modern knowledge is being applied to African problems. The author has compressed as many as possible of the salient facts of this monumental study into his *The Future of Colonial Peoples.* Princeton: Princeton University Press, 1944. Pp. 62.

HERSKOVITS, MELVILLE J. *Dahomey: An Ancient West African Kingdom.* 2 vols. New York: J. J. Augustin, 1938. NcD, NcU, NcC.
In the words of the author, this work "aims at extending our knowledge of primitive life in general, and of the culture . . . described in particular. In addition, it is intended to provide material for those students of New World Negro culture who wish to know more fully the mode of life of the peoples from whom were drawn the ancestors of the Negroes who today inhabit the Americas."

HERSKOVITS, MELVILLE J. "The Ancestry of the American Negro," *American Scholar,* VIII (Winter, 1938), 84-94. NcD, NcU.
Concerning our neglect of the African background of the American Negro, the largest of our minority groups.

HERSKOVITS, MELVILLE J. *The Myth of the Negro Past.* New York: Harper and Brothers, 1941. Pp. xiv, 374. NcD, NcU, NcC.
The author undertakes to prove that the widely accepted beliefs about Negro inferiority are largely unsubstantiated by anthropological and other scientific data.

HOERNLÉ, R. F. ALFRED. *South African Native Policy and the Liberal Spirit.* Cape Town: Lovedale Press, 1939. Pp. xiv, 190. NcD, NcU.
An analysis of the liberal spirit in relation to white domination in South Africa.

HOLLOWAY, JOHN EDWARD. *American Negroes and South African Bantu.* Pretoria: Carnegie Visitors' Grants Committee, 1935. Pp. 26. NcD, NcU.
A South African compares the racial situation in South Africa and the United States with special reference to educational policy.

HUBERICH, CHARLES HENRY. *The Political and Legislative History of Liberia.* 2 vols. New York: Central Book Co., 1947. Pp. 1733. NcD.

A documentary history of the constitution, laws and treaties of Liberia from the earliest settlements to the establishment of the Republic, a sketch of the activities of the American Colonization Societies, a commentary on the Constitution of the Republic and a survey of the political and social legislation from 1847 to 1944.

HUGGINS, WILLIAM NATHANIEL, and JACKSON, JOHN G. *A Guide to Studies in African History. Directive Lists for Schools and Clubs.* New York: Federation of History Clubs, 1934. Pp. vii, 98. NcD.
This guide contains a series of problems for an extensive one-year course in African history.

JOHNSTON, SIR HARRY HAMILTON. *A History of the Colonization of Africa by Alien Races.* Rev. ed. Cambridge: Cambridge University Press, 1930. Pp. xiii, 319. NcD. NcU.
The essential facts on the conquest and partition of Africa by European states. Important material and maps on the slave trade, Christian missions, and other subjects.

KINGSLEY, MARY H. *Travels in West Africa, Congo, Français, Corisco and Cameroons.* New York: The Macmillan Co., 1897. Pp. xvi, 743. NcD, NcU.
A classic account of the general state and manner of life in Lower Guinea.

KINGSLEY, MARY H. *West African Studies.* 2nd ed. London: Macmillan and Co., 1901. Pp. xxxii, 507. NcD.
This, one of the world's great books, is an attempt to humanize the natives of Africa to the people of Europe and America.

KIRK, JOHN H. "Comparison of Race Relations in South Africa and the Southern States," *Social Forces,* XIII (October, 1934), 104-11. NcD, NcU, NcC.
Similar in some ways there also are many important differences, e.g., in the degree of economic competition between the races, in the status of the mulatto, in the problem of miscegenation, and in the personal safety and economic and educational opportunity of the black man.

KLINGBERG, FRANK J. "The Rise of the Negro in Africa," in *Africa, the Near East and the War.* Berkeley: University of California Press, 1943. NcD, NcU.
Africa is primarily and primordially Negro.

LEYS, NORMAN. *The Colour Bar in East Africa.* London: The Hogarth Press, 1941. Pp. 160. NcD, NcU.
"In both Rhodesias and in Kenya an African's life is so beset by colour bars that the moment he leaves his village home he meets them at every turn. In Nyasaland there are perhaps rather fewer, in Tanganyika fewer still and in Uganda fewest of all, hardly any in fact."

OJIKE, MBONU. *I Have Two Countries.* New York: The John Day Co., 1947. Pp. viii, 208. NcD.
An American-trained African returned to his native country with a liberal education in race relations.

OLIVIER, SYDNEY HALDANE. *The Anatomy of African Misery.* London: L. and V. Woolf, 1927. Pp. 234. NcD.
The principle under which America decreed the abolition of slavery has never been assimilated by South Africa.

OLIVIER, SYDNEY HALDANE. *White Capital and Coloured Labour.* New ed. London: L. and V. Woolf, 1929. Pp. 348. NcD, NcU.

First published in 1906 this book deals with industrialism and the race problem in Africa. A standard work.

ORDE-BROWNE, GRANVILLE ST. JOHN. *The African Labourer*. London: Humphrey Milford, 1933. Pp. viii, 240. NcD, NcU.
A practical discussion by the Head of the Labour Department of Tanganyika.

ROBESON, ESLANDA GOODE. *African Journey*. New York: The John Day Co., 1945. Pp. 187. NcD, NcU, NcC.
The wife of Paul Robeson discovers the rich cultures of the Negroes of Africa.

SCHAPERA, I., ed. *Western Civilization and the Natives of South Africa: Studies in Culture Contact*. London: George Routledge and Sons, 1934. Pp. xiv, 312. NcD, NcU.
Twelve important papers and a bibliography.

SELIGMAN, CHARLES GABRIEL. *Races of Africa*. London: T. Butterworth, Ltd., 1930. Pp. 256. NcD, NcU.
African peoples and their cultures from the most primitive to the most advanced.

THURNWALD, RICHARD. *Black and White in East Africa: The Fabric of a New Civilization*. London: G. Routledge and Sons, Ltd., 1935. Pp. xxii, 419. NcD, NcU.
A study of the "problems emerging from the contact between black and white in Africa and the ensuing processes of adaptation."

WESTERMANN, DIEDRICH. *The African Today and Tomorrow*. Rev. ed. London: Oxford University Press, 1939. Pp. xvi, 355, NcD, NcU, NcC.
The ethnic composition of the African people, their language, and various aspects of their culture.

WOODSON, CARTER G. *The African Background Outlined; or, Handbook for the Study of the Negro*. Washington: The Association for the Study of Negro Life and History, 1936. Pp. viii, 478. NcD, NcU, NcC.
A compilation of information on African life, culture, and history, supplemented by a topical study outline with selected references.

YOUNG, T. CULLEN. "A Good Village," *Africa*, VII (January, 1934), 89-96. NcD, NcU.
The moral order of an African native village.

IV. The Negro in America

APTHEKER, HERBERT. *Essays in the History of the American Negro*. New York: International Publishers, 1945. Pp. viii, 216. NcD, NcU, NcC.
According to the author of this collection of previously published essays, "the desire for freedom is the central theme, the motivating force, in the history of the American Negro people."

APTHEKER, HERBERT. *The Negro People in America*. New York: International Publishers, 1946. Pp. 80. NcD, NcU.
A critique of Myrdal's *An American Dilemma*.

BECKER, JOHN LEONARD. *The Negro in American Life*. New York: Julian Messner, 1944. Pp. 53. NcD, NcU, NcC.
Pictures illustrating the Negro's contributions to American life and living since first coming to this country.

BONTEMPS, ARNA. *The Story of the Negro*. New York: A. A. Knopf, 1948. Pp. 239. NcD.
An excellent book, principally for high school students. The illustrations are by Raymond Lufkin.

BRAWLEY, BENJAMIN G. *A Social History of the American Negro*. New York: The Macmillan Co., 1921. Pp. xv, 420. NcD, NcU.
Negro history as a revelation of the Negro's strivings and aspirations. The history of a people conscious of common purposes and a common cause.

BRAWLEY, BENJAMIN G. *A Short History of the American Negro*. New York: The Macmillan Co., 1931. Pp. xvii, 311. NcD, NcU, NcC.
Suitable for junior and senior high schools.

BROWN, INA C. *The Story of the American Negro*. New York: Friendship Press, 1936. Pp. 208. NcD, NcU, NcC.
A simple chronological story of the American Negro told in words suitable for an elementary reading public.

BROWN, INA C. "The Background of American Race Relations," *National Survey of the Higher Education of Negroes: Socio-Economic Approach to Educational Problems*. Washington: U. S. Government Printing Office, 1942. Misc. No. 6, Vol. I, Chap. II. NcD, NcU, NcC.
Possibly the best short statement of the matter to be found in the literature.

BROWN, WILLIAM WELLS. *The Black Man: His Antecedents, His Genius, and His Achievements*. New York: T. Hamilton, 1863. Pp. 312. NcD, NcU.
Significant as the work of perhaps the first American Negro to become professionally interested in the history of his people.

CARPENTER, MARIE ELIZABETH. *The Treatment of the Negro in American History Textbooks*. Menasha, Wisconsin: George Banta Publishing Co., c. 1941. Pp. 137. NcD, NcU, NcC.
"A comparison of changing textbook content, 1826 to 1939, with developing scholarship in the history of the Negro in the United States."

DUBOIS, W. E. B. *The Gift of Black Folks: The Negroes in the Making of America*. Boston: Stratford Publishing Co., 1924. Pp. iv, 349. NcD, NcU, NcC.
"The Negro elements in the mosaic of American civilization."

EPPSE, MERL R. *A Guide to the Study of the Negro in American History.* Nashville, Tennessee: National Educational Publishing Company, 1943. Pp. 181. NcD, NcU, NcC.
A study guide.

EPPSE, MERL R. *The Negro, Too, in American History.* Chicago: National Educational Publishing Co., 1943. Pp. xxii, 591. NcD, NcU, NcC.
A Negro discusses the Negro's part in American history and reflects his own intense race consciousness.

FRANKLIN, JOHN HOPE. *From Slavery to Freedom: A History of American Negroes.* New York: A. A. Knopf, 1947. Pp. 679. NcD, NcU, NcC.
The author views the story of the Negro as a chapter in the struggle of mankind for freedom and equality.

FULLER, THOMAS OSCAR. *Pictorial History of the American Negro.* Memphis, Tennessee: Pictorial History, Inc., 1933. Pp. xxiii, 375. NcD, NcU, NcC.
The author details the progress of the American Negro along social, educational, political, economic, artistic, and religious lines. There are a large number of illustrations.

GORDON, ASA H. *The Georgia Negro, a History.* Ann Arbor, Michigan: Edwards Brothers, Inc., 1937. Pp. xv, 426. NcD, NcU.
"An attempt to write and arrange the material . . . so that it may be used as a supplementary or parallel text in United States and Negro history in the white and colored high schools and junior colleges of the state."

GREENE, LORENZO J. *The Negro in Colonial New England.* New York: Columbia University Press, 1942. Pp. 404. NcD, NcU, NcC.
A well-documented account.

HERSKOVITS, MELVILLE J. "The Social History of the Negro," in C. Murchison, ed., *A Handbook of Social Psychology,* pp. 207-67. Worcester, Mass.: Clark University Press, 1935. NcD.
From Africa to the New World.

ILLINOIS Writer's Program. *Cavalcade of the American Negro.* Chicago: Diamond Jubilee Exposition Authority, 1940. Pp. 95. NcD, NcU, NcC.
An outline of the Negro's progress in America, compiled by the workers of the Writers' program of the Work Projects Administration.

JOHNSON, CHARLES S. *The Negro in American Civilization.* New York: Henry Holt and Company, 1930. Pp. xiv, 538. NcD, NcU, NcC.
This work is the result of a conference of members representing sixteen organizations interested in the welfare of the Negro. The first part, by Dr. Johnson, is a factual presentation of the life of the Negro in America. Part two, by various authors, discusses the Negro in industry, Negro health and mortality, citizenship, and race relations.

JOHNSON, CHARLES S. "The Negro," *American Journal of Sociology,* XLVII, (May, 1942), 854-64. NcD, NcU, NcC.
The depression, the advent of the New Deal, and the war emergency have profoundly changed the economic condition of the Negro during the past decade.

JOHNSON, GUION G. *A Social History of the Sea Islands, with Special Reference to St. Helena Island, South Carolina.* Chapel Hill: The University of North Carolina Press, 1930. Pp. 245. NcD, NcU, NcC.
Ends with the close of the Reconstruction period. Subsequent history of the island is treated in T. J. Woofter, Jr., *Black Yeomanry* and G. B. Johnson, *Folk Culture on St. Helena Island.*

30 RACE AND REGION

JOHNSTON, SIR HARRY HAMILTON. *The Negro in the New World.* New York: The Macmillan Co., 1910. Pp. xxix, 499. NcD, NcU.
One of the better-known older references.

PIERSEL, W. G. "Regional Study of the Negro; Comparison in Six Regions of Population, Urbanization, Marriage and Family, Education, Social and Economic Status," *Social Forces,* XIX (March, 1941), 390-401. NcD, NcU, NcC.
A brief survey of Negro life in the six regions of the United States as they are defined in Odum's *Southern Regions.* Comparative data are presented for population, urbanization, sex, children, schooling and literacy, professional life, and economy.

REID, IRA DE A., director. *The Negro in New Jersey.* Report of a Survey by the Interracial Committee of the New Jersey Conference of Social Work in Cooperation with the State Department of Institutions and Agencies. Newark, N. J., 1932. Pp. 116. NcD, NcU.
A survey made "to ascertain the social and economic status of the Negro population of New Jersey."

REUTER, EDWARD B. *The American Race Problem. A Study of the Negro.* Rev. ed. New York: Thomas Y. Crowell Co., 1938. Pp. xiii, 430. NcD, NcU, NcC.
Probably the best-known textbook on the subject.

ROUSSÈVE, CHARLES BARTHELEMY. *The Negro in Louisiana: Aspects of His History and His Literature.* New Orleans, Louisiana: The Xavier University Press, 1937. Pp. xvii, 212. NcD, NcU, NcC.
The Negro's achievements "within the very State which may be called the center of yesterday's slavery in the Deep South."

SCHOMBURG, ARTHUR A. "The Negro Digs Up His Past," *Survey,* LIII (March 1, 1925), 670-72. NcD, NcU.
"The Negro historian today digs under the spot where his predecessor stood and argued."

SHACKELFORD, JANE D. *The Child's Story of the Negro.* Washington, D. C.: Associated Publishers, 1938. Pp. xi, 219. NcD, NcU, NcC.
Supplementary history of the American Negro from his African background to the present. Biographical sketches of noted Negroes are included.

SWIFT, HILDEGARDE HOYT. *North Star Shining.* New York: William Morrow and Co., 1947. Pp. 44. NcD, NcC.
The full page illustrations in this interesting book on Negro life in America were done by Lynd Ward. The text is written in free verse.

TANNENBAUM, FRANK. *Slave and Citizen: The Negro in the Americas.* New York: A. A. Knopf, 1947. Pp. xi, 128. NcD, NcU, NcC.
The lot of the Negro in Latin America and in English America compared.

THOMAS, WILLIAM HANNIBAL. *The American Negro: What He Was, What He Is, and What He May Become.* New York: The MacMillan Co., 1901. Pp. xxv, 440. NcD, NcU, NcC.
"A frank and candid expression of the attitude of the American mulatto toward the American Negro at the time this volume was published."

VAN DEUSEN, JOHN G. *The Black Man in White America.* Washington, D. C.: Associated Publishers, 1944. Pp. 381. NcD, NcU, NcC.
". . . notable for its countless newsy facts."

VIRGINIA Writers' Program. *The Negro in Virginia.* New York: Hastings House, 1940. Pp. xii, 380. NcD, NcU, NcC.

Sponsored by the Hampton Institute. The Negro in Virginia from 1619 to the present. An informative and interesting book.

WEATHERFORD, W. D. *The Negro from Africa to America.* New York: George H. Doran and Co., 1924. Pp. 487. NcD, NcU, NcC.

A summary account of the life and progress of the Negro from his African background through the slave period in America to the present.

WEATHERFORD, W. D., and JOHNSON, CHARLES S. *Race Relations: Adjustment of Whites and Negroes in the United States.* Boston: D. C. Heath and Co., 1934. Pp. x, 590. NcD, NcU, NcC.

A textbook on the philosophy of race relations, slavery, and the contemporary situation.

WESLEY, CHARLES H., ed. *The Negro in the Americas.* Washington, D. C.: The Graduate School, Howard University, 1940. Pp. 86. NcD, NcU, NcC.

Chapters on the Negro in the British and French West Indies, Brazil, Spanish America, Haiti, the United States, and Canada.

WILLIAMS, GEORGE WASHINGTON. *History of the Negro Race in America from 1619 to 1880.* 2 vols. New York: G. P. Putnam's Sons, 1883. NcD, NcU, NcC.

Perhaps the first effort made by a Negro to separate Negro history from general American history.

WOODSON, CARTER G. *The Story of the Negro Retold.* Washington: Associated Publishers, 1935. Pp. viii, 369. NcD, NcU, NcC.

A textbook of Negro American history for high-school pupils.

WOODSON, CARTER G. *The Negro in Our History.* 9th ed., rev. and enl. Washington: Associated Publishers, 1947. Pp. xxx, 691. NcD, NcU, NcC.

The history of the Negro as a neglected chapter in the history of the American people.

YOUNG, DONALD R., ed. *The American Negro, Annals of the American Academy of Political and Social Science,* CXL (November, 1928). Pp. viii, 359. NcD, NcU, NcC.

"We are here trying to present not new facts hitherto unpublished but rather a series of surveys of the most significant studies and information brought forth in the past few years."

V. The Slave Trade

BANCROFT, FREDERIC. *Slave-Trading in the Old South*. Baltimore, Md.: J. H. Furst Co., 1931. Pp. 415. NcD, NcU, NcC.

It was in the slave trade, rather than in slave-holding, that slavery became an abstract relation divested of all human associations, restraints, and inhibitions. Bancroft shows how men could be, and were, treated as commodities of trade.

BUXTON, THOMAS. *The African Slave Trade*. New York: S. W. Benedict, 1840. Pp. vi, 259. NcD, NcU.

Contains some especially interesting documents.

CAREY, HENRY CHARLES. *The Slave Trade, Domestic and Foreign*. Philadelphia: H. C. Baird, *c.* 1853. Pp. 426. NcD, NcU.

Carey argued that progress in commerce and in industry was incompatible with the maintainance of slavery.

COLLINS, WINFIELD H. *The Domestic Slave Trade of the Southern States*. New York: Broadway Publishing Co., 1904. Pp. iii, 154. NcD, NcU.

A study of the manner in which Negro slave labor was distributed in the Old South.

DONNAN, ELIZABETH, ed. *Documents Illustrative of the History of the Slave Trade to America*. 4 vols. Washington, D. C.: Carnegie Institution of Washington, 1930. NcD, NcU, NcC.

The documents are chronologically arranged and each section is headed by a historical essay.

DUBOIS, W. E. B. *The Supression of the African Slave-Trade to the United States of America, 1638-1870*. New York: Longmans, Green and Co., 1896. Pp. xi, 335. NcD, NcU. NcC.

An old but still important reference.

SPEARS, JOHN RANDOLPH. *The American Slave-Trade; An Account of Its Origin, Growth and Supression*. New York: Charles Scribner's Sons, 1900. Pp. xvii, 232. NcD, NcU.

A history compiled from public documents, biographies, and other sources of original information. Grew from a study of the American navy.

VI. The Plantation

ALEXANDER, DONALD C. *The Arkansas Plantation, 1920-1942*. New Haven: Yale Univeristy Press, 1943. Pp. 118. NcD, NcU, NcC.

A historical analysis of the development of Federal agricultural policy and a description of the changes in the plantation itself.

ALLEN, JAMES S. *The Negro Question in the United States*. New York: International Publishers, 1936. Pp. 224. NcD, NcU, NcC.

The thesis of this Marxian analysis is that "it is not the plantation legend but rather the plantation itself that continues to cast its shadow over the South; the old system has never died."—Malcolm Cowley.

BLALOCK, H. W. *Plantation Operations of Landlords and Tenants in Arkansas*. University of Arkansas, Agricultural Experiment Station Bulletin, No. 339. Fayetteville, Arkansas, May, 1937. Pp. 45. NcD.

A description of the plantation system in the State with special reference to the incomes and standards of living of the plantation workers.

BOEKE, JULIUS HERMAN. *The Structure of Netherlands Indian Economy*. New York: Institute of Pacific Relations, 1942. Pp. x, 201. NcD, NcU.

In this study race problems and race relations appear as incidents in the expansion of Western economy.

BRANNEN, CLAUDE O. *Relation of Land Tenure to Plantation Organization, with Developments Since 1920*. Fayetteville, Arkansas, 1928. Part I of this study was published by the United States Department of Agriculture, Bulletin No. 1269 (1924). Pp. v, 85. NcU.

A cross section picture, as of 1920, of the plantation as a whole with some indication of trends in labor supply and conditions affecting staple crop production.

EDWARDS, ALLEN D. *Beaverdam: A Rural Community in Transition*. Virginia Agricultural Experiment Station Bulletin, No. 340 (May, 1942). Pp. 64. NcD, NcU.

A study of the transition from plantation to farm in a Virginia community.

GAINES, FRANCIS P. *The Southern Plantation: A Study in the Development and Accuracy of a Tradition*. New York: Columbia University Press, 1924. Pp. vii, 243. NcD, NcU, NcC.

The contrast between the Southern plantation of fact and of fiction. A survey of the literature.

GRAY, LEWIS C. "Southern Agriculture, Plantation System, and the Negro Problem," *Annals of the American Academy of Political and Social Science*, XL (March, 1912), 90-99. NcD, NcU.

Underlying both Southern agriculture and the so-called race problem is the plantation system.

GRAY, LEWIS C. "Economic Efficiency and Competitive Advantages of Slavery Under the Plantation System," *Agricultural History*, IV (April, 1930), 31-47. NcD, NcU.

"This essay is devoted to an interpretation of the competitive superiority which enabled slavery to displace other forms of labor."

HOLLEY, WILLIAM C., WINSTON, ELLEN, and WOOFTER, T. J., JR. *The Plantation South, 1934-1937.* Federal Works Agency, Work Projects Administration, Division of Research, Research Monograph XXII. Washington, 1940. Pp. xxii, 124. NcD, NcU.
A resurvey of the plantation areas in the Southeast covered in the earlier investigation by T. J. Woofter, Jr., and others in *Landlord and Tenant on the Cotton Plantation.*

JOHNSON, CHARLES S. *Shadow of the Plantation.* Chicago: The University of Chicago Press, 1934. Pp. xxiv, 214. NcD, NcU, NcC.
The contemporary remnants of a feudal society in Macon County, Alabama.

KELLER, ALBERT G. *Colonization: A Study of the Founding of New Societies.* Boston: Ginn and Co., 1908. Pp. xii, 632. NcD, NcU, NcC.
Colonies are classified as *farm* colonies and *plantation* colonies, each detemined by climatic conditions. The plantation type of colony is invariably an interracial colony with race problems.

LANDIS, BENSON Y., and HAYNES, GEORGE E. *Cotton-Growing Communities.* New York: Federal Council of Churches of Christ in America, Department of Race Relations, Interracial Publications, Study No. 1 (1934), pp. 43; Study No. 2 (1935), pp. 47. NcD, NcU.
Study No. 1 deals with nine rural communities and thirty plantations in Alabama. Study No. 2 deals with ten rural communities and ten plantations in Arkansas.

McBRIDE, GEORGE M. "Plantation," *Encyclopaedia of the Social Sciences,* XII, 148-53. NcD, NcU.
A good statement of the characteristics of the institution.

MYRDAL, GUNNAR. *An American Dilemma.* 2 vols. (Vol. I, Chaps. 10, 11, and 12). New York: Harper and Brothers, 1944. NcD, NcU, NcC.
The changing role of the Negro in the Southern plantation economy.

NIXON, CLARENCE. *Forty Acres and Steel Mules.* Chapel Hill: The University of North Carolina Press, 1938. Pp. 98. NcD, NcU.
A study of the effects of impending agricultural mechanization upon the people of the plantation South.

PERCY, WILLIAM A. *Lanterns on the Levee.* New York: A. A. Knopf, 1941. Pp. 347. NcD, NcU, NcC.
The autobiography and reflections of a Mississippi patrician. Mr. Percy's life story is also the story of a Southern plantation area.

PHILLIPS, ULRICH B. "The Economics of the Plantation," *South Atlantic Quarterly,* II (July, 1903), 231-36. NcD, NcU.
An early article by an author who later became an authority on the history of the South. He here argues for the return and continuation of the plantation as the best unit for Southern agriculture and because it produced "the fine type of the Southern gentlemen of the old regime."

PHILLIPS, ULRICH B. "The Plantation as a Civilizing Factor," *Sewanee Review,* XII (July, 1904), 257-67. NcD, NcU.
The slave plantations of Virginia and the West Indies contrasted.

PHILLIPS, ULRICH B. "The Decadence of the Plantation System," *Annals of the American Academy of Political and Social Science,* XXXV (January, 1910), 37-41. NcD, NcU.
"The plantation system formed . . . the industrial and social frame of government in the black belt communities, while slavery was a code of written

laws enacted for the furtherance of that system's purposes." The author argues that retention of the plantation system is both expedient and inevitable for a long time in the future.

RAPER, ARTHUR F. "The Role of Agricultural Technology in Southern Social Change," *Social Forces*, XXV (October, 1946), 21-30. NcD, NcU, NcC.
The staple crops of Southern agriculture have been among the least mechanized crops in the nation but drastic changes are coming.

RAPER, ARTHUR F., and REID, IRA DE A. *Sharecroppers All*. Chapel Hill: The University of North Carolina Press, 1941. Pp. x, 281. NcD, NcU, NcC.
"Against a rural plantation background is placed a timely study of urban expressions of the plantation economy."

STONE, ALFRED H. "A Plantation Experiment," *Quarterly Journal of Economics*, XIX (February, 1905), 270-87. NcD, NcU. Also in Stone, *Studies in the American Race Problem* (Chap. IV). New York: Doubleday Page and Co., 1908. NcD, NcU.
Describes the failure of a six-year "experiment" on a plantation in Mississippi intended to build up an "assured tenantry."

THOMPSON, EDGAR T. "Mines and Plantations and the Movements of Peoples," *American Journal of Sociology*, XXXVII (January, 1932), 603-11. NcD, NcU, NcC.
"The organization of a plantation is much like that of a coal mine," says J. Russell Smith.

THOMPSON, EDGAR T. "Population Expansion and the Plantation System," *American Journal of Sociology*, XLI (November, 1935), 314-26. NcD, NcU.
An outline of the plantation cycle.

THOMPSON, EDGAR T. "The Plantation: the Physical Basis of Traditional Race Relations in the South." Chap. VII in Edgar T. Thompson, ed., *Race Relations and the Race Problem*. Durham: Duke University Press, 1939. NcD, NcU, NcC.
The plantation is defined and described as (1) a settlement, (2) an industrial, (3) a political, and (4) a cultural institution.

THOMPSON, EDGAR T. "The Planter in the Pattern of Race Relations in the South," *Social Forces*, XIX (December, 1940), 244-52. NcD, NcU, NcC.
"Without the planter there either would have been no race problem in the South or it would have assumed an altogether different form."

THOMPSON, EDGAR T. "The Climatic Theory of the Plantation," *Agricultural History*, XV (January, 1941), 49-60. NcD, NcU.
The climatic theory, like other sentiments, beliefs, and attitudes connected with the plantation system, must be understood as a product of forces working within the system itself, as an important part of that system, but not as an explanation of it.

THOMPSON, EDGAR T. "Comparative Education in Colonial Areas, With Special Reference to Plantation and Mission Frontiers," *American Journal of Sociology*, XLVIII (May, 1943), 82-93. NcD, NcU, NcC.
The plantation and the agricultural mission have different histories and conflicting ideologies, but they develop in similar environments; and in adjusting to the permanent elements in the environment, like geography and climate, they eventually become very similar institutions.

UNITED STATES, Bureau of the Census. *Plantation Farming in the United States*. Washington, D. C.: U. S. Government Printing Office, 1916. Pp. 40. NcD.

Special studies and analyses of returns derived from the statistics contained in Chap. XII, "Plantations of the South," of Vol. V of the 1910 Census, the first census since the Civil War to count the plantation as a separate unit.

WOOFTER, THOMAS J., JR. *Landlord and Tenant on the Cotton Plantation.* Works Progress Administration, Research Monograph V. Washington, D. C.: Works Progress Administration, Division of Social Research, 1936. Pp. xxxiii, 288. NcD, NcU.
A valuable statistical and analytical study of 646 plantations in the Southeast.

2. HISTORY

BALLAGH, JAMES C. *White Servitude in the Colony of Virginia.* Johns Hopkins University Studies in Historical and Political Science, Series XIII, VI-VII (1895). Pp. 99. NcD, NcU.
A standard work on the subject.

BARROW, DAVID C., JR. "A Georgia Plantation," *Scribner's Monthly,* XXI (April, 1881), 830-36. NcD, NcU.
An important article showing with the aid of two very interesting maps the transition from slavery to freedom on a single plantation.

BASSETT, JOHN SPENCER, ed. *The Southern Plantation Overseer as Revealed in His Letters.* Northampton, Massachusetts: Printed for Smith College, 1925. Pp. vii, 280. NcD, NcU, NcC.
A study made through the medium of a series of naïve letters written by a succession of overseers on the plantation of President Polk. It was the overseer who, perhaps even more than the planter, epitomized the formal and objective aspect of the plantation as a political institution.

BURWELL, LETITIA M. (PAGE THACKER, pseud.) *Plantation Reminiscences.* Owensboro, Ky. (?), 1878. Pp. 69. NcD.
One of the best reminiscences of ante-bellum plantation life.

COULTER, ELLIS M. "A Century of a Georgia Plantation," *Mississippi Valley Historical Review,* XVI (December, 1929) 334-46. NcD, NcU.
An account of the rise, progress, and decline of a plantation in Georgia organized soon after the War of 1812.

CURLEE, ABIGAIL. "The History of a Texas Slave Plantation," *Southwestern Historical Quarterly,* XXVI (October, 1922), 79-127. NcD, NcU.
General conditions of agriculture in Texas between 1831 and 1836, and life on the plantation.

DAVIS, EDWIN A., ed. *Plantation Life in the Florida Parishes of Louisiana, 1836-1846, as Reflected in the Diary of Bennet H. Barrow.* New York: Columbia University Press, 1943. Pp. xvi, 457. NcD, NcU.
Barrow's diary shows the actual day-by-day life of an ante-bellum Southern planter.

DEVEREUX, (MRS.) MARGARET. *Plantation Sketches.* Cambridge: Privately Printed at the Riverside Press, 1906. Pp. 168. NcD, NcU.
"I have drawn from memory a few pen sketches of plantation life, based upon actual events, in which are recorded some of the good and even noble traits of character which were brought forth under the yoke of slavery."

DODD, WILLIAM E. "The Plantation and Farm Systems in Southern Agriculture," *The South in the Building of the Nation, V (Economic History, 1607-1865),* 73-80. Richmond: The Southern Historical Publication Society, 1909. NcD, NcU.
Planter and farmer in the South before the Civil War.

DOUGLAS, PAUL H. *American Apprenticeship and Industrial Education.* Columbia University Studies in History, Economics and Public Law, XCV, No. 2. New York: Columbia University Press, 1921. Pp. 348. NcD, NcU.
Early English and American apprenticeship is important in the history of indentured servitude and slavery.

EASTERBY, J. H., ed. *The South Carolina Rice Plantation, as Revealed in the Papers of Robert F. W. Allston.* Chicago: The University of Chicago Press, 1945. Pp. xxi, 478. NcD, NcU.
"These papers throw a great deal of light on the daily life and problems of a rice planter and his family and the routine of plantation economy."

EVERETT, MARY. "Texan Plantation: Then and Now," *Sewanee Review,* XLIV (October, 1936), 386-404. NcD, NcU.
A Texas plantation before and after the Civil War.

FLANDERS, RALPH B. "Two Plantations and a County of Ante-Bellum Georgia," *Georgia Historical Quarterly,* XII (March, 1928), 1-37. NcD, NcU.
A prize-winning paper on two plantations, each representative of a type, in ante-bellum Georgia.

FLANDERS, RALPH B. *Plantation Slavery in Georgia.* Chapel Hill: The University of North Carolina Press, 1933. Pp. x, 326. NcD, NcU, NcC.
The "foundations of slavery in Georgia" are described and the development of the plantation regime up to the Civil War is traced.

FLEMING, WALTER L. "Plantation Life in the South," *Journal of American History,* III (April-July, 1909) 233-46. NcD, NcU.
On the relations which existed between Jefferson Davis and his slaves on his Mississippi plantation.

FREYRE, GILBERTO. *Brazil: An Interpretation.* New York: A. A. Knopf, 1945. Pp. 179. NcD, NcU, NcC.
Chapter II presents an interesting comparison between the historical Brazilian and Southern plantation systems.

GAYARRE, CHARLES. "A Louisiana Sugar Plantation of the Old Regime," *Harper's New Monthly Magazine,* LXXIV (March, 1887), 606-21. NcD, NcU, NcC.
An account of the plantation of Jean Etienne de Bore, the grandfather of the writer, in Louisiana.

GILMAN, (MRS.) CAROLINE HOWARD. *Recollections of a Southern Matron.* New York: Harper and Brothers, 1838. Pp. vii, 272. NcD, NcU.
"The single work which stands out as best of all interpretations of Carolina plantation life. . . . A chronicle of reality thinly concealed under the guise of fiction."

GRAY, LEWIS C. *History of Agriculture in the Southern United States to 1860.* 2 vols. Carnegie Institution of Washington Publications, No. 430. Washington: Carnegie Institution of Washington, 1933. NcD, NcU, NcC.
Parts III and IV of Vol. I describe the genesis and development of the plantation system as an agency for the colonial expansion of European capitalism.

HERRICK, CHEESMAN A. *White Servitude in Pennsylvania.* Philadelphia: J. J. McVey, 1926. Pp. ix, 330. NcD, NcU.
This study reveals the divergent evolution, in different environments, of two similar institutions, i.e., servitude and slavery.

HOFSTADLER, R. "U. B. Phillips and the Plantation Legend," *Journal of Negro History,* XXIX (April, 1944), 109-24. NcD, NcU, NcC.
The author takes exception to both the method and the conclusions of Phillips' plantation studies.

JONES, GEORGE NOBLE. *Florida Plantation Records from the Papers of George Noble Jones.* Edited by Ulrich Bonnell Phillips and James David Glunt. St. Louis: Missouri Historical Society, 1927. Pp. 605. NcD, NcU.
The most complete and minute account of life and problems of an antebellum Southern plantation yet published.

KANE, HARNETT T. *Plantation Parade.* New York: William Morrow and Co., 1945. Pp. vi, 342. NcD, NcU.
A series of biographies of some of old Louisiana's most prominent planter families.

KEMBLE, FRANCES. *Journal of a Residence on a Georgia Plantation in 1838-39.* New York: Harper and Brothers, 1864. Pp. 434. NcD, NcU, NcC.
The diary of a famous actress. Her husband's Georgia plantation was of that darker aspect of Negro slavery, the absentee landlord, overseer system, as contrasted with the milder domestic slavery elsewhere.

LEIGH, (MRS.) FRANCES BUTLER. *Ten Years on a Georgia Plantation Since the War.* London: R. Bentley & Son, 1883. Pp. xi, 347. NcD, NcU.
The daughter of Frances Kemble describes conditions on the plantation during Reconstruction.

MOORE, WILBERT E., and WILLIAMS, ROBIN M. "Stratification in the Ante-Bellum South," *American Sociological Review,* VII (June, 1942), 343-51. NcD, NcU.
Some broader implications of well-known facts.

PHILLIPS, ULRICH B. *Plantation and Frontier Documents: 1649-1863.* (Vols. I and II of *A Documentary History of American Industrial Society*). Cleveland: Arthur H. Clark Co., 1909. NcD, NcU, NcC.
"In preparing this collection of documents the policy has been as far as possible to use material combining three qualities in each instance, rareness, unconsciousness, and faithful illustration. The purpose is to show the most saliently characteristic features of southern industrial society, through the writings not only of contemporaries, but preferably of actual participators who wrote with no expectation that what they wrote would be published."

PHILLIPS, ULRICH B. "Plantations With Slave Labor and Free," *American Historical Review,* XXX (July, 1925), 738-53. NcD, NcU, NcC.
The Southern plantation with slave labor and free compared and contrasted with the sugar beet estates of the West. Argues that the plantation arose as a necessary and inevitable adjustment to a situation.

POSTL, KARL (CHARLES SEALSFIELD, pseud.). *The Cabin Book; or, Sketches of Life in Texas.* Translated from the German by C. F. Mersch. New York: J. Winchester, 1844. Pp. 155. NcD. *The Cabin Book; or National Characteristics.* Translated from the German by Sarah Powell. London: Ingram, Cooke and Co., 1852. Pp. 296. NcD.
These books belong "to the literature of the pioneer age when the plantation frontier was being extended into rough and remote zones."

RAVENEL, HENRY WILLIAM. "Recollections of Southern Plantation Life," *Yale Review,* XXV (June, 1936), 748-77. N.S. NcD, NcU.
These "recollections," edited by Marjorie Mendenhall, picture life on the ancestral Ravenel plantation near Charleston, South Carolina.

SAXON, LYLE. *Old Louisiana.* New York: The Century Company, 1929. Pp. xvi, 388. NcD, NcU, NcC.
A book of footnotes to history. The chronicle of two centuries of Louisiana plantation life. Reproduces about one-sixth of the diary of Lestant Prudhomme,

a naïve document disclosing the planter's assumption of superiority and master-ship with a patrician's quietude.

SCISCO, L. D. "The Plantation Type of Colony," *American Historical Review*, VIII (January, 1903), 260-70. NcD, NcU.

A valuable article showing the historical connections between the Southern plantation, the Maryland manor, the Dutch patroon of New Netherland, and the New England town.

SMEDES, (MRS.) SUSAN DABNEY. *A Southern Planter*. 4th ed. New York: J. Pott and Co., 1890. Pp. 341. NcD, NcU, NcC.

The author's father with his family and slaves migrated from Virginia to Mississippi. This is an account of a gentleman planter on a rough frontier.

SMITH, ALICE RAVENEL HUGER, and SASS, HERBERT RAVENEL. *A Carolina Rice Plantation of the Fifties*. New York: William Morrow and Co., 1936. Pp. xii, 97. NcD, NcU.

Reproduction of thirty water color paintings by Alice R. Huger Smith and the memoirs of her father, D. E. Huger Smith, with narrative by Ravenel Sass.

STEPHENSON, WENDELL H. *Isaac Franklin, Slave Trader and Planter of the Old South*. Baton Rouge, La.: Louisiana State University Press, 1938. Pp. xi, 368. NcD, NcU, NcC.

"A document of Negro history . . . [and] a socio-economic story of the plantation regime."

STONEY, SAMUEL G. *Plantations of the Carolina Low Country*. Charleston, South Carolina: The Carolina Art Association, 1939. Pp. 243. NcD, NcU.

An illustrated description and account of the old plantations of the Carolina Low Country.

TODD, JOHN REYNARD, and HUTSON, FRANCIS M. *Prince William's Parish and Plantations*. Richmond, Virginia: Garrett and Massie, 1935. Pp. xxiii, 265. NcD.

This beautiful volume with a series of well-chosen reproductions of photo-graphs preserves the records of a part of the South Carolina lowlands.

3. FICTION

ALEXANDER, LILLIE M. *Candy*. New York: Dodd, Mead and Co., 1934. Pp. 310. NcD, NcU, NcC.

A story of life among Negroes on a South Carolina cotton plantation.

BASSO, HAMILTON. *Cinnamon Seed*. New York: Charles Scribner's Sons, 1934. Pp. 379. NcD.

A faithful and realistic picture of modern life on a Louisiana plantation.

CARUTHERS, WILLIAM ALEXANDER. *The Cavaliers of Virginia; or, The Recluse of Jamestown. An Historical Romance*. 2 vols. New York: Harper, 1834-35. NcD, NcU.

Caruthers was the first to include in his novels the founders of the plantation system in Virginia "so that the light of other days might add to the glory of the present."

CHAPIN, (MRS.) SALLIE. *Fitz-Hugh St. Clair, the South Carolina Rebel Boy; or, It's No Crime to Be Born a Gentleman*. 2nd ed. Philadelphia: Claxton, 1873. Pp. 252. NcD, NcU.

"The fiercest note of unreconstructed sentiment in a vindication of the Carolina plantation."

CHESTNUTT, CHARLES W. *The Conjure Woman*. Boston: Houghton Mifflin and Co., 1899. Pp. 299. NcD, NcU, NcC.

Seven tales of old North Carolina plantation life told in dialect.

COOKE, JOHN ESTEN. *The Virginia Comedians; or, Old Days in the Old Dominion.* 2 vols. New York: D. Appleton and Co., 1854. NcD, NcU.
The foremost work of an ante-bellum novelist who "brought to relative perfection the glorification of the past."

DEFOE, DANIEL. "Life of Colonel Jack." Vol. I in *The Novels and Miscellaneous Works of Daniel Defoe.* London: G. Bell and Sons, 1891-96. NcD, NcU.
Defoe was "capitivated by the idea of Virginia as a land of beginning again for unfortunate Englishmen and his plantation, though wholly unlike the later literary image, contained certain romantic figures and episodes."

EDWARDS, HARRY STILLWELL. *Eneas Africanus.* Macon, Ga.: J. W. Burke Co., 1940. Pp. 40. NcD, NcU.
The humorous story of black Eneas who traveled through seven states over a period of eight years.

FREEMAN, (MRS.) MARY ELEANOR. *The Heart's Highway: A Romance of Virginia in the Seventeenth Century.* New York: Doubleday, Page and Co., 1900. Pp. 308. NcD, NcU.
Catches something of the spirit of the pre-Revolutionary plantations.

GILMORE, JAMES ROBERTS (EDMUND KIRKE, pseud.). *Among the Pines; or, South in Secession-Time.* New York: J. R. Gilmore, 1862. Pp. 310. NcD, NcU.
Old South Carolina plantation society, rich and idle.

GILMORE, JAMES ROBERTS (EDMUND KIRKE, pseud.). *My Southern Friends.* New York: Carleton, 1863. Pp. 308. NcD, NcU.
A novel contrasting two North Carolina plantations, one good, the other bad.

GLASGOW, ELLEN. *The Deliverance: A Romance of the Virginia Tobacco Fields.* New York: Doubleday, Page and Co., 1904. Pp. vii, 543. NcD, NcU, NcC.
The principal character, forced to work as a common laborer on the plantation his family had owned for generations, ends by repossessing the estate.

GLASGOW, ELLEN. *Barren Ground.* New York: Grosset and Dunlap, 1925. Pp. 511. NcD, NcU, NcC.
The story of meager lives in rural Virginia shown along with the possibility of inner enrichment and growth.

GLASGOW, ELLEN. *The Battle-Ground.* Garden City: Doubleday, Doran and Co., 1936. Pp. vii, 512. NcD, NcU.
The beginning of a new and realistic attitude in plantation fiction. The interest of the author "is in the extinction of the plantation and the cavalier types in the face of new conditions."

GODCHAUX, ELMA. *Stubborn Roots.* New York: The Macmillan Co., 1936. Pp. 404. NcD.
This novel deals exclusively with the lives of the various members of the self-contained, isolated sugar cane plantation in Louisiana.

HARRISON, CONSTANCE CARY. *Flower de Hundred: The Story of a Virginia Plantation.* New York: The Century Company, 1899. Pp. 301. NcD, NcU.
"One of the fullest studies of plantation life just before the Civil War."

HUGGINS, CLELIE BENTON. *Point Noir.* Boston: Houghton Mifflin Co., 1937. Pp. 532. NcD, NcU, NcC.
A story of a gloomy plantation in Louisiana, the home of a wealthy neurotic Creole family.

JOHNSTON, MARY. *Lewis Rand*. Boston: Houghton Mifflin Co., 1908. Pp. viii, 510. NcD, NcU, NcC.
The caste structure of Virginia in the late Jeffersonian period.

KENNEDY, JOHN PENDLETON. *Swallow Barn; or, A Sojourn in the Old Dominion*. New York: Harcourt, Brace and Co., 1929. Pp. xxxiv, 422. NcD, NcU.
Here the plantation is used for the first time solely for its own glamorous qualities—the big house, the old furniture, the gardens, the pattern of society.

MERCIER, ALFRED. *L'Habitation Saint-Ybars; ou, Maîtres et Esclaves en Louisiane, récit social*. Novelle-Orléans: Imprimerie Franco-Américaine, 1881. Pp. 234. NcD, NcU.
A novel of life on a Louisiana plantation owned by Creoles about the time of the Civil War. Much of the story is autobiographical and contains many pages of dialogue in the Creole dialect.

MITCHELL, MARGARET. *Gone With The Wind*. New York: The Macmillan Co., 1936. Pp. 1037. NcD, NcU, NcC.
A best-seller whole-heartedly in the Southern tradition.

MUNZ, CHARLES CURTIS. *Land Without Moses*. New York: Harper and Brothers, 1938. Pp. 370. NcD.
The stark insecurity of the sharecropper system is shown in this novel.

PAULDING, JAMES KIRKE. *Westward Ho!* 2 vols. New York: J. and J. Harper, 1832. NcD, NcU.
A significant early novel linking Virginia and Kentucky.

POSTL, KARL (CHARLES SEALSFIELD, pseud.). *Life in the New World; or Sketches of American Society*. Translated from the German by G. C. Hebbe and James Mackay. New York: J. Winchester, 1844. Pp. 349. NcD.
A series of seven stories bound in one volume. "A work of uncommon realism."

SIMMS, WILLIAM GILMORE. *Life in America; or, The Wigwam and the Cabin*. Aberdeen: G. Clark and Son, 1848. Pp. 311. NcD, NcU.
In this collection of stories, Simms gives glimpses of the plantation life of lower South Carolina.

TROUBETZKOY, AMÉLIE RIVES CHANLER. *Virginia of Virginia, a Story*. New York: Harper and Brothers, 1888. Pp. 222. NcD, NcU.
A story of Virginia with characterizations of Negroes and whites and their relationships on the plantation.

TUCKER, St. GEORGE. *Hansford: A Tale of Bacon's Rebellion*. Richmond: G. M. West, 1857. NcU. Republished under the title *The Devoted Bride; or, Faith and Fidelity*. Philadelphia: T. B. Peterson and Brothers, 1878. Pp. 356. NcD.
The action of the story develops upon a colonial plantation described as "a little independent barony."

VII. The American Negro Population

FRY, CHARLES LUTHER. "The Negro in the United States: a Statistical Statement," *Annals of the American Academy of Political and Social Science*, CXL (November, 1928), 26-35. NcD, NcU, NcC.
The elementary facts concerning the number of Negroes, their increase and distribution.

GOVER, MARY. "Increase of the Negro Population in the United States," *Human Biology*, I (May, 1929), 263-73. NcD, NcU.
American Negroes have more than held their own with whites biologically.

HOLMES, SAMUEL JACKSON. "The Increasing Growth-Rate of the Negro Population," *American Journal of Sociology*, XLII (September, 1936), 202-14. NcD, NcU.
"The restriction of immigration, the decline in the birth rate among whites, the reduction of the Negro death rate, and the increasing opportunities for employment in industry in the United States would seem to favor an increase in the Negro population."

LORIMER, FRANK, and OSBORN, FREDERICK. *Dynamics of Population. Social and Biological Significance of Changing Birth Rates in the United States.* New York: The Macmillan Co., 1934. Pp. xiii, 461. NcD, NcU.
An important study of the trend of the national population.

MYRDAL, GUNNAR. *An American Dilemma.* 2 vols. (Vol. I, Chap. 7, "Population"). New York: Harper and Brothers, 1944. NcD, NcU, NcC.
Except for the first decade of the nineteenth century and the 1930's the proportion of Negroes in the population of the United States has been steadily declining.

SMITH, T. LYNN. "A Demographic Study of the American Negro," *Social Forces*, XXIII (March, 1945), 379-87. NcD, NcU, NcC.
" . . . a summary of the data concerning the demographic situation and trends among the American Negro population."

UNITED STATES, Bureau of the Census. *Negroes in the United States.* Bulletin No. 8. Washington: U. S. Government Printing Office, 1904. Pp. 333. NcU.
In addition to a number of tables not published in the twelfth or previous censuses, this volume contains an important analysis of population and vital statistics by Walter F. Willcox, and an important section on the Negro farmer by W. E. B. DuBois. This is the first census study of the Negro for the nation as a whole.

UNITED STATES, Bureau of the Census. *Negroes in the United States.* Bulletin No. 129. Washington: U. S. Government Printing Office, 1915. Pp. 207. NcD.
Based on the thirteenth census and contains statistics on population, occupations, agriculture, mortality, and religious affiliation.

UNITED STATES, Bureau of the Census. *Negro Population, 1790-1915.* Washington: U. S. Government Printing Office, 1918. Pp. 844. NcD, NcU.
Growth and Geographic Distribution: 1790-1910; Migration Displacement and Segregation; Physical Characteristics; Vital Statistics; Educational and Social Statistics; Economic Statistics; General Tables.

UNITED STATES, Bureau of the Census. *Negroes in the United States, 1920-1932.* Washington: U. S. Government Printing Office, 1935. Pp. xvi, 845. NcD, NcU, NcC.
Supplements the census volume "Negro Population in the United States, 1790-1915," published in 1918.
UNITED STATES, Bureau of the Census. *Negro Population, 1930. A Listing of the 695 Cities and Urban Places Having 1,000 or More Negro Inhabitants.* Washington: U. S. Government Printing Office, 1935. Pp. 6. NcD.
Negroes are not only moving to town, they are moving to the big towns.
UNITED STATES, National Resources Committee. *The Problems of a Changing Population.* Washington: U. S. Government Printing Office, 1938. Pp. iv, 306. NcD, NcU.
The Negro and other minority groups are considered in relation to general population trends.
WILLCOX, WALTER F. *Studies in American Demography.* (Chap. 8, "Statistics of Race"). Ithaca, New York: Cornell University Press, 1940. NcD, NcU, NcC.
A survey of race as a census classification by a foremost authority.

VIII. The Racial Balance of Births and Deaths

ALLEN, RUTH. *The Labor of Women in the Production of Cotton.* Austin: University of Texas, 1931. Pp. 285. NcD, NcU.

A comparative study of white, Negro, and Mexican women agricultural workers in Texas. The Mexican woman has a willingness to accept a lower standard of living than either the white or the Negro woman. This fact coupled with her willingness to bear children in larger numbers are factors in the ability of the Mexicans to compete successfully in the production of cotton.

BURNEY, L. E. "Control of Syphilis in a Southern Rural Area," *American Journal of Public Health,* XXIX (September, 1939), 1006-14. NcD, NcU, NcC.

The low incomes of both white and Negro families in the rural plantation South make public provision for the treatment of syphilis necessary.

CLEMENTS, FORREST. "Racial Differences in Mortality and Morbidity," *Human Biology,* III (September, 1931), 397-419. NcD, NcU.

Comparative data on Negroes, Indians, and native-born whites are presented.

CORNELY, PAUL B., and ALEXANDER, VIRGINIA M. "The Health Status of the Negro in the United States," *Journal of Negro Education,* VIII (July, 1939), 359-75. NcD, NcU, NcC.

"A comparison of the health progress of the Negro as compared with that of the white group during the past two decades and a consideration of the progress being made in the United States to meet the health problems of the Negro."

DAVIS, MICHAEL MARKS. "Problems of Health Service for Negroes," *Journal of Negro Education,* VI (July, 1937), 438-49. NcD, NcU, NcC.

"Race relations in the South accentuate the economic problem of the Negro by limiting his access to existing medical facilities and services."

DEADERICK, WILLIAM HEISKELL, and THOMPSON, LOYD. *The Endemic Diseases of the Southern States.* Philadelphia: W. B. Saunders Co., 1916. Pp. 546. NcD, NcU.

The diseases considered are: malaria, blackwater fever, pellagra, amebic dysentery, and hookworm.

DICKENS, DOROTHY, and FORD, ROBERT N. "Geophagy (dirt-eating) Among Mississippi Negro School Children," *American Sociological Review,* VII (February, 1942), 59-65. NcD, NcU.

Twenty-five per cent of the children studied were known dirt-eaters. The authors believe that dirt-eating may be due to an iron deficiency or to a cultural trait.

DOULL, JAMES A. "Comparative Racial Immunity to Diseases," *Journal of Negro Education,* VI (July, 1937), 429-37. NcD, NcU, NcC.

"The whole subject of comparative racial immunity to disease is a field of research which has been but little tilled."

DUBLIN, LOUIS I. "Life, Death and the Negro," *American Mercury,* XII (September, 1927), 37-45. NcD, NcU, NcC.

A rearward and a forward look at our Negro population. A population of only fourteen and a half million for the year 2000 is predicted.

DUBLIN, LOUIS I. "The Health of the Negro," *Annals of the American Academy of Political and Social Science,* CXL (November, 1928), 77-85. NcD, NcU, NcC.
Based upon data collected by the Metropolitan Life Insurance Company over a period of many years.

EZDORF, RUDOLPH HERMAN VON. *Malaria in the United States: its Prevalence and Geographic Distribution,* pp. 1603-24. Public Health Service Reprint No. 277, or P. H. Reports, Vol. 30, No. 22. Washington: U. S. Government Printing Office, 1915. NcD, NcU.
A study based upon the replies to a circular inquiry addressed to all doctors and state health officers in eight Southern states. The report covered the period from 1910 to 1915.

FRAZIER, E. FRANKLIN. "Psychological Factors in Negro Health," *Social Forces,* III (March, 1925), 488-90. NcD, NcU, NcC.
Chronic ill-health "affords the Negro that defense against self-depreciation that is intolerable."

GARVIN, C. H. "Immunity to Disease Among Dark Skinned People," *Opportunity,* IV (August, 1926), 242-45. NcU.
There is a difference in susceptibility to disease between races of men, but there is no absolute racial immunity to any disease.

GIBSON, JOHN M. "Black Man and the Great White Plague," *Social Forces,* XIV (May, 1936), 585-90. NcD, NcU, NcC.
Tuberculosis, a rarity among Negroes prior to the Civil War, now is responsible for the death of one-tenth of the Negroes dying in the United States. The disease among Negroes is definitely curable but the chief difficulty is that of getting the Negro patient in time to effect a cure.

GOVER, MARY. *Mortality Among Negroes in the United States.* Public Health Bulletin, No. 174. Washington: U. S. Government Printing Office, 1928. Pp. vi, 63. NcD, NcU, NcC.
Based upon the 1920 census report.

GOVER, MARY. "Trend of Mortality Among Southern Negroes Since 1920," *Journal of Negro Education,* VI (July, 1937), 276-88. NcD, NcU, NcC.
Mortality among Negroes in the ten Southern states of the Registration Area of 1920 has declined from 16.2 in 1922 to 15.8 per 1,000 in 1932, or 2.5 per cent.

HAZEN, H. H. "A Leading Cause of Death Among Negroes: Syphilis," *Journal of Negro Education,* VI (July, 1937), 310-21. NcD, NcU, NcC.
Concludes that among the poorer classes syphilis is twice as prevalent among Negroes as among whites.

HAZEN, H. H. *Syphilis in the Negro.* Washington: U. S. Government Printing Office, 1942. Pp. ix, 96. NcD,
There is a disposition to identify the syphilis problem in the United States with the Negro race.

"THE Health Status and Health Education of Negroes in the United States," *Journal of Negro Education,* Vol. VI, No. 3 (July, 1937). NcD, NcU, NcC.
The sixth Yearbook of the *Journal.* Thirty-three articles and a bibliography devoted to a critical survey of the health status, health facilities, and health education of Negroes in the United States.

HOFFMAN, FREDERICK LUDWIG. *Race Traits and Tendencies of the American Negro.* Publications of the American Economic Association, XI, 1-3. New York: The Macmillan Co., 1896. Pp. 329. NcD, NcU.

The first extensive research into Negro mortality trends. The author thought that gradual extinction was only a question of time.

HOFFMAN, FREDERICK LUDWIG. *Malaria in Virginia, North Carolina, and South Carolina.* New York: The Prudential Press, 1933. Pp. 30. NcD, NcU.

Statistics showing the decrease in the death rate due to malaria in these three states.

HOLMES, SAMUEL JACKSON. "The Principal Causes of Death Among Negroes: a General Comparative Statement," *Journal of Negro Education,* VI (July, 1937), 289-302. NcD, NcU, NcC.

From the standpoint of biological survival the most formidable enemies of the Negro are tuberculosis, respiratory infections, venereal disease, uterine cancer, and intestinal disorders of infancy.

HOLMES, SAMUEL JACKSON. *The Negro's Struggle for Survival: A Study in Human Ecology.* Berkeley: University of California Press, 1937. Pp. xii, 296. NcD, NcU, NcC.

A study made from the point of view of one who observes the struggle for survival between two rival species inhabiting the same territory.

HOLMES, SAMUEL JACKSON. "The Trend of the Racial Balance of Births and Deaths," in Edgar T. Thompson, ed., *Race Relations and the Race Problem.* Durham: Duke University Press, 1939. NcD, NcU, NcC.

" . . . the fate of the Negroes will be decided on the farms and in the small villages of the Southern states. The future development of agriculture in the South will have much to do in deciding this issue."

HOLMES, SAMUEL JACKSON, and PARKER, S. L. "The Stabilized Natural Increase of the Negro," *Journal of the American Statistical Association,* XXVI (June, 1931), 159-71. N. S. No. 174. NcD, NcU.

Unlike the whites, the Negroes of the United States owe relatively little of their increase to immigration from abroad. The rural South has prevented the actual decrease in the Negro population.

JONES, R. FRANK, and PRICE, KLINE A. "The Incidence of Gonorrhea Among Negroes," *Journal of Negro Education,* VI (July, 1937), 364-76. NcD, NcU, NcC.

Although the incidence is high "gonorrhea is not a peculiar element magically attaching itself to Negroes alone."

KLASSEN, PETER P. "Differential Reproduction Rates of the White and Negro Populations in Selected Areas of the South," *Southwestern Social Science Quarterly,* XX (September, 1939), 193-204. NcD, NcU.

"Due to the factor of better industrial opportunities in the Northern states, the decrease of our total white northern population to a point below the permanent replacement level and the increase of certain southern groups to a point considerably above the permanent replacement level, there has been an extensive migration of southern people to the North."

LEWIS, JULIAN H. *The Biology of the Negro.* Chicago: The University of Chicago Press, 1942. Pp. xvii, 433. NcD, NcU, NcC.

"A study of the physical and biological constitution of Negroes, American and African, and their reaction to disease."

MOSSELL, SADIE T. "The Standard of Living Among One Hundred Negro Migrant Families in Philadelphia," *Annals of the American Academy of Political and Social Science,* XCVIII (November, 1921), 173-218. NcD, NcU.

A statistical study of the standard of living of this group with a discussion of the obstacles to a maintenance of a fair standard and how these could be counteracted in regard to the whole migratory movement to Philadelphia.

NATIONAL Tuberculosis Association. *Report of the Committee on Tuberculosis Among Negroes.* New York: National Tuberculosis Association, 1937. Pp. 77. NcD.

A five-year study and what it accomplished.

ORNSTEIN, GEORGE G. "The Leading Causes of Death Among Negroes: Tuberculosis," *Journal of Negro Education,* VI (July, 1937), 303-9. NcD, NcU, NcC.

High incidence of tuberculosis among Negroes is not to be accounted for as a racial characteristic but as an effect of environmental conditions.

SEBRELL, W. H. "The Nature of Nutritional Diseases Occurring in the South," *The Milbank Memorial Fund Quarterly,* XVII (October, 1939), 358-66. NcD, NcU.

Scurvy, beriberi, nutritional edema, and nutritional anemia occur throughout the South but pellagra is the most widespread deficiency disease in the region.

STILES, CHARLES WARDELL. "Hookworm Disease in Its Relation to the Negro," *United States Public Health and Marine Hospital Service.* Reprint No. 36 from the *Public Health Reports,* Vol. XXIV, No. 31 (July 30, 1909), pp. 1083-89. NcD.

Concludes that the Negro presents relative immunity to the direct effects of hookworm infection when compared with whites.

STITT, EDWARD RHODES. "Our Disease Inheritance from Slavery," *United States Naval Medical Bulletin,* XXVI (October, 1928), 801-17. NcD, NcU.

Discusses (1) diseases among the Indians, (2) diseases introduced by European colonists, and (3) diseases probably introduced from Africa.

TANDY, ELIZABETH C. *Infant and Maternal Mortality Among Negroes.* Washington: Department of Labor, Children's Bureau, Bureau Publication No. 243, 1937. Pp. 34. NcD, NcU.

In the area studied the rural infant mortality rate for 1933-1935 was 56 per 1,000 for white infants and 80 per 1,000 for Negro infants.

IX. The Negro Physical Type

BARNES, IRENE. "The Inheritance of Pigmentation in the American Negro," *Human Biology*, I (September, 1929), 321-81. NcD, NcU.
How is pigmentation in the American Negro inherited? How does it behave in race crosses?

COBB, W. MONTAGUE. "The Physical Constitution of the American Negro," *Journal of Negro Education*, III (July, 1934), 340-88. NcD, NcU, NcC.
A critical review of the results of investigations.

COBB, W. MONTAGUE. "Physical Anthropology of the American Negro," *American Journal of Physical Anthropology*, XXIX (June, 1942), 113-223. NcD, NcU.
One of the most important discussions of the subject.

HERSKOVITS, MELVILLE J. "Some Physical Characteristics of the American Negro Population," *Journal of Social Forces*, VI (September, 1927), 93-98. NcD, NcU, NcC.
Concludes that the American Negro is evolving a new physical type.

HERSKOVITS, MELVILLE J. *The Anthropometry of the American Negro*. New York: Columbia University Press, 1930. Pp. xi, 283. NcD, NcU.
Measurements and descriptions of American Negroes.

HRDLIČKA, ALEŠ. "Anthropology of the American Negro: Historical Notes," *American Journal of Physical Anthropology*, X (April-June, 1927), 205-35. NcD, NcU.
A review of the most important literature dealing with the physical anthropology of the Negro.

HRDLIČKA, ALEŠ. "The Full-Blood American Negro," *American Journal of Physical Anthropology*, XII (July-September, 1928), 15-53. NcD, NcU.
A study of the physical anthropology of the full-blood American Negro as a base for the study of other full and mixed stocks.

HUBER, ERNST. *Evolution of Facial Musculature and Facial Expression*. Baltimore: The Johns Hopkins Press, 1931. Pp. xii, 184. NcD.
Includes a comparison of facial musculature and expression in different human races. Maintains that the Negro has a less differentiated mimetic musculature.

JOHNSON, CHARLES S., and BOND, HORACE M. "The Investigation of Racial Differences Prior to 1910," *Journal of Negro Education*, III (July, 1934), 328-39. NcD, NcU, NcC.
Indices of race have been introduced at points in time where the cultural use of "scientific facts" becomes expedient.

"THE Physical and Mental Abilities of the American Negro," *Journal of Negro Education*, Vol. III, No. 3 (July, 1934). NcD, NcU, NcC.
The third Yearbook of the *Journal* containing fifteen articles and a bibliography.

TODD, T. WINGATE. "Entrenched Negro Physical Features," *Human Biology*, I (January, 1929), 57-69. NcD, NcU.
Some so-called Negro physical traits are said to disappear rapidly in race mixture. Others persist tenaciously.

X. White and Negro Intelligence

ARLITT, ADA HART, "On the Need for Caution in Establishing Race Norms," *Journal of Applied Psychology*, V (June, 1921), 179-83. NcD, NcU.
" . . . there is more likeness between children of the same social status but different race than between children of the same race but of different social status."

BRIGHAM, CARL C. *A Study of American Intelligence.* Princeton: Princeton University Press, 1923. Pp. xxv, 210. NcD, NcU.
An analysis of the data from the intelligence tests administered to United States Army conscripts in the First World War. The author's interpretation of the data, later repudiated by him, supported the thesis of the racial superiority of the Nordic stock.

BRIGHAM, CARL C. "Intelligence Tests of Immigrant Groups," *Psychological Review*, XXXVII (March, 1930), 158-65. NcD, NcU.
"This review has summarized some of the more recent test findings which show that comparative studies of various national and racial groups may not be made with existing tests. . . . In particular one of the most pretentious of these comparative racial studies—the writer's own—was without foundation."

BRUCE, MYRTLE. "Factors Affecting Intelligence Test Performance of Whites and Negroes in the Rural South," *Archives of Psychology*, Vol. XXXVI, No. 252 (July, 1940). Pp. 100. NcD, NcU.
In tests administered in a rural community in Virginia whites scored higher than Negroes but both whites and Negroes scored lower than the national average.

DANIEL, ROBERT P. *A Psychological Study of Delinquent and Non-Delinquent Negro Boys.* New York: Columbia University Press, 1932. Pp. vi, 59. NcD, NcU.
Such characteristics as emotional stability, personal attitudes, ethical judgment, and trustworthiness were studied.

FERGUSON, GEORGE OSCAR, JR. *The Psychology of the Negro: An Experimental Study.* Columbia University Contributions to Philosophy and Psychology, Vol. XXV, No. 1. New York: Science Press, 1916. Pp. 138. NcD.
Investigations for this study were made in 1914 upon pupils in three Virginia cities. The author concludes that "in view of all the evidence it does not seem possible to raise the scholastic attainment of the Negro to an equality with that of the white. It is probable that no expenditure of time and money would accomplish this end."

GARTH, THOMAS R. "A Review of Racial Psychology," *Psychological Bulletin*, XXII (June, 1925), 343-64. NcD, NcU.
A very complete review of the literature.

GARTH, THOMAS R. *Race Psychology.* New York: McGraw-Hill Book Co., 1931. Pp. xiv, 260. NcD, NcU.
A survey of the problem of racial differences in mentality.

GARTH, THOMAS R. "The Hypothesis of Racial Difference," *Journal of Social Philosophy*, II (April, 1937), 224-31. NcD, NcU.

Concludes that differences are the result of one of two factors, the factor of selection or the factor of nurture.

GRAY, C. Y., and BINGHAM, C. W. "A Comparison of Certain Phases of Musical Ability of Colored and White Public School Pupils," *Journal of Educational Psychology*, XX (October, 1929), 501-6. NcD, NcU.

The Seashore Test of Musical Ability when administered to 258 Negro and 219 white school children in two Texas communities showed superiority in the whites in the measures for pitch, intensity, time, and musical memory. Scores for consonance were approximately equal. Scores for rhythm not given.

HIRSCH, NATHANIEL D. "A Study of Natio-Racial Mental Differences," *Genetic Psychology Monographs*, Vol. I, Nos. 3 and 4 (May and July, 1926), 239-406. NcD, NcU.

A study of the mental capacity and anthropomorphic characteristics of some of the national and ethnic groups living in the United States.

JENKINS, MARTIN D. "The Mental Ability of the American Negro," *Journal of Negro Education*, VIII (July, 1939), 511-20. NcD, NcU, NcC.

A summary of the findings of various intelligence tests.

JENKINS, MARTIN D. "The Intelligence of Negro Children," *Educational Method*, XIX (November, 1939), 106-12. NcD, NcU.

Critical analysis of research methodology in this field.

JOHNSON, GUY B. "A Summary of Negro Scores on the Seashore Music Talent Tests," *Journal of Comparative Psychology*, XI (April, 1930), 383-93. NcD, NcU.

Tests administered to North Carolina Negroes in sense of pitch, sense of intensity, and sense of time show no conclusive evidence either of inferiority or superiority to whites. The prescribed Seashore technique is not fully adequate when applied to Negro subjects in the South.

KLINEBERG, OTTO. *Negro Intelligence and Selective Migration.* New York: Columbia University Press, 1935. Pp. 66. NcD, NcU.

Concludes that equalizing the environments of Negroes and whites would completely eliminate the so-called inferiority of Negro intelligence.

KLINEBERG, OTTO. "Experimental Studies of Negro Personality," in Otto Klineberg, ed., *Characteristics of the American Negro.* New York: Harper and Brothers, 1944. NcD, NcU, NcC.

A summary and evaluation of results obtained from the administration of tests of intelligence and personality.

LONG, HOWARD H. "The Intelligence of Colored Elementary Pupils in Washington, D. C.," *Journal of Negro Education*, III (April, 1934), 205-22. NcD, NcU, NcC.

" . . . the wonder is not that the colored children of Washington fail to equal the whites in I. Q. score, but that their I.Q.'s are as high as they are."

McGRAW, MYRTLE BRYAN. "A Comparative Study of a Group of Southern White and Negro Infants," *Genetic Psychology Monographs*, Vol. X, No. 1 (July, 1931). Pp. 105. NcD, NcU.

"It is significant that even with very young subjects when environmental factors are minimized, the same type and approximately the same degree of superiority is evidenced on the part of the white subjects as that found among other groups."

MAYO, MARION JACOB. "The Mental Capacity of the American Negro," *Archives of Psychology*, Vol. IV, No. 28 (November, 1913). Pp. iii, 70. NcD, NcU.

A comparative study of relative efficiency in scholarship of white and Negro pupils in New York City high schools. In the view of the author there is a measurable degree of superiority on the part of the white pupils.

MEAD, MARGARET. "The Methodology of Racial Testing: Its Significance for Sociology," *American Journal of Sociology,* XXXI (March, 1926), 657-67. NcD, NcU.

The author stresses the importance of giving careful consideration to the factors of language, education, and social status in interpreting the results of intelligence tests.

NATHANSON, YALE S. "The Musical Ability of the Negro," *Annals of the American Academy of Political and Social Science,* CXL (November, 1928), 186-90. NcD, NcU, NcC.

There is no evidence to permit us to evaluate the musical ability of the Negro as definitely inferior or superior to the musical talent of the Caucasian.

PETERSON, JOSEPH. "The Comparative Abilities of White and Negro Children," *Comparative Psychology Monographs,* Vol. I, No. 5 (July, 1923). Pp. 141. NcD, NcU.

" . . . there seems to be a fair degree of evidence to indicate, though there is not yet proof of it, that the chief deficiencies of the negroes do lie along the line of abstract thinking, logical analysis, and mental reconstruction."

PETERSON, JOSEPH. "Basic Considerations of Methodology in Race Testing," *Journal of Negro Education,* III (July, 1934), 403-10. NcD, NcU, NcC.
Criticizes traditional methods of race testing.

PETERSON, JOSEPH, and LANIER, LYLE H. "Studies in the Comparative Abilities of Whites and Negroes," *Mental Measurement Monographs,* No. 5 (February, 1929). Pp. vi, 156. NcD, NcU.

The authors feel their studies establish the "enormous and reliable superiority of whites over Negroes."

PRICE, J. ST. CLAIR. "Negro-White Differences in General Intelligence," *Journal of Negro Education,* III (July, 1934), 424-52. NcD, NcU, NcC.

Demonstrates the inadequacy of our measurement of the intelligence of the Negro.

STRONG, ALICE C. "Three Hundred Fifty White and Colored Children Measured by the Simon-Binet Scale of Intelligence: A Comparative Study," *Pedagogical Seminary,* XX (December, 1913), 485-515. NcD, NcU.

A report on the first application of the Binet tests to white and Negro school children. In Columbia, South Carolina, where the tests were given, white mill children scored midway between Negro children and white city children.

TANSER, H. A. *The Settlement of Negroes in Kent County, Ontario, and a Study of the Mental Capacity of Their Descendents.* Chatham, Ontario, Canada: The Shepard Publishing Co., 1939. Pp. 187. NcD, NcU, NcC.

Whites are found to be superior to Negroes in every test, but the writer advises caution in the interpretation of the results.

WITTY, P. A., and JENKINS, M.A. "The Case of B........, a Gifted Negro Girl," *Journal of Social Psychology,* VI (February, 1935), 117-24. NcD, NcU.

A Negro girl of apparently unmixed stock whose I. Q. falls in the very highest range.

WOODWORTH, ROBERT S. "Racial Differences in Mental Traits," *Science,* XXXI (February, 1910), 171-86. N.S. NcD, NcU, NcC.

Racial differences in sensory powers, mental and motor performances, and intelligence are slight.

WOODWORTH, ROBERT S. "Comparative Psychology of Races," *Psychological Bulletin*, XIII (October 15, 1916), 388-97. NcD, NcU.

A review of the literature.

WOOFTER, THOMAS J., JR. "Difficulties in Measuring Racial Mental Traits," *Social Forces*, XIII (March, 1935), 415-18. NcD, NcU, NcC.

The careless interpretations of the results of psychological tests have led to conclusions not in harmony with the facts.

XI. The Races on the Land

ALLEN, JAMES S. "The Struggle for Land During the Reconstruction Period,"
Science and Society, I (Spring, 1937), 378-401. NcD.
The story of the failure of the post-bellum movement in the South to con-
fiscate and partition the plantations.

BANKS, E. M. *The Economics of Land Tenure in Georgia.* Columbia University Studies in History, Economics, and Public Law, Vol. XXIII, No. 1
(1905). Pp. 142. NcD, NcU.
A study of the changes in relations between men and land in Georgia. Using
such sources as original tax records, Banks shows that the number of landholders
among the whites increased from 1873 to 1902 by 56 per cent, the period of
change being the greatest before 1880.

BIZZELL, WILLIAM B. *Farm Tenancy in the United States. A Study of the
Historical Development of Farm Tenancy and Its Economic and Social Consequences on Rural Welfare, with Special Reference to Conditions in the
South and Southwest.* Texas Agricultural Experiment Station Bulletin, No.
278 (April, 1921). Pp. 408. NcD, NcU.
A comprehensive survey of farm tenancy conceived as essentially a feudal
product.

BROOKS, R. P. "A Local Study of the Race Problem: Race Relations in the
Eastern Piedmont Region of Georgia," *Political Science Quarterly,* XXVI
(June, 1911), 193-221. NcD, NcU.
Population changes, loss of a common ideology, loss of control, and a reduc-
tion in the size of land and farm units all seem to go together and to react
upon each other to effect social change.

COLVIN, ESTHER M., and FOLSOM, JOSEPH C., comps. *Agricultural Labor
in the United States, 1915-1935.* U. S. Department of Agriculture, Bureau of
Agricultural Economics, Bibliography No. 64. Pp. vii, 493. NcD.
A selected list of references.

COMAN, KATHARINE. "The Negro as a Peasant Farmer," *American Statistical Association Publications*, IX (June, 1904), 39-54. N.S., No. 66. NcD,
NcU.
"Neither the wage system nor the métayer system can be regarded as the ulti-
mate solution of the Southern labor problem. Nowhere is Mill's classic conten-
tion for the economic advantages of peasant proprietorship better exemplified.
The African is endowed with a land hunger like that of the French peasantry."

DUBOIS, W. E. B. *The Negro Landholder in Georgia.* U. S. Department of
Labor, Bulletin No. 35. Washington: U. S. Government Printing Office, 1901.
Pp. 130. NcD, NcU.
Showing the gradual acquisition of landed property by Georgia Negroes from
the Civil War until the time of this study.

FORTUNE, T. THOMAS. *Black and White: Land, Labor and Politics in the
South.* New York: Fords, Howard and Hulburt, 1884. Pp. iv, 310. NcD,
NcU, NcC.
The author, a Negro born in Florida before the Civil War, was one of the
first to call attention to the importance of the land as the physical basis of
slavery and share-cropping.

GOTTLIEB, MANUEL. "The Land Question in Georgia During Reconstruction," *Science and Society*, III (Summer, 1939), 356-88. NcD.
A discussion of the freedman's desire and struggle for land. Important historical facts are brought together.

HAINES, HAROLD H. *The Callaghan Mail 1821-1859. A Book Featuring the Lives of William Callaghan and his Slave, Isaac Crawford*. Hannibal, Missouri: The Author, 1944. Pp. 70. NcD.
Master and slave on a thinly settled frontier opposed the Indians, cleared the land, built the cabins, and planted the crops together.

HARTMAN, WILLIAM ALBERT, and WOOTEN, H. H. *Georgia Land Use Problems*. University of Georgia Experiment Station Bulletin No. 191, May, 1935. Pp. 195. NcD.
Character of land ownership as related to land use problems in the Old Plantation Piedmont Cotton Belt. Economic and social status of farm operators in this area. Illustrated with charts and maps.

HARTSHORNE, RICHARD. "Racial Maps of the United States," *Geographical Review*, XXVIII (April, 1938), 276-88. NcD, NcU.
Maps showing the proportion of Negroes, Mexicans, Indians, Orientals, and foreign-born whites to the total population, by counties. Accompanying text.

HOLLINGSHEAD, A. B. "Changes in Land Ownership as an Index of Succession in Rural Communities," *American Journal of Sociology*, XLIII (March, 1938), 764-77. NcD, NcU, NcC.
A point of view for the study of racial competition for the land.

HULBERT, ARCHER BUTLER. *Soil; Its Influence on the History of the United States, with Special Reference to Migration and the Scientific Study of Local History*. New Haven: Yale University Press, 1930. Pp. x, 227. NcD, NcU.
A study of the role of the soil in the process of land settlement. The various kinds of soil and vegetation constitute the molds in which different types of economics and social structures are developed.

JOHNSON, CHARLES S., EMBREE, EDWIN R., and ALEXANDER, WILL W. *The Collapse of Cotton Tenancy: Summary of Field Studies and Statistical Surveys, 1933-1935*. Chapel Hill: The University of North Carolina Press, 1935. Pp. ix, 81. NcD, NcU, NcC.
The present situation in the South is described as "our greatest social humiliation," and cotton tenancy is pictured as possibly even worse than slavery.

LEWIS, EDWARD E. "Recent Farm-Ownership Changes in the Cotton Belt and Their Significance for Migration," *Social Forces*, XIII (December, 1934), 238-44. NcD, NcU, NcC.
During the period studied farm ownership tended to increase among both whites and Negroes but with increase more widespread among Negroes than among whites.

LEWIS, EDWARD E. "Some Pre-Depression Land Tenure Changes in the South and Their Current Significance," *American Economic Review*, XXVI (September, 1936), 441-50. NcD, NcU, NcC.
"The depression of 1923-1934 marked quite definitely the termination of the period of non-agricultural opportunity for the Negro such as he enjoyed in the war and post-war years. The incentives for remaining in or returning to agriculture were thus vastly increased for the Negro as compared with the white farmer."

MENDENHALL, MARJORIE S. "The Rise of Southern Tenancy," *Yale Review*, XXVII (September, 1937), 110-29. NcD, NcU.

Share-tenancy did not originate in an upward change of status for Negroes after the Civil War; it originated in a downward change of status for whites long before the war.

POE, CLARENCE H. "What Is Justice Between the White Man and the Black Man in the Rural South?" in *Lectures and Addresses on the Negro in the South.* Publications of the University of Virginia, Phelps-Stokes Fellowship Papers, No. 1, Chap. 4. NcD, NcU.

In this address, delivered about 1914, Dr. Poe argued that the segregation of the races in the rural South was a matter of simple justice to the laboring white farmer. His arguments were denied by G. T. Stephenson in the *South Atlantic Quarterly,* XIII (April, 1914), 107-17, and by W. D. Weatherford in the *Survey,* XXXIII (January 2, 1915), 375-77. NcD, NcU.

PRICE, A. GRENFELL. *White Settlers in the Tropics.* New York: American Geographical Society, 1939. Pp. xiii, 311. NcD, NcU.

Dr. Price uses sample type areas like Queensland, Florida, the Caribbean, South Africa, and Panama to study the question of what does and what does not constitute a "white man's country."

RAPER, ARTHUR F. *Preface to Peasantry: A Tale of Two Black Belt Counties.* Chapel Hill: The University of North Carolina Press, 1936. Pp. xiii, 423. NcD, NcU, NcC.

A study of two representative counties in the Black Belt of Georgia with suggestions for a new land policy of restoration and rehabilitation.

RAPER, ARTHUR F. *Tenants of the Almighty.* New York: The Macmillan Co., 1943. Pp. xii, 403. NcD, NcU, NcC.

Dr. Raper's reporting and Jack Delano's photographs of Greene County, Georgia, tell a deeply human story.

ROBERTS, ELIZABETH MADOX. *The Time of Man.* New York: The Viking Press, 1926. Pp. 397. NcD, NcU, NcC.

A richly indigenous novel of tenant farming in Kentucky.

SPELLMAN, C. L. "A Negro Community in Action," *Rural Sociology,* X (June, 1945), 174-87. NcD, NcU.

Whites live in this community, but the white and Negro areas are not coterminous.

STEARNS, CHARLES. *The Black Man of the South and the Rebels.* New York: American News Company, 1872. Pp. xiii, 562. NcD, NcU.

It is the purpose of the author "to portray in these pages . . . the necessities of the Southern freedman, and then to show that these necessities cannot be effectually provided for without making him, among other things, the industrious owner of the land he cultivates."

THOMAS, WILLIAM HANNIBAL. *Negro Problems: Land and Education.* Boston: Wallace Spooner, 1890. Pp. 71. NcD.

The author advocated Negro land proprietorship through leases with the right of subsequent purchase.

THOMPSON, EDGAR T. "The Natural History of Agricultural Labor in the South." Chap. IV in David K. Jackson, ed., *American Studies in Honor of William K. Boyd.* Durham, North Carolina: Duke University Press, 1940. NcD, NcU, NcC.

The Southern plantation arose to deal with a labor problem which was capable of no complete and satisfactory solution, but which had to be faced.

UNITED STATES, Bureau of the Census. *The Negro Farmer in the United States.* Fifteenth Census of the United States: 1930 Census of Agriculture. Washington: U. S. Government Printing Office, 1933. Pp. 84. NcD, NcU.
A monograph covering the Negro farmer's migrations and agricultural status.
UNITED STATES, Special Committee on Farm Tenancy. *Farm Tenancy.* Prepared Under the Auspices of the National Resources Committee. Washington: U. S. Government Printing Office, 1937. Pp. viii, 108. NcD, NcU.
This report of the President's Committee emphasizes the insecurity of fully one-half the farm population of the United States, especially in the South.
VANCE, RUPERT B. *How the Other Half is Housed: A Pictorial Record of Sub-Minimum Farm Housing in the South.* Southern Policy Papers, No. 4. Chapel Hill: The University of North Carolina Press, 1936. Pp. 16. NcD, NcU.
Photographs picturing houses inhabited by tenants and squatters.
VANCE, RUPERT B. *Farmers Without Land.* Public Affairs Pamphlets No. 12. New York, 1937. Pp. 32. NcD, NcU.
A clear and brief account of the growth and nature of agricultural tenancy in the South.
VANCE, RUPERT B. "Racial Competition for the Land," in Edgar T. Thompson, ed., *Race Relations and the Race Problem.* Durham: Duke University Press, 1939. NcD, NcU, NcC.
"Land ownership and land occupancy have . . . in interracial situations the world over become matters of conflict and of political action designed to restrict competition."
WHITE, R. CLYDE. "Cotton and Some Aspects of Southern Civilization," *Journal of Social Forces,* II (September, 1924), 651-54. NcD, NcU, NcC.
There is no significant correlation between cotton culture and the percentage of Negroes in the various cotton producing states. Neither is the correlation between cotton and illiteracy significant. On the other hand, cotton culture is favorable to tenancy, and tenancy and illiteracy go together.
WOODSON, CARTER G. *The Rural Negro.* Washington: The Association for the Study of Negro Life and History, 1930. Pp. xvi, 265. NcD, NcU, NcC.
A description of conditions among Negroes in a Southern rural section. Covers farming, health, tenancy and peonage, industry and trade, religion, education, and recreation.
WORK, MONROE N. "Racial Factors and Economic Forces in Land Tenure in the South," *Social Forces,* XV (December, 1936), 205-15. NcD, NcU, NcC.
The facts show a shrinkage of the black belt area and a somewhat more even distribution of the Negro population over the entire South.
ZEICHNER, OSCAR. "The Legal Status of the Agricultural Laborer in the South," *Political Science Quarterly,* LV (September, 1940), 412-28. NcD, NcU, NcC.
An analysis of some of the legislation affecting white and Negro tenants in certain Southern states enacted since 1865.

XII. The Poor White

BREWER, WILLIAM M. "Poor Whites and Negroes in the South Since the Civil War," *Journal of Negro History*, XV (January, 1930), 26-37. NcD, NcU, NcC.

"The poor white, under the leadership of demagogic politicians and with the connivance of the capitalists, is determined to render the Negro politically innocuous and economically subordinate."

BROWN, WILLIAM O. "Role of the Poor Whites in Race Contacts of the South," *Social Forces*, XIX (December, 1940), 258-68. NcD, NcU, NcC.

An analysis of the role of the economically disinherited white man in the pattern of Southern race relations.

BUCK, PAUL H. "The Poor Whites of the Ante-Bellum South," *American Historical Review*, XXXI (October, 1925), 41-54. NcD, NcU, NcC.

The poor whites of the South were not so much exploited as superfluous.

CALDWELL, ERSKINE. *Tobacco Road*. New York: Grosset and Dunlap, 1932. Pp. 241. NcD, NcU, NcC.

"Tobacco Road is strong meat. Too ludicrous for any free pity, too pitiful for any whole laughter, in it the people move from first to last like the still hungry but half rotten dead."

CRAVEN, AVERY O. "Poor Whites and Negroes in the Ante-Bellum South," *Journal of Negro History*, XV (January, 1930), 14-25. NcD, NcU, NcC.

A view of the Negro as a co-dweller with the plain white people in the lower rounds of life. There is a striking similarity between the way of life of the poor white and that of the Negro before the Civil War. In both groups women and children worked, households were unstable, religion was emotional, laziness was universal.

DOOB, LEONARD W. "Poor Whites: A Frustrated Class." Appendix I in John Dollard, *Caste and Class in a Southern Town*. New Haven: Yale University Press, 1937. NcD, NcU, NcC.

A discussion of the present status, knowledge, attitudes, and frustrations of poor whites near Southern Town.

"FLORIDA 'CRACKERS.'" *Littell's Living Age*, Fifth Series, CLIX (December, 1883), 625-29. NcD, NcU.

A picture of the poor whites of the Florida swamps.

GRAFFENRIED, CLAIRE DE. "The Georgia Cracker in the Cotton Mills," *Century Magazine*, XLI (February, 1891), 483-98. NcD, NcU, NcC.

The picture drawn is fifty years old but is still authentic.

HOLLANDER, A. N. J. DEN. *De Landelijke Arme Blanken in het Zuiden der Vereenigde Staten: een Sociaal-Historische en Sociografische Studie*. Groningen: J. B. Wolters', 1933. Pp. xiv, 517. NcD, NcU.

A good review of this important work on the Southern poor white may be found in *Social Forces*, XIV (March, 1936), 441-44.

HOLLANDER, A. N. J. DEN. "The Tradition of 'Poor Whites,' " in W. T. Couch, ed., *Culture in the South*. Chapel Hill: The University of North Carolina Press, 1935. NcD, NcU.

Hollander emphasizes the differentiation between the relatively large number of non-slaveholding white people (the yeomanry) and the "poor whites," and discusses the origin of the conception that all non-slaveholding people of the ante-bellum South were "poor whites."

HUNDLEY, DANIEL ROBINSON. *Social Relations in Our Southern States* (Chap. VII, "Poor White Trash"). New York: Henry B. Price, 1860. NcD. NcU.

An ante-bellum planter is puzzled to comprehend for what purpose "the miserable" wretches were even allowed to obtain a footing in this country.

McILWAINE, SHIELDS. *The Southern Poor White from Lubberland to Tobacco Road.* Norman: University of Oklahoma Press, 1939. Pp. xxv, 274. NcD, NcU, NcC.

The literary history of the poor white from William Byrd's *History of the Dividing Line* to Erskine Caldwell's *Tobacco Road.*

MELL, MILDRED R. *A Definitive Study of the Poor Whites of the South.* Ph.D. dissertation, University of North Carolina, 1938. Pp. 313. NcU.

The poor whites of the ante-bellum South were those whites who had no recognized place in the division of labor.

MELL, MILDRED R. "Poor Whites of the South," *Social Forces*, XVII (December, 1938), 153-67. NcD, NcU, NcC.

The poor white class of the South consisted of that class of rural whites who were not integrated into the dominant agricultural economy of the region.

MILLER, CAROLINE H. *Lamb in His Bosom.* New York: Harper and Brothers, 1933. Pp. 345. NcD, NcU.

A novel of poor white life in the back country of Georgia in pre-Civil War days.

THE Poor White Problem in South Africa. 5 vols. Stellenbosch: Pro Ecclesia-Drukkery, 1932. NcD, NcU.

This elaborate study of the poor whites of South Africa was largely financed by the Carnegie Corporation of New York. No comparable work on the poor whites of the South has ever been undertaken.

QUEEN, STUART A., and GRUENER, JENELLE POWE. *Social Pathology* (Chap. 17, "Poor Whites"). New York: Thomas Y. Crowell Co., 1940. NcD, NcC.

Class barriers are considered from the point of view of social pathology.

SANDERS, IRWIN T. "Bulgarians and Southern Rural Whites in Contrast," *Social Forces*, XIX (October, 1940), 88-94. NcD, NcU, NcC.

"The Bulgarian peasant is primarily identified with the village culture and secondarily with newer national culture in process of development. The Southern white is identified with a regional culture but not with a folk culture."

SHUGG, ROGER W. *Origins of Class Struggle in Louisiana. A Social History of White Farmers and Laborers During Slavery and After, 1840-1875.* University: Louisiana State University Press, 1939. Pp. x, 372. NcD, NcU.

"In these essays an attempt is made to isolate the white farmers and laborers of Louisiana as a class in order to analyze their situation and condition in a society that passed through war from slave to free labor."

TANNENBAUM, FRANK. "The South Buries Its Anglo-Saxons," *Century Magazine*, CVI (June, 1923), 205-15. NcD, NcU.

On the isolation, the paternalism, and the control of textile mill villages in the South. The workers are white, but employer attitudes toward them are not so different from those of the white planter toward his Negro tenants.

WESTON, GEORGE M. *The Poor Whites of the South.* Washington: Buell and Blanchard, 1856. NcD, NcU.

A letter to the New York *Tribune*, February 1, 1856, by a Northern writer. The letter brings out the connection between the poor whites and the beginnings of Southern industrialism.

XIII. The Negro in the City

BERCOVICI, KONRAD. *Around the World in New York.* New York: The
Century Co., 1924. Pp. 416. NcD, NcU, NcC.
The various minority groups, including the Negro, in their urban environments. Polyglot and polychrome peoples reacting upon one another against the
background of American civilization.

BONTEMPS, ARNA, and CONROY, JACK. *They Seek a City.* New York:
Doubleday, Doran and Co., 1945. Pp. xvii, 266. NcD, NcU, NcC.
Apparently all peoples suffering discrimination seek cities and promised lands.

BOYD, WILLIAM K. *The Story of Durham: City of the New South.* Durham,
N. C.: Duke University Press, 1925. Pp. xi, 345. NcD, NcU, NcC.
The appeal of this book is not dependent upon one's interest in the particular
community of Durham. Durham, without an ante-bellum history, is portrayed
as a typical "city of the New South." Chapter on the Negro concludes that
contributions to the development of the city "have not been confined to
one race."

BRINTON, HUGH P. *The Negro in Durham: A Study of Adjustment to Town
Life.* Ph.D. dissertation, University of North Carolina, 1930. Pp. 465. NcU.
Negro progress in Durham, N. C., exemplifies the changing status of the race
in the New South.

BURGESS, ERNEST W. "Residential Segregation in American Cities," *Annals
of the American Academy of Political and Social Science,* CXL (November,
1928), 105-15. NcD, NcU, NcC.
In Northern cities generally the bulk of the Negro population lives immediately adjacent to the central business district. Negro areas are frequently in
close proximity to (1) Italian settlements, and (2) vice areas.

CHENAULT, LAWRENCE ROYCE. *The Puerto Rican Migrant in New York
City.* New York: Columbia University Press, 1938. Pp. xii, 190. NcD, NcU.
Puerto Ricans, finding it increasingly difficult to eke out an existence in their
home island, and unable to compete with Negro labor in the other islands of
the West Indies, have migrated in large numbers to New York City to settle
in and near Harlem and in Brooklyn. Their problems of adjustment to an urban
environment are similar to those of Southern Negroes.

DONALD, HENDERSON H. "The Urbanization of the American Negro," in
George Peter Murdock, ed., *Studies in the Science of Society Presented to
A. G. Keller,* pp. 181-99. New Haven: Yale University Press, 1937. NcD,
NcU, NcC.
"Despite its inevitable attendant maladjustments, urbanization promises in
time to secure for the Negro a higher status in American society."

DRAKE, ST. CLAIR, and CAYTON, HORACE R. *Black Metropolis: A Study
of Negro Life in a Northern City.* New York: Harcourt, Brace and Co.,
1945. Pp. xxxiv, 809. NcD, NcU, NcC.
An important book presenting material to be found nowhere else.

DUBOIS, W. E. B. "The Upbuilding of Black Durham," *World's Work,* XXIII
(January, 1912), 334-38. NcD, NcU.
Durham, North Carolina, "has distinctly encouraged the best type of black
man by active aid and passive tolerance. What accounts for this? I may be
overemphasizing facts, but I think not, when I answer in a word: Trinity Col-

[59]

lege. The influence of a Southern institution of high ideals; with a president
and professors who have dared to speak out for justice toward black men; with
a quarterly journal, the learning and catholicism of which is well known—this
has made white Durham willing to see black Durham rise."

DUBOIS, W. E. B. *The Philadelphia Negro: A Social Study.* Together with a
special report on domestic service by I. Eaton. Publications of the University of Pennsylvania Series in Political Economy and Public Law, No. 14.
Philadelphia: University of Pennsylvania Press, 1899. Pp. xx, 520. NcD, NcU.
An early but still significant survey of the Negro in the Northern city.

EDWARDS, PAUL K. *The Southern Urban Negro as a Consumer.* New York:
Prentice-Hall, Inc., 1932. Pp. xxiv, 323. NcD, NcU, NcC.
This book is primarily a study of the economics of merchandizing, but the
fact that the Negro consumer is to some extent set apart in our social system
forces into consideration cultural factors which students of merchandizing
usually take for granted.

FRAZIER, E. FRANKLIN. "Occupational Classes Among Negroes in Cities,"
American Journal of Sociology, XXXV (March. 1930), 718-38. NcD, NcU.
The most significant differentiation of the population into occupational classes
has occurred since the Civil War. The growth of cities is mainly responsible
for this.

FRAZIER, E. FRANKLIN. "Negro Harlem: an Ecological Study," *American
Journal of Sociology,* XLIII (July, 1937), 72-88. NcD, NcU, NcC.
Harlem, in contrast to the Negro community in Chicago, has developed out
from a center in a radial pattern similar to the pattern of growth of a self-
contained city.

FRAZIER, E. FRANKLIN. "The Impact of Urban Civilization Upon Negro
Family Life," *American Sociological Review,* II (October, 1937), 609-18.
NcD, NcU.
The effect of the city on various Negro family heritages.

GLICK, CLARENCE. "The Position of Racial Groups in Occupational Structures," *Social Forces,* XVI (December, 1947), 206-11. NcD, NcU, NcC.
An analysis of the changing racial division of labor accompanying urbanization in two plantation societies, Hawaii and the South.

"HARLEM," *Survey,* Vol. LIII, No. 11 (March 1, 1925). NcD, NcU.
". . . a dramatic flowering of a new race spirit is taking place close at home—
among American Negroes, and the stage of that new episode is Harlem." A
symposium in three parts: (1) The greatest Negro community in the world,
(2) The Negro expresses himself, and (3) Black and White—studies in race
contacts.

HOUCK, THOMAS H. *A Newspaper History of Race Relations in Durham,
North Carolina, 1910-1940.* M.A. thesis, Duke University, 1941. Pp. 193. NcD.
Race relations studied as news.

JOHNSON, CHARLES S. *Negro Housing.* Report of the Committee on Negro
Housing. Washington: The President's Conference on Home Building and
Home Ownership, 1932. Pp. xiv, 282. NcD, NcU, NcC.
"So closely have the terms *alleys* and *Negroes* been associated that in the minds
of most of the older citizens they are inseparable."

JOHNSON, JAMES WELDON. *Black Manhattan.* New York: A. A. Knopf,
1930. Pp. xvii, 284. NcD, NcU, NcC.
The story of the Negro in New York City from colonial times to the present.

JONES, WILLIAM HENRY. *The Housing of Negroes in Washington, D. C.: A Study in Human Ecology.* Washington, D. C.: Howard University Press, 1929. Pp. 191. NcD, NcU.

The most interesting parts of this study are the author's remarks on alleys and the changes that are taking place in them.

KAHEN, HAROLD I. "The Validity of Anti-Negro Restrictive Covenants: A Reconsideration of the Problem," *The University of Chicago Law Review,* XII (February, 1945), 198-213. NcD, NcU, NcC.

"Judicial failure to abandon a rule so costly in its social consequences to the community at large will ultimately require legislative correction unless abominable housing for Negroes, and the pernicious effects of such conditions on the general community, are to be accepted as a permanent condition of American life."

KENNEDY, LOUISE V,ENABLE. *The Negro Peasant Turns Cityward.* Columbia University Studies in History, Economics and Public Law, No. 329. New York: Columbia University Press, 1930. Pp. 270. NcD, NcU, NcC.

The difficulties that befall the Negro in his new environment.

KISER, CLYDE VERNON. *Sea Island to City: A Study of St. Helena Islanders in Harlem and Other Urban Centers.* Columbia University Studies in History, Economics and Public Law, No. 368. New York: Columbia University Press, 1932. Pp. 272. NcD, NcU.

The trend toward the urbanizing of the colored population will have a significance for the Negro "second in importance only to emancipation."

LEE, GEORGE W. *Beale Street: Where the Blues Began.* New York: Robert O. Ballou, 1934. Pp. 296. NcU, NcC.

The "main street of Negro America" where it is always Saturday night.

LONG, HERMAN H., and JOHNSON, CHARLES S. *People vs. Property: Race Restrictive Covenants in Housing.* Nashville, Tennessee: Fisk University Press, 1947. Pp. 107. NcD, NcU.

An examination of some of the social effects of residential segregation.

McKAY, CLAUDE. *Harlem: Negro Metropolis.* New York: E. P. Dutton and Co., Inc., 1940. Pp. xi, 262. NcD, NcU, NcC.

Harlem—"a flock of luxuriant, large-lipped orchids spreading over the sides of a towering rock, the color of African life . . . boldly splashed . . . upon the north end of Manhattan."

McNEIL, ELAINE OGDEN, and CAYTON, HORACE R. "Research on the Urban Negro," *American Journal of Sociology,* XLVII (September, 1941), 176-83. NcD, NcU, NcC.

By devising indices of fixed status and free competition, Negro-white relations in various societies may be directly compared. It would then be possible to bring into one general framework the studies of the caste-like societies of the Deep South and of the urban societies of the Northern cities.

NATIONAL Urban League. *Source Materials on the Urban Negro in the United States, 1910-1938.* 2nd ed. New York: National Urban League, 1939. Pp. 37. NcD, NcU.

A bibliography.

OGDEN, MARY E. *The Chicago Negro Community: A Statistical Description.* Chicago: Work Projects Administration, 1939. Pp. xvii, 247. NcD, NcU.

A mimeographed monograph providing a rich source of statistical data on the Negro in a metropolitan area.

OTTLEY, ROI. *New World A-Coming:Inside Black America.* Boston: Houghton Mifflin Co., 1943. Pp. vi, 364. NcD, NcU, NcC.

A picture of the Negro's world with Harlem at its center presented by a Negro newspaperman.

PORCH, MARVIN E. *The Philadelphia Main Line Negro: A Social, Economic, and Education Survey.* Ed. D. thesis, Temple University, Philadelphia, 1938. Pp. 125. NcD, NcU.

The nativity, spatial distribution, occupational status, social and civic organizations, housing accommodations, criminality, health conditions, etc., of 6083 Main Line Negroes.

REID, IRA DE A. "Mirrors of Harlem—Investigations and Problems of America's Largest Colored Community," *Journal of Social Forces,* V (June, 1927), 628-34. NcD, NcU, NcC.

Harlem was Dutch, then Irish, then Jewish, and is now Negro. It is neither slum nor ghetto, resort nor colony. It is just the greatest Negro city in the world.

ROSS, FRANK A. "Urbanization and the Negro," *Publications of the American Sociological Society,* XXVI (August, 1932), 115-28. NcD, NcU.

The rate of urbanization for the United States as a whole has been diminishing for some time, but the rate for Negroes has been increasing. The present drift is toward Southern urban centers and toward the larger metropolitan areas of the North.

SHANNON, ALEXANDER H. *The Negro in Washington: A Study in Race Amalgamation.* New York: W. Neale, 1930. Pp. 332. NcD, NcU.

There is no place in American life for the Negro, according to the author of this book, and the only solution of the problem is to remove him from the country.

SPAULDING, CHARLES C. "Business in Negro Durham," *Southern Workman,* LXVI (December, 1937), 364-68. NcD, NcU, NcC.

The president of the North Carolina Mutual Life Insurance Company tells about the development of Negro business in Durham.

THURMAN, WALLACE. *Negro Life in N. Y.'s Harlem.* Little Blue Book No. 494. Girard, Kansas: Haldeman Julius Publications, 1928. Pp. 64. NcU. Brief and very interesting.

WARNER, ROBERT AUSTIN. *New Haven Negroes: A Social History.* New Haven: Yale University Press, 1940. Pp. xiv, 309. NcD, NcU, NcC.

The life story of a Northern Negro community told from colonial times to the present day.

WASHINGTON, BOOKER T. "Durham, North Carolina, a City of Negro Enterprises," *Independent,* LXX (March 30, 1911), 642-50. NcD, NcU.

When the Negro educator visited Durham in 1910, he said, "Of all the Southern cities I have visited, I found here the sanest attitude of the white people toward the black."

WEAVER, ROBERT. *The Negro Ghetto.* New York: Harcourt, Brace and Co., 1948. Pp. xviii, 404. NcD, NcU.

"This book is about residential segregation in the North."

WIRTH, LOUIS. *The Ghetto.* Chicago: The University of Chicago Press, 1928. Pp. xvi, 306. NcD, NcU, NcC.

The history of the ghetto in general and the Chicago ghetto in particular. The Jewish character has been molded by the isolation of the ghetto which becomes finally less a locality than a state of mind. This study is a model for the understanding of racial ghettos generally.

WOOFTER, THOMAS J., JR., et al. *Negro Problems in Cities.* Garden City, N. Y.: Doubleday, Doran and Co., 1928. Pp. 285. NcD, NcU, NcC.

A study of Negro neighborhoods, housing, schools, and recreation in seven Northern and nine Southern cities.

XIV. The Negro in the American Economy

BAILER, LLOYD H. "The Negro Automobile Worker," *Journal of Political Economy*, LI (October, 1943), 415-28. NcD, NcU, NcC.
Why has the Negro, more or less suddenly, become a focal point of strife in the automobile industry?

BEECHER, JOHN. "Share Croppers' Union in Alabama," *Social Forces*, XIII (October, 1934), 124-32. NcD, NcU, NcC.
A communist effort to organize Negro and white sharecroppers of the South got under way in Alabama in 1931. What followed was described by the press as a race war.

BRAZEAL, BRAILSFORD R. *The Brotherhood of Sleeping Car Porters*. New York: Harper and Brothers, 1946. Pp. xiv, 258. NcD, NcU, NcC.
A well-documented and readable account of the efforts of A. Philip Randolph and his colleagues to build a strong union.

BROWN, WILLIAM G. "The White Peril: The Immediate Danger of the Negro," *North American Review*, CLXXIX (December, 1904), 824-41. NcD, NcU.
The rise of white competition against the Negro in the South.

CARPENTER, NILES, and ASSOCIATES. "Nationality, Color, and Economic Opportunity in the City of Buffalo," *University of Buffalo Studies*, Vol. V, No. 4 (June, 1927). Monographs in Sociology No. 2. Pp. 194. NcD, NcU.
Negroes and white immigrants are clearly disadvantaged as compared with the native white in America. In spite of certain very important advantages held by the Negro over the white immigrant he does not advance as rapidly. The disability of color difference more than offsets the Negro's initial advantage.

CAYTON, HORACE R., and MITCHELL, GEORGE S. *Black Workers and the New Unions*. Chapel Hill: The University of North Carolina Press, 1939. Pp. xviii, 473. NcD, NcU, NcC.
A study of the new fields of industry into which Negroes are moving where new social and technical skills are essential to their survival. Highly significant as marking a shift from caste to class feeling are the emerging new relations of black and white workers in single unions.

CONSUMERS' Income in the United States. Washington: U. S. Government Printing Office, 1938. Pp. vii, 104. NcD, NcC.
In 1935-1936 the average annual income of the Negro family was one-third to one-half that of white families. The median annual family income for white families in the Southern rural areas was $1,100 as compared with $480 for Negro families in the same areas.

DUTCHER, DEAN. *The Negro in Modern Industrial Society: An Analysis of Changes in the Occupations of Negro Workers, 1910-1920*. Lancaster, Pa., 1930. Pp. xiv, 137. NcD, NcU.
Traces Negro population trends from Emancipation to 1930 with a description of the Negro's adjustment to industry. Included are statistics on Negro women in various occupations, including domestic service.

EDWARDS, ALBA M. "The Negro as a Factor in the Nation's Labor Force," *American Statistical Association Journal*, XXXI (September, 1936), 529-40. NcD, NcU.

Statistics presented to show that between 1910 and 1930 there was a gradual upward trend in the social-economic status of Negro gainful workers.

EDWARDS, ALBA M. *A Socio-Economic Grouping of the Gainful Workers of the United States.* Washington: U. S. Government Printing Office, 1938. Pp. vi, 264. NcU.

Gainful workers of 1930 in social-economic groups by color, nativity, age, and sex, by industry, with comparative statistics for 1920 and 1910. Contains valuable data for the study of the racial division of labor in the United States.

EVERETT, FAYE PHILIP, ed. *The Colored Situation: A Book of Vocational and Civic Guidance for the Negro Youth.* Boston: Meador Publishing Co., 1936. Pp. 312. NcD, NcU, NcC.

This book is intended to assist Negro youth in the choice of vocations and professions.

FELDMAN, HERMAN. *Racial Factors in American Industry.* New York: Harper and Brothers, 1931. Pp. xvi, 318. NcD, NcU, NcC.

Presents data concerning working conditions, employment, social and economic status of Negroes, Orientals, Mexicans, and European immigrants in American industries.

FLEMING, WALTER L. *The Freedmen's Savings Bank: A Chapter in the Economic History of the Negro Race.* Chapel Hill: The University of North Carolina Press, 1927. Pp. 170. NcU.

Deals with an early phase of the economic history of the African freedman.

FRANKLIN, CHARLES LIONEL. *The Negro Labor Unionist of New York: Problems and Conditions Among Negroes in the Labor Unions in Manhattan.* New York: Columbia University Press, 1936. Pp. 417. NcD, NcU, NcC.

A factual analysis and history of the Negro worker of New York City in relation to labor union membership and organization.

GANNETT, HENRY. "Occupations of the Negro," *John F. Slater Occasional Papers,* No. 6 (1895). Pp. 16. NcU.

This study of the occupational status of the Negro as shown in the census statistics for 1890 provides an excellent basis for studying changes in that status at the present time.

GARDNER, BURLEIGH B. *Human Relations in Industry.* Chicago: Richard D. Irwin, 1945. Pp. xi, 307. NcD, NcU.

A systematic investigation of industry considered as a system of human relations. The role of Negroes and other minority groups in industry is considered in Chaper XI.

GREENE, LORENZO J., and WOODSON, CARTER G. *The Negro Wage Earner.* Washington: The Association for the Study of Negro Life and History, 1930. Pp. xiii, 388. NcD, NcU, NcC.

A survey of the Negro in various occupations from the days of slavery to the present. There is an especially valuable background chapter on "Occupations Prior to Emancipation."

HALL, EGERTON ELLIOTT. *The Negro Wage Earner of New Jersey.* New Brunswick, New Jersey: School of Education, Rutgers University, 1935. Pp. 115. NcD.

A study of occupational trends in New Jersey, of the effect of unequal racial distribution in the occupations, and of the implications for education and guidance.

HARMON, JOHN H., JR., LINDSAY, ARNETT G., and WOODSON, CARTER G. *The Negro as a Business Man.* Washington, D. C.: The Association for the Study of Negro Life and History, 1929. Pp. v, 111. NcD, NcU.

Negro bankers and insurance men from the Civil War to the present.

HARRIS, ABRAM L. "Economic Foundations of American Race Division," *Social Forces*, V₁ (March, 1927), 468-78. NcD, NcU, NcC.

Historically the Negro has been held apart and subordinated, not merely as an individual, but as a race, a social whole. He was not enslaved because of his complexion but because his labor was wanted.

HARRIS, ABRAM L. *The Negro As Capitalist: A Study of Banking and Business Among American Negroes*. Philadelphia: The American Academy of Political and Social Science, 1936. Pp. xii, 205. NcD, NcU, NcC.

The author treats of the uncertain economic foundation of the Negro upper class.

HAYES, LAURENCE J. W. *The Negro Federal Government Worker*. Washington: The Graduate School, Howard University, 1941. Pp. 156. NcD, NcU.

A survey of practices with reference to the hiring and classifying of Negro workers and the extent and nature of discrimination against them.

HAYNES, GEORGE EDMUND. *The Negro at Work in New York City: A Study in Economic Progress*. Columbia University Studies in History, Economics and Public Law, Vol. 49, No. 3, 1912. Pp. 158. NcD, NcU.

Facts on migration, wage-earners and businessmen.

HERBST, ALMA. *The Negro in the Slaughtering and Meat-Packing Industry in Chicago*. Boston: Houghton Mifflin Co., 1932. Pp. xxiii, 182. NcD, NcU.

A study of Negro workmen in the slaughtering and meat-packing industry in Chicago emphasizing their entrance into the industry, the work they perform, their conditions of employment, their efficiency and reliability.

HILL, T. ARNOLD. "Present Status of Negro Labor," *Opportunity*, VII (May, 1929), 143-45. NcU.

The extent to which jobs heretofore regarded as "Negro jobs" are being filled by whites.

HILL, T. ARNOLD. "Negroes in Southern Industry," *Annals of the American Academy of Political and Social Science*, CLIII (January, 1931), 170-81. NcD, NcU, NcC.

An intensified economic interracial competition is impending if not already here. To survive, Negroes must become more efficient and more vocation-conscious.

HILL, T. ARNOLD. "Social Significance to Minority Groups of Recent Labor Developments," *National Conference of Social Work* (64th session, 1937), 399-408. NcD, NcU.

In this article Mr. Hill notes that "the chief social achievement that has taken root among Negroes as the result of recent labor developments has been their willingness to organize and advance their own cause."

HUGHES, EVERETT C. "Race Relations in Industry." Chap. VI in William F. Whyte, ed., *Industry and Society*. New York: McGraw-Hill Book Co., 1946. NcD.

"Wherever it has gone—and industry is always moving into new parts of the world—it has put some new combination of the peoples of the earth at work together."

JOHNSON, CHARLES S. "The Conflict of Caste and Class in an American Industry," *American Journal of Sociology*, XLII (July, 1936), 55-65. NcD, NcU.

Southern Negro labor made its earliest significant shift from field to factory in the manufacture of tobacco and long held a monopoly in this field of labor. But with each advance in machinery there has been an increase of white labor in the tobacco industries.

JOHNSON, CHARLES S. "Negroes in the Railway Industry," *Phylon*, Part I,
Vol. III (First Quarter, 1942), 5-14; Part II, Vol. III (Second Quarter,
1942), 196-205. NcD, NcU, NcC.
Part I deals with the employment of Negroes in the railway industry as
affected by economic conditions and processes. Part II presents the problems of
special segments of the Negro railway labor group.

JOHNSON, KEITH WHITAKER. *Racial Division of Labor and the American
Negro: A Statistical Study of the Occupational Distribution of the Four
Major Race and Nativity Groups in the United States, with Particular Dis-
cussion of the Negro*. Ph.D. dissertation, Duke University, 1943. Pp. vii,
260. NcD.
A factual study.

KAPLAN, A. D. H., and WILLIAMS, FARTH M. "Family Income and Expenditure in the Southeastern Region, 1935-36," *United States Department
of Labor, Bureau of Labor Statistics, Bulletin 647*, I (1939), 1-520; II (1940),
1-298. NcD, NcU.
Volume I is an analysis of how native white and Negro families in five southeastern cities obtain their incomes and how much they have available for current family living. Volume II examines the manner in which these incomes are
spent in three of the cities.

KISER, VERNON BENJAMIN. *Occupational Changes Among Negroes in
Durham, North Carolina*. M. A. thesis, Duke University, 1942. Pp. vii, 137.
NcD.
Occupations won and lost by Durham Negroes since 1890.

LAING, JAMES T. "The Negro Miner in West Virginia," *Social Forces*, XIV
(March, 1936), 416-22. NcD, NcU, NcC.
"Here Negroes occupy a unique position; more Negro miners work in the coal
mines of West Virginia than in those of any other state. Although they formed
only 6.6 per cent of the population of the State in 1930 they constituted 21.8
per cent of all miners."

LEAP, W. L. "The Standard of Living of Negro Farm Families in Albemarle
County, Virginia," *Social Forces*, XI (December, 1932), 258-62. NcD, NcU,
NcC.
Statistics are presented which require much more interpretation than the
author gives.

McKENZIE, RODERICK D. "Cultural and Racial Differences as Bases of Hu-
man Symbiosis." Chap. VI in Kimball Young, ed., *Social Attitudes*. New
York: Henry Holt and Co., 1931. NcD, NcU.
Racial divisions of labor illustrated in British Malaya, Hawaii, and Alaska.

MILLER, KELLY. "The Negro as a Workingman," *American Mercury*, VI
(November, 1925), 310-13. NcD, NcU, NcC.
The issue of race is deeper than that of wages, and the good sense of the
Negro workingman arrays him on the side of capital rather than with labor
because the employer, looking only to production, has little prejudice against
color, whereas the white laborer is suspicious of the black as a potential
competitor.

MITCHELL, GEORGE S. "The Negro in Industry," *American Scholar*, IV
(Summer, 1935), 316-25. NcD, NcU.
"Is mixed unionism a way out of prejudice, interracial violence, and industrial
and agricultural serfdom in the South?"

MITCHELL, GEORGE S. "The Negro in Southern Trade Unionism," *Southern
Economic Journal*, II (January, 1936), 26-33. NcD, NcU.

Occupationally the Negro has been locked in agricultural and personal service. Southern trade unionism in the past has been a device for the movement of white artisans into Negro jobs but recently, in some Southern areas, mixed trade unionism has been advancing.

MYRDAL, GUNNAR. *An American Dilemma.* 2 vols. (Vol. I, Chaps. 13, 14, 16, 17, 18, 19, and Appendix 6). New York: Harper and Brothers, 1944. NcD, NcU, NcC.

What will be the Negro's economic lot in post-war America? What was his lot in pre-war America?

NEGRO Women in Industry. U. S. Department of Labor, Bulletin of the Woman's Bureau, No. 20. Washington: U. S. Government Printing Office, 1922. Pp. v, 65. NcD.

A study of some of the problems connected with the entrance of Negro women into industry.

NORTHRUP, HERBERT R. "The Tobacco Workers International Union," *The Quarterly Journal of Economics,* LVI (August, 1942), 606-26. NcD, NcU, NcC.

Conditions in the tobacco industry do not favor organized labor. There is a sharp division of labor between whites and Negroes and more than half the workers of each race are women.

NORTHRUP, HERBERT R. *Organized Labor and the Negro.* New York: Harper and Brothers, 1944. Pp. xviii, 312. NcD, NcU, NcC.

A carefully documented study of labor union policies regarding Negro membership in eleven basic industries.

PAYNTER, JOHN H. *Horse and Buggy Days With Uncle Sam.* New York: Margent Press, 1943. Pp. xiii, 190. NcD, NcC.

A first-hand picture of the early Negro messenger. The author served as a clerk in the U. S. Department of Internal Revenue.

PIER, HELEN LOUISE, and SPALDING, MARY LOUISA. "Negro: A Selected Bibliography," *Monthly Labor Review,* XXII (January, 1926), 216-44. NcD, NcU.

Bibliography on the Negro in industry and Negro health.

PINCHBECK, RAYMOND B. *The Virginia Negro Artisan and Tradesman.* Publications of the University of Virginia Phelps-Stokes Fellowship Papers, No. 7. Richmond: The William Byrd Press, Inc., 1926. Pp. 146. NcD, NcU.

". . . the past and the present condition of Virginia Negroes in the skilled trades."

POWDERMAKER, HORTENSE, and SEMPER, JOSEPH. "Education and Occupation Among New Haven Negroes," *Journal of Negro History,* XXIII (April, 1938), 200-15. NcD, NcU, NcC.

A detailed analysis of the relations between education, jobs, and wages of high-school graduates from 1924 to 1936.

REUTER, EDWARD B. "Competition and the Racial Division of Labor." Chap. II in Edgar T. Thompson, ed., *Race Relations and the Race Problem.* Durham, North Carolina: Duke University Press, 1939. NcD, NcU, NcC.

"In the future, and in a measure in the present, the struggle for existence, as it works itself out in the caste and bi-racial order, tends to favor the Negro."

ROSS, MALCOLM. *All Manner of Men.* New York: Harcourt, Brace and Co., 1948. Pp. 314. NcD.

The story of an effort to change the racial division of labor in the United States, told by the former chairman of the FEPC.

SCOTT, ESTELLE HILL. *Occupational Changes among Negroes in Chicago.* Chicago: Work Projects Administration, 1939. Pp. xvi, 259. NcD, NcU.

A mimeographed monograph providing valuable material on occupational changes among Negroes in a metropolitan area.

SPERO, STERLING D., and HARRIS, ABRAM L. *The Black Worker: The Negro and the Labor Movement.* New York: Columbia University Press, 1931. Pp. x, 509. NcD, NcU, NcC.

A descriptive and analytical study of the Negro in relation to the American labor movement.

STERNER, RICHARD. *The Negro's Share: A Study of Income, Consumption, Housing and Public Assistance.* New York: Harper and Brothers, 1943. Pp. xii, 433. NcD, NcU, NcC.

Here are brought together the data concerning occupational employment trends, size of families and of income, habits of food consumption, housing conditions, and the Negro's relation to the whole Federal social security program.

STONE, ALFRED H. "The Economic Future of the Negro—The Factor of White Competition." Chap. V in *Studies in the American Race Problem.* New York: Doubleday Page and Co., 1908. NcD, NcU.

Stone argues that the Negro has invariably failed, both in the North and in the South, when faced with white competition. This chapter compares Italian and Negro agricultural labor in Mississippi.

UNITED STATES, Department of the Interior. Office of the Adviser on Negro Affairs. *The Urban Negro Worker in the United States, 1925-1936.* 2 vols. Washington: U. S. Government Printing Office, 1938-39. NcD, NcC.

Vol. I, prepared by Ira de A. Reid, is an analysis of the training, types, and conditions of employment, and the earnings of 200,000 skilled and white-collar Negro workers. Vol. II, prepared by Robert C. Weaver, is a study of male Negro skilled workers in the United States between 1930 and 1936.

WEAVER, ROBERT C. *Negro Labor: A National Problem.* New York: Harcourt, Brace and Co., 1946. Pp. xiv, 329. NcD, NcU, NcC.

The story of Negro labor during the last war and the outlook for the years to come.

WESLEY, CHARLES H. *Negro Labor in the United States, 1850-1925. A Study in American Economic History.* New York: The Vanguard Press, 1927. Pp. xiii, 343. NcD, NcU, NcC.

A survey of the Negro worker throughout American history and a consideration of his part in the modern labor movement.

WOODSON, CARTER G. "The Negro Washerwoman, a Vanishing Figure," *Journal of Negro History,* XV (July, 1930), 269-77. NcD, NcU, NcC.

"She was the all but beast of burden of the aristocratic slaveholder, and in freedom she continued at this hard labor as a bread winner of the family."

XV. The Negro in Domestic Service

ANDERSON, MARY. "The Plight of Negro Domestic Labor," *Journal of Negro Education*, V (January, 1936), 66-72. NcD, NcU, NcC.
As Negro men are re-employed or secure wage increases their wives and daughters will not be forced to sell their services so cheaply.

BROWN, JEAN COLLIER. *The Negro Woman Worker.* U. S. Department of Labor, Bulletin of the Women's Bureau, No. 165. Washington: U. S. Government Printing Office, 1938. Pp. v, 17. NcD, NcU.
An attractive and readable bulletin summarizing the present problems of America's 2,000,000 Negro women workers.

COX, OLIVER C. "Marital Status and Employment of Women, with Special Reference to Negro Women," *Sociology and Social Research*, XXV (November, 1940), 157-65. NcD, NcU.
"In the United States the Negro married woman is a worker; white married women are 'home-makers.' "

EATON, ISABEL. "Special Report on Negro Domestic Service in the Seventh Ward," in W. E. B. DuBois, *The Philadelphia Negro*. Publications of the University of Pennsylvania, Series in Political Economy and Public Law, No. 14. Philadelphia, 1899. Pp. 425-509. NcD, NcU.
An old but still important investigation of male and female Negro servants in Philadelphia.

FLEMING, WALTER L. "The Servant Problem in a Black Belt Village," *Sewanee Review*, XIII (January, 1905), 1-17. NcD, NcU.
On the trials and tribulations of white employers of Negro servants in Auburn, Alabama.

GILMORE, HARLAN W., and WILSON, LOGAN. "The Employment of Negro Women as Domestic Servants in New Orleans," *Social Forces*, XXII (March, 1944), 318-23. NcD, NcU, NcC.
A factual investigation of some of the conditions under which Negro domestics in New Orleans work.

HARLAN, HOWARD H. *Zion Town: A Study in Human Ecology.* Charlottesville: University of Virginia, 1935. Pp. 65. NcD, NcU.
Zion Town is an outlying Negro community in the city of Richmond. Its relation to a neighboring white community is found to be that of a servant's reservation.

HAYNES, ELIZABETH ROSS. "Two Million Negro Women at Work," *Southern Workman*, LI (February, 1922), 64-72. NcD, NcU, NcC.
Negro women in (1) domestic and personal service, (2) agriculture, and (3) manufacturing industries.

HAYNES, ELIZABETH ROSS. "Negroes in Domestic Service in the United States," *Journal of Negro History*, VIII (October, 1923), 384-442. NcD, NcU, NcC.
Negroes furnish a larger percentage of domestic workers than any other racial or national group in the United States.

THE Negro in Richmond, Virginia. Richmond Council of Social Agencies. Negro Welfare Survey Committee. Richmond, 1929. Pp. viii, 136. NcD, NcU.
A portion of this survey reports on results of questionnaires addressed to white housewives and Negro servants.

REED, RUTH. "The Negro Women of Gainesville, Georgia," *Bulletin of the University of Georgia*, Vol. XXII, No. 1 (December, 1921), 1-61. NcD, NcU.
A report on a house-to-house canvas during which Negro servants and white mistresses were interviewed.

ROEBUCK, JULIAN. *Domestic Service; With Particular Attention to the Negro Female Servant in the South.* M.A. thesis, Duke University, 1944. Pp. ii, 143. NcD.
An analysis of the domestic servant situation in the South.

SALMON, LUCY MAYNARD. *Domestic Service.* New York: The Macmillan Co., 1897. Pp. xxiv, 307. NcD.
A standard work on the problem which has been called "the great American question."

STIGLER, GEORGE J. *Domestic Servants in the United States, 1900-1940.* New York: National Bureau of Economic Research, 1946. Pp. 44. NcD.
Statistical analysis of number, characteristics, wages, etc.; and of factors affecting income of servants.

WATSON, AMEY E. "Domestic Service," *Encyclopaedia of the Social Sciences*, V, 198-205. NcD, NcU.
The coming of alternate forms of occupation especially for women, plus the stigma that has attached itself to domestic service, are factors in the universal "servant problem."

WINSLOW, THYRA SAMTER. "Treasure," *American Mercury*, XXVIII (February, 1933), 149-52. NcD, NcU, NcC.
The ways and habits of a colored maid whose mistress is a Southern white woman living in New York.

XVI. Race Conflict

1. General

BREARLEY, H. C. "The Pattern of Violence." Chap. XXXI in W. T. Couch, ed., *Culture in the South*. Chapel Hill: The University of North Carolina Press, 1935. NcD, NcU.

Violence, the author suggests, is not merely a fact but a tradition in the part of the United States lying below "the Smith and Wesson line."

BREARLEY, H. C. "Ba-ad Nigger," *South Atlantic Quarterly*, XXXVIII (January, 1939), 75-81. NcD, NcU, NcC.

As a local hero and a racial demi-god the "bad" Negro enjoys prestige and esteem.

BREARLEY, H. C. "The Negro's New Belligerency," *Phylon*, V (Fourth Quarter, 1944), 339-445. NcD, NcU, NcC.

". . . in recent months the Negro's usual protests have become a mighty chorus of discord."

BROWN, WILLIAM O. "Culture Contact and Race Conflict." Chap. III in E. B. Reuter, ed., *Race and Culture Contacts*. New York: McGraw-Hill Book Co., 1934. NcD, NcU, NcC.

Brown describes the stages in the natural history of race conflict.

DAVIS, ALLISON. "Caste, Economy and Violence," *American Journal of Sociology*, LI (July, 1945), 7-15. NcD, NcU, NcC.

Race relations in the South are caste relations except on the economic level. Increasing interracial conflict and violence indicate that Negroes are beginning to compete more effectively with whites.

DETWEILER, FREDERICK G. "The Rise of Modern Race Antagonisms," *American Journal of Sociology*, XXXVII (March, 1932), 738-47. NcD, NcU, NcC.

Ancient civilizations such as those of Greece and Rome had apparently very little social discrimination based upon color or race, but such discrimination developed with the impact of Western nations on the other peoples of the world.

DOLLARD, JOHN. "Hostility and Fear in Social Life," *Social Forces*, XVII (October, 1938), 15-26. NcD, NcU, NcC.

The author distinguishes between rational and irrational components in race prejudice. Discussion by Franz Alexander, pp. 27-29.

HANDMAN, MAX. "Ku Klux Klan," *Encyclopaedia of the Social Sciences*, VIII, 606-9. NcD, NcU.

"The modern Ku Klux Klan has very little in common with the original Klan except the name."

JOHNSON, CHARLES S. *To Stem This Tide*. Boston: The Pilgrim Press, 1943. Pp. x, 142. NcD, NcU, NcC.

A survey of racial tension areas in the United States.

JOHNSON, GUY B. "A Sociological Interpretation of the New Ku Klux Movement," *Social Forces*, I (May, 1923), 440-45. NcD, NcU, NcC.

Both the old and the new Ku Klux Klan movements sprang up in the year following the close of a war, both were defensive secret societies, and both originated in the South.

JOHNSON, GUY B. "Patterns of Race Conflict." Chap. V in Edgar T. Thompson, ed., *Race Relations and the Race Problem.* Durham: Duke University Press, 1939. NcD, NcU, NcC.

Types of behavior in the South which have produced race conflict are classified as: the pattern of insolence; the pattern of insubordination; the pattern of attack on the persons or property of whites; and ,the pattern of concerted action. A new era of conflict is considered almost inevitable.

KOHN, HANS. "Race Conflict," *Encyclopaedia of the Social Sciences,* XIII, 36-41. NcD, NcU.

"Race relations today present more dangerous features in the field of inter-human relations than any other point of conflict."

MECKLIN, JOHN M. *Democracy and Race Friction: A Study in Social Ethics.* New York: The MacMillan Company, 1921. Pp. xi, 273. NcD, NcU, NcC.

A study of the conflict between the legal status and the actual social status of racial groups in America.

MECKLIN, JOHN M. *The Ku Klux Klan: A Study of the American Mind.* New York: Harcourt, Brace and Co., 1924. Pp. 244. NcD, NcU, NcC.

While the Klan is dangerous and undesirable, the psychological and sociological factors which brought it into being are worth studying and this book attempts to understand them.

MEYER, AGNES E. *Journey Through Chaos.* New York: Harcourt, Brace and and Co., 1944. Pp. xvii, 388. NcD, NcU.

A report on delinquency, race conflict, bad housing, and other evidences of chaos on the Amercian homefront in wartime.

MURRAY, GILBERT. "Satanism and the World Order," *Century Magazine,* C (July, 1920), 289-99. NcD, NcU.

"The spirit of unmixed hatred toward the existing world order is perhaps more rife today than it has been for a thousand years."

ROBINSON, BERNARD F. "War and Race Conflicts in the United States," *Phylon,* IV (Fourth Quarter, 1943), 311-27. NcD, NcU, NcC.

The author suggests a causal relationship between each of the major wars of the United States—the Revolutionary War, the Civil War, and the two World Wars—and the rise of each of the major types of Negro-white conflict—slave insurrections, lynchings, and race riots.

STONE, ALFRED H. "Is Race Friction Between Blacks and Whites in the United States Growing and Inevitable?" *American Journal of Sociology,* XIII (March, 1908), 676-97. NcD, NcU.

"All racial problems are distinctly problems of racial distribution."

TANNENBAUM, FRANK. "The Ku Klux Klan: Its Social Origin in the South," *Century Magazine,* CV (April, 1923), 873-82. NcD, NcU.

It is the dead monotony of Southern small town life which makes the occasional lynching possible. The seed-bed of the Ku Klux Klan is a situation where people are starved emotionally and crave excitement.

WECKLER, J. E., and HALL, THEO E. *The Police and Minority Groups: A Program to Improve Relations Between Different Racial, Religious, and National Groups.* Chicago: International City Managers' Association, 1944. Pp. iv, 20. NcD.

Emphasis is placed on police techniques for preventing riots and violence.

2. SLAVE INSURRECTIONS

APTHEKER, HERBERT. *Negro Slave Revolts in the United States, 1526-1860.* New York: International Publishers, 1939. Pp. 72. NcD, NcU.

This little booklet contains a table showing the date and location of slave plots and revolts in the United States.

APTHEKER, HERBERT. *American Negro Slave Revolts.* New York: Columbia University Press, 1943. Pp. 409. NcD, NcU, NcC.
Slave rebellions occurred frequently during the whole span of American history from the years of original settlement to the Civil War.

CARROLL, JOSEPH C. *Slave Insurrections in the United States, 1800-1865.* Boston: Chapman and Grimes, 1938. Pp. 229. NcD, NcU.
A much better book on slave insurrections will some day be written, but this book evidences the increasing interest in insurrections accompanying the growth of race consciousness among Negroes.

COFFIN, JOSHUA. *An Account of Some of the Principal Slave Insurrections.* New York: Anti-Slavery Society, 1860. Pp. 36. NcD.
An abolitionist justification of slave insurrections.

CROMWELL, JOHN W. "The Aftermath of Nat Turner's Insurrection," *Journal of Negro History,* V (April, 1920), 208-34. NcD, NcU, NcC.
Nat Turner's insurrection marked a turning point in the history of Southern Negro slavery.

DREWRY, WILLIAM S. *Slave Insurrections in Virginia, 1830-1865: The Southampton Insurrection.* Washington: The Neals Co., 1900. Pp. 201. NcD, NcU.
An account of the Nat Turner insurrection.

JAMES, C. L. R. *A History of Negro Revolt.* London: Fact Ltd., 1938. Pp. 97. NcD.
A left-wing version of Negro revolt in San Domingo, the United States, and Africa.

JAMES, C. L. R. *The Black Jacobins: Toussaint L'Ouverture and the San Domingo Revolution.* New York: Dial Press, 1938. Pp. xvi, 328. NcD, NcU, NcC.
A contribution to the history of the class and race struggle in the Caribbean.

NEWCOMB, COVELLE. *Black Fire: A Story of Henri Christophe.* New York, Toronto: Longmans, Green and Company, 1940. Pp. xii, 275. NcD.
A fictional biography of Henri Christophe, black king of Haiti, and his struggle against the French. Written for boys from eight to ten.

WISH, HERVEY. "American Slave Insurrections Before 1861," *Journal of Negro History,* XXII (July, 1937), 299-320. NcD, NcU, NcC.
This article discusses the effects of slave insurrections on the whites.

3. THE FIGHT FOR FREEDOM

APTHEKER, HERBERT. *The Negro in the Abolitionist Movement.* New York: International Publishers, 1941. Pp. 48. NcD, NcU.
It is strange that Negro abolitionist leadership has been so greatly neglected by students.

BARNES, GILBERT HOBBS. *The Antislavery Impulse, 1830-1844.* New York: D. Appleton-Century Co., 1933. Pp. ix, 298. NcD, NcU, NcC.
An important work on the anti-slavery movement in America. According to the author the movement received its inspiration from the Great Revival of the West rather than from New England.

BASSETT, JOHN SPENCER. *Anti-Slavery Leaders of North Carolina.* Baltimore: The Johns Hopkins Press, 1898. Pp. 74. NcD, NcU, NcC.
The leaders dealt with here are Helper, Hedrick, Goodloe, Caruthers, and Lane.

BUCKMASTER, HENRIETTA (pseud.). *Let My People Go.* New York: Harper and Brothers, 1941. Pp. xii, 398. NcD, NcU, NcC.
The story of how thousands of Negro slaves were bootlegged to freedom over the underground railroad. The Negro began to rebel against slavery in the

person of the fugitive slave, but the movement eventually assumed the proportions of a great national crusade.

CROW, MARTHA F. *Harriet Beecher Stowe.* New York: D. Appleton and Co., 1914. Pp. xi, 310. NcD.
One of the best works that have been written about the author of *Uncle Tom's Cabin.* The book is an insightful account of Mrs. Stowe's personal and domestic life.

CURTIS, ANNA L. *Stories of the Underground Railroad.* New York: The Island Workshop Press Co-op, Inc., 1941. Pp. 115. NcD, NcU.
Material on the part played by the Negro himself in the struggle for freedom. For less sophisticated readers.

CURTIS, CLARA K. *Fighters for Freedom.* Rochester: Clara K. Curtis, 1933. Pp. 168. NcU.
Seven short historical stories showing the conditions that led to the anti-slavery movement in America.

HELPER, HINTON ROWAN. *The Impending Crisis of the South: How to Meet It.* New York: A. B. Burdick, 1860. Pp. x, 420. NcD, NcU, NcC.
A famous anti-slavery appeal to the poor whites of the South by one of their number.

LLOYD, ARTHUR Y. *The Slavery Controversy, 1831-1860.* Chapel Hill: The University of North Carolina Press, 1939. Pp. xi, 337. NcD, NcU, NcC.
A "new light upon the slavery controversy as a part of the sectional struggle preceding the Civil War."

MILLER, ALPHONSE B. *Thaddeus Stevens.* New York: Harper and Brothers, 1939. Pp. xi, 440. NcD, NcU, NcC.
A biography of the "sinister patriot," one of the most belligerent of the Negro's advocates.

NUERMBERGER, RUTH K. *The Free Produce Movement.* Durham: Duke University Press, 1942. Pp. ix, 147. NcD, NcU, NcC.
A Quaker protest against slavery.

PHILLIPS, ULRICH B. "The Slavery Issue in Federal Politics." Vol. IV, pp. 382-422 in *The South in the Building of the Nation.* Richmond, Va.: The Southern Historical Publication Society, 1909. NcD, NcU.
A survey of slavery in relation to national politics in the ante-bellum period.

POLLARD, EDWARD A. *The Anti-Slavery Men of the South.* Reprinted from *The Galaxy,* Vol. XVI (September, 1873), 329-41. NcD, NcU.
Before about 1830 probably most of the opposition to slavery centered in the South.

ROBERT, JOSEPH CLARKE. *The Road from Monticello.* Durham: Duke University Press, 1941. Pp. ix, 127. NcD, NcU, NcC.
A study of the Virginia Slavery Debate of 1832.

SIEBERT, WILBUR H. *The Underground Railroad: From Slavery to Freedom.* New York: The Macmillan Co., 1898. Pp. xxv, 478. NcD, NcU.
Included is an important map of underground railways.

STILL, WILLIAM. *The Underground Railroad.* Philadelphia: Porter and Coates, 1872. Pp. 780. NcD, NcU.
The Negro author of this book was connected with the anti-slavery office in Philadelphia. Material for the book came from notes made on the runaway Negroes who came through Philadelphia. The book is the "official" account of the underground railroad.

SWIFT, HILDEGARDE HOYT. *The Railroad to Freedom: A Story of the Civil War.* New York: Harcourt, Brace and Co., 1932. Pp. xix, 364. NcD, NcU, NcC.
The stirring story of Harriet Tubman and her work in connection with the underground railroad.

TYLER, ALICE FELT. *Freedom's Ferment: Phases of American Social History to 1860.* Minneapolis: The University of Minnesota Press, 1944. Pp. x, 608. NcD, NcU, NcC.
A study of cults, utopias, and humanitarian crusades, all of which indirectly, and many of which directly, involve Negroes.

WASHINGTON, JOHN E. *They Knew Lincoln.* New York: E. P. Dutton & Co., 1942. Pp. 244. NcD, NcU, NcC.
Pictures of Lincoln as he appeared to Negroes who knew him.

WESLEY, CHARLES H. *The Collapse of the Confederacy.* Washington: Associated Publishers, 1937. Pp. xiii, 225. NcD, NcU, NcC.
This book by a Negro historian contributes, among other things, a discussion of the effect of the failure of the Confederacy to employ Negroes in the military service.

WILEY, BELL I. *Southern Negroes, 1861-1865.* New Haven: Yale University Press, 1938. Pp. viii, 366. NcD, NcU, NcC.
A study of the attitude of the slave toward freedom. It is Professor Wiley's thesis that slave disloyalty was the rule during the Civil War and loyalty the exception.

4. THE RECONSTRUCTION PERIOD

ALLEN, JAMES S. *Reconstruction: The Battle for Democracy* (1865-76). New York: International Publishers, 1937. Pp. 256. NcD, NcU.
The way a communist sees it.

BEALE, HOWARD K. "On Rewriting Reconstruction History," *American Historical Review,* XLV (July, 1940), 807-27. NcD, NcU, NcC.
Both Northern and Southern writings on Reconstruction have been dominated by sectional feeling. It is time for younger American historians to restudy the period.

COULTER, ELLIS M. *The Civil War and Readjustment in Kentucky.* Chapel Hill: The University of North Carolina Press, 1926. Pp. 468. NcD, NcU.
A comprehensive and well-documented study of post-Civil War adjustments in Kentucky.

DUBOIS, W. E. B. *Black Reconstruction.* New York: Harcourt, Brace and Co., 1935. Pp. 746. NcD, NcU, NcC.
A reconstruction of Reconstruction history from the point of view of the Negro proletariat.

FLEMING, WALTER L. *Civil War and Reconstruction in Alabama.* New York: Columbia University Press, 1905. Pp. xxiii, 815. NcD, NcU.
One of the earliest and most comprehensive of the studies of Reconstruction.

FLEMING, WALTER L. *Documentary History of Reconstruction, Political, Military, Social, Religious, Educational and Industrial, 1865 to Present Time.* 2 vols. Cleveland, Ohio: The Arthur H. Clarke Co., 1906-1907. NcD, NcU.
A valuable collection of documents, most of them bearing upon the relations between the races in the South during the period of Reconstruction.

HAMILTON, J. G. DE ROULHAC. *Reconstruction in North Carolina.* Columbia University Studies in History, Economics, and Public Law, No. 141. 1914. Pp. x, 683. NcD, NcU, NcC.
One account of a stormy period in North Carolina history.

HENRY, ROBERT SELPH. *The Story of Reconstruction.* Indianapolis: The
    Bobbs-Merrill Co., 1938. Pp. 633. NcD, NcU.
The author speaks of "the antagonism of races, cultivated for political profit."

HORN, STANLEY F. *Invisible Empire: The Story of the Ku Klux Klan,
    1866-1871.* Boston: Houghton Mifflin Co., 1939. Pp. x, 434. NcD, NcU.
Italy had its Carbonari, Ireland its Fenians, the late colonial period in America
its Liberty Boys, and the South its Ku Klux Klan. This is the story of the
Klan between 1866 and 1871.

SIMKINS, FRANCIS B., and WOODY, ROBERT H. *South Carolina During
    Reconstruction.* Chapel Hill: The University of North Carolina Press, 1932.
    Pp. xiv, 610. NcD, NcU, NcC.
Includes an account of the social and economic revolution which resulted
from the change to free labor.

TAYLOR, ALRUTHEUS A. *The Negro in South Carolina During the Recon-
    struction.* Washington, D. C.: Association for the Study of Negro Life and
    History, 1924. Pp. iv, 341. NcD, NcU.
Taylor has put the matter of this controversial subject in a different context.
He has included the sort of material which, while not minimizing the actual disorder and corruption of the period, at least makes these things somewhat more
intelligible.

TAYLOR, ALRUTHEUS A. *The Negro in the Reconstruction of Virginia.*
    Washington, D. C.: Association for the Study of Negro Life and History, 1926.
    Pp. iv, 300. NcD, NcU.
The story of Reconstruction in Virginia from the point of view of the freedman, the beneficiary as well as the victim.

TAYLOR, ALRUTHEUS A. *The Negro in Tennessee, 1865-1880.* Washington,
    D. C.: Associated Publishers, 1941. Pp. 306. NcD, NcU, NcC.
A study of Reconstruction in Tennessee.

WHARTON, VERNON LANE. *The Negro in Mississippi, 1865-1890.* Ph.D. dis-
    sertation, University of North Carolina, 1939. Pp. 544. NcU.
Presents some important new facts of significance for Reconstruction history.

5. LYNCHINGS AND RIOTS

AMES, JESSIE D. *The Changing Character of Lynching. Review of Lynch-
    ing, 1931-1941, With a Discussion of Recent Developments in This Field.*
    Atlanta, Ga.: Commission on Interracial Cooperation, 1942. Pp. ix, 70. NcD,
    NcU.
Lynchings are becoming fewer in number and mobs are becoming smaller.
Lynchings are concentrating in the Southeast and mobs are dropping their claims
of chivalry. Lynchings for minor offenses are on the increase, and it is becoming
more and more difficult to say exactly what a lynching is.

BERNARD, LUTHER LEE. "Mob," *Encyclopaedia of the Social Sciences,* X,
    552-54. NcD, NcU, NcC.
A brief analysis of rebellious behavior.

CANTRIL, HADLEY. *The Psychology of Social Movements* (Chap. IV, "The
    Lynching Mob"). New York: John Wiley and Sons, 1941. NcD, NcU, NcC.
An effort "to translate the objective descriptions of lynching mobs into their
probable subjective psychological counterparts."

CHADBOURN, JAMES HARMON. *Lynching and the Law.* Chapel Hill: The
    University of North Carolina Press, 1933. Pp. xi, 221. NcD, NcU, NcC.
A treatment of the legal aspects of lynching. Proposals for additional legislation.

CHICAGO Commission on Race Relations. *The Negro in Chicago: A Study of Race Relations and A Race Riot* (1920-1922). Chicago: The University of Chicago Press, 1922. Pp. xxiv, 672. NcD, NcC.

This study of a race riot in Chicago "is unique in one respect: more than any previous study it has succeeded (a) in uncovering the sources of racial friction, and (b) in showing the effects of these sometimes obscure irritations upon public opinion."

COKER, FRANCIS W. "Lynching," *Encyclopaedia of the Social Sciences*, IX, 639-43. NcD, NcU.

Lynching is not to be confused with the extra-legal punishment of criminals in early frontier society. It is not a substitute for law and order. It is rather a protest against the uncertainties and delays of the law as well as a low form of recreation for the lynchers.

COLLINS, WINFIELD H. *The Truth About Lynching and the Negro in the South*. New York: The Neale Publishing Co., 1918. Pp. 163. NcD, NcU.

The author pleads that the South be made safe for the white race.

COX, OLIVER C. "Lynching and the Status Quo," *Journal of Negro Education*, XIV (Autumn, 1945), 576-88. NcD, NcU, NcC.

Among other things this important article describes the stages in the lynching cycle.

CUTLER, JAMES ELBERT. *Lynch Law: An Investigation into the History of Lynching in the United States*. New York: Longmans, Green and Co., 1905. Pp. xiv, 287. NcD, NcU, NcC.

One of the most important books on the subject. "The purpose of the investigation has not been primarily to write the history of lynching, but to determine from the history the causes for the prevalence of the practice, to determine what the social conditions are under which lynch-law operates, and to test the validity of the arguments which have been advanced in justification of lynching."

EATON, CLEMENT. "Mob Violence in the Old South," *The Mississippi Valley Historical Review*, XXIX (December, 1942), 351-70. NcD, NcU.

After 1830 mob violence gradually subsided in the North but reached its greatest intensity in the South.

HAYDEN, HARRY. *The Story of the Wilmington Rebellion*. Wilmington, N. C.: Privately printed, 1936. Pp. 32. NcD, NcU.

A brief account by a sympathizer with the white side in the riot and the events leading up to it.

LEE, ALFRED McCLUNG, and HUMPHREY, NORMAN DAYMOND. *Race Riot*. New York: The Dryden Press, 1943. Pp. xi, 143. NcD, NcU, NcC.

An eyewitness account of the riot in Detroit and a practical program suggested to prevent riots.

LOCKE, ALAIN. "Harlem: Dark Weather-Vane," *Survey Graphic*, XXV (August, 1936), 457-62, 493-95. NcD, NcU, NcC.

Harlem after the riot of 1935.

MYRDAL, GUNNAR. *An American Dilemma*. 2 vols. (Vol. I, Chap. 27, "Violence and Intimidation"). New York: Harper and Brothers, 1944. NcD, NcU, NcC.

Ordinarily conservatism ranges itself on the side of strict law enforcement but in the South racial conservatism is allied with illegality. Lynching and other forms of intimidation flow from this fact.

PRUDEN, DURWARD. "A Sociological Study of a Texas Lynching," *Studies in Sociology*, I (1936), 3-9. NcD.

A revealing account of the lynching of a Negro laborer near Leeville, Texas, in 1930.

RAPER, ARTHUR F. *The Tragedy of Lynching.* Chapel Hill: The University of North Carolina Press, 1933. Pp. viii, 499. NcD, NcU, NcC.
A study of both the victims and the lynchers. An analysis of the economic, social, and cultural factors involved in lynching.

RATLIFF, B. A. "In the Delta: The Story of a Man Hunt," *Atlantic Monthly,* CXXV (April, 1920), 456-61. NcD, NcU.
A vivid account by an observer.

SANCTON, THOMAS. "Race Clash," *Harper's Magazine,* CLXXX (January, 1944), 135-40. NcD, NcU, NcC.
An incident showing how race riots are made.

SHAY, FRANK. *Judge Lynch: His First Hundred Years.* New York: Ives Washburn, 1938. Pp. 288. NcD, NcU, NcC.
A well-documented record of one hundred years of lynching in the United States with a brief account of its origin and a survey of the present legislation designed to prevent it.

SMELLIE, K. "Riot," *Encyclopaedia of the Social Sciences,* XIII, 386-88. NcD, NcU.
Rioting, in one of its aspects, has been a form of recreation for the poor of some of our large cities.

THIRTY Years of Lynching in the United States, 1889-1918. New York: National Association for the Advancement of Colored People, 1919. Pp. 105. NcU, NcC.
Contains statistical tables, the story of one hundred lynchings, and a chronological list, by states, of persons lynched in the United States.

WHITE, WALTER F. *Rope and Faggot: A Biography of Judge Lynch.* New York: A. A. Knopf, 1929. Pp. xiii, 272. NcD, NcU, NcC.
A consideration of the various factors in lynching—economic, race prejudice, religion, sex, politics, journalism, etc.

YOUNG, ERLE FISKE. "The Relation of Lynching to the Size of Political Areas," *Sociology and Social Research,* XII (March-April, 1928), 348-53. NcD, NcU.
A discussion based upon the observation "that the Southern counties with large populations are relatively freer from race violence than those with smaller populations."

6. THE NEGRO IN LAW AND IN THE COURTS

ANDREWS, HENRY L. *Racial Distinctions in the Courts of North Carolina.* M.A. thesis, Duke University, 1933. Pp. 139. NcD.
Race distinctions in the police court, before the justice of the peace, in the recorder's court, the superior court, and the supreme court.

CATTERALL, HELEN T., ed. *Judicial Cases Concerning American Slavery and the Negro.* 5 vols. Washington: The Carnegie Institution of Washington, 1926-37. NcD, NcU, NcC.
These volumes contain an abundance of useful documentary material pertinent to an understanding of the social order of the Old South derived from the decisions of the highest courts. Faced with concrete problems jurists were in process of formulating "a political and social philosophy by which they could uphold an established institution and yet maintain standards of justice."

GUILD, JUNE PURCELL. *Black Laws of Virginia: A Summary of the Legislative Acts of Virginia Concerning Negroes from Earliest Times to the Present*. Richmond, Virginia: Whittet & Shepperson, 1936. Pp. 249. NcD, NcU.
Virginia laws speaking for themselves.

HURD, JOHN CODMAN. *The Law of Freedom and Bondage in the United States*. 2 vols. Boston: Little, Brown and Co.; New York: D. Van Nostrand, 1858-62. NcD, NcU.
An exhaustive study of the backgrounds and history of the law governing freedom and slavery until the American Civil War.

KONVITZ, MILTON R. *The Constitution and Civil Rights*. New York: Columbia University Press, 1947. Pp. x, 254. NcD, NcU.
A comprehensive consideration of the law of civil rights.

MANGUM, CHARLES S., JR. *The Legal Status of the Negro*. Chapel Hill: The University of North Carolina Press, 1940. Pp. viii, 436. NcD, NcU, NcC.
"A review of the statutes and cases which concern the relations of the white and colored races since the Civil War."

MYRDAL, GUNNAR. *An American Dilemma*. 2 vols. (Vol. I, Chaps. 24, 25, and 26). New York: Harper and Brothers, 1944. NcD, NcU, NcC.
The author quotes DuBois as saying, ". . . the Negro is coming more and more to look upon law and justice, not as protecting safeguards, but as sources of humiliation and oppression."

RAPER, ARTHUR F. "A Day at Police Court," *Phylon*, V (Third Quarter, 1944), 225-32. NcD, NcU, NcC.
Some differences in attitudes and treatment when members of the two races face "His Honesty" in a Southern court.

SELLIN, THORSTEN. "Race Prejudice in the Administration of Justice," *American Journal of Sociology*, XLI (September, 1935), 212-17. NcD, NcU.
In America the judiciary is largely composed of whites of old American stock. The influence of race and nationality prejudice in judges is revealed through a comparative study of the average length of sentences—definite and indeterminate—of native-born white, foreign-born white, and Negro prisoners.

STEPHENSON, GILBERT T. *Race Distinctions in American Law*. New York: D. Appleton and Co., 1910. Pp. xiv, 388. NcD, NcU, NcC.
A study of legal color-lines.

STROUD, GEORGE M. *A Sketch of the Laws Relating to Slavery in the Several States of the United States of America*. Philadelphia: Henry Longstreth, 1856. Pp. vii, 180. NcD, NcU.
Contains material of very great importance.

STYLES, FITZHUGH L. *Negroes and the Law*. Boston: Christopher Publishing House, 1937. Pp. xi, 320. NcD, NcU, NcC.
"A manual of the rights of the Negro under the law."

TO Secure These Rights: The Report of the President's Committee on Civil Rights. Washington: U. S. Government Printing Office, 1947. Pp. xii, 178. NcD, NcU, NcC.
Many people participating in the controversy which has developed around this report apparently have not read it.

WARSOFF, LOUIS A. *Equality and the Law*. New York: Liveright Publishing Corporation, 1938. Pp. x, 324. NcD.
"It will be the purpose of this book to consider the state of due process and equality in the United States prior to 1866 as well as the debates in Congress

and the temper of the people at the time of the Fourteenth Amendment's formulation, in an endeavor to determine what scope the equal protection clause was intended by its framers to have and how much of a departure it represented from pre-existing concepts. In its second half the study will turn to the interpretation given the clause by the courts and to a comparison of its development with the intent of its framers."

7. THE NEGRO IN POLITICS

ALILUNAS, LEO. "Legal Restrictions on the Negro in Politics," *Journal of Negro History*, XXV (April, 1940), 152-202. NcD, NcU, NcC.
A review of (1) Negro suffrage policies prior to 1915, (2) the rise of the "white primary" movement, (3) judicial cases which developed as a result of this movement, and (4) the political participation of the Negro in the South and North.

BASSETT, JOHN SPENCER. "Suffrage in the State of North Carolina, 1776-1861," *American Historical Association Report* (1895), pp. 269-85. NcD, NcU.
"The degree in which we understand the conditions of suffrage in a State will be a measure of the appreciation of the politics of that State. It is with a view of getting this appreciation of the politics of North Carolina that the present treatment of suffrage has been undertaken."

GOSNELL, HAROLD F. "The Chicago 'Black Belt' as a Political Battleground," *American Journal of Sociology*, XXXIX (November, 1935), 329-41. NcD, NcU.
The free exercise of the suffrage is one of the symbols of the changed status of the Negro in the Northern city.

GOSNELL, HAROLD F. *Negro Politicians*. Chicago: The University of Chicago Press, 1935. Pp. xxxi, 404. NcD, NcU, NcC.
A study of the political struggles of a minority group in an American metropolitan community. It appears that present economic interests are having more influence on Negroes than past political sentiment.

LEWINSON, PAUL. *Race, Class and Party: A History of Negro Suffrage and White Politics in the South*. New York: Oxford University Press, 1932. Pp. x, 302. NcD, NcU, NcC.
A history of Negro suffrage and white politics in the South which attempts to make clear the interaction between the racial question and the white class and party struggle.

LITCHFIELD, EDWARD H. "A Case Study of Negro Political Behavior in Detroit," *Public Opinion Quarterly*, V (June, 1941), 267-74. NcD, NcU.
At last the Negro is becoming politically average.

LOGAN, RAYFORD W., ed. *The Attitude of the Southern White Press Toward Negro Suffrage, 1932-1940*. Washington: The Foundation Publishers, 1940. Pp. xii, 115. NcD, NcU, NcC.
An examination of thirty-six Southern white newspapers over a period of eight years shows "a continuous intolerance in the Deep South and a growing tolerance in the Border States."

MABRY, WILLIAM A. *The Negro in North Carolina Politics Since Reconstruction*. Durham, N. C.: Duke University Press, 1940. Pp. vii, 87. NcD, NcU, NcC.
This study centers around the Populist-Republican fusion campaign of the 1890's when Negroes, courted by all parties, perhaps held the balance of power.

MOON, HENRY LEE. *Balance of Power: The Negro Vote*. New York: Doubleday and Co., 1948. Pp. 256. NcD.

In national elections Negroes tend to divide at the polls in much the same way as the rest of the nation. This book is an analysis of the history and prospects of Negro suffrage in the United States.

MYRDAL, GUNNAR. *An American Dilemma.* 2 vols. (Vol. I, Part V). New York: Harper and Brothers, 1944. NcD, NcU, NcC.
The relative lack of an independent civil service and of a firm legal pattern in public administration in America and especially in the South has greatly enhanced the importance of the ballot. In such a situation a disfranchised group like the Southern Negro group is especially disadvantaged.

NABRIT, JAMES M., JR. "Disabilities Affecting Suffrage Among Negroes," *Journal of Negro Education,* VIII (July, 1939), 383-94. NcD, NcU, NcC.
"The states which enjoy the most unhampered exercise of the right of suffrage and impose the fewest number of restrictions are the states which are furtherest advanced economically, educationally, and socially."

NOWLIN, WILLIAM F. *The Negro in American National Politics.* Boston: The Stratford Co., 1931. Pp. 148. NcD, NcU, NcC.
A study of the part played by the American Negro in national politics since 1868.

PORTER, KIRK H. *A History of Suffrage in the United States.* Chicago: The University of Chicago Press, 1918. Pp. xi, 260. NcD, NcU.
A history of the vigorous fight made since 1776 to secure the suffrage for some large and discontented groups in the general population. Negro suffrage is considered in this wider context.

SHUGG, ROGER W. "Negro Voting in the Ante-Bellum South," *Journal of Negro History,* XXI (October, 1936), 357-64. NcD, NcU, NcC.
Where suffrage was defined by property and not by race, eligible Negroes voted as a matter of course.

SIMKINS, FRANCIS B. *The Tillman Movement in South Carolina.* Durham: Duke University Press, 1926. Pp. ix, 274. NcD, NcU, NcC.
A scholarly study of the career of Ben Tillman and the upsurge of white democracy in South Carolina in the 1890's and after.

SMITH, SAMUEL DENNY. *The Negro in Congress,* 1870-1901. Chapel Hill: The University of North Carolina Press, 1940. Pp. xiii, 160. NcD, NcU, NcC.
"A survey of the careers of twenty-two Negroes who served in Congress during and immediately after Reconstruction, and an evaluation of their achievements."

SMITH, W. R. "Negro Suffrage in the South." Chap. X in *Studies in Southern History and Politics.* New York: Columbia University Press, 1914. NcD, NcU.
A good brief summary.

WEEKS, STEPHEN BEAUREGARD. "The History of Negro Suffrage in the South," *Political Science Quarterly,* IX (December, 1894), 671-703. NcD, NcU.
This article contains much useful information.

WOOFTER, THOMAS J., JR. "Race in Politics: An Opportunity for Original Research," *Social Forces,* VII (March, 1929), 435-38. NcD, NcU, NcC.
Four phases for study: (1) the historical treatment of the Reconstruction period and the disfranchisement movement; (2) the present political status of the Negro both in the North and in the South; (3) the problems of the Negro office-holder; (4) the effects of the political situation on the thinking of the white South.

8. RACE CONSCIOUSNESS

BARTON, REBECCA CHALMERS. *Race Consciousness and the American Negro: A Study of the Correlation Between the Group Experience and the Fiction of 1900-1930.* Copenhagen: Arnold Busck, 1934. Pp. 299. NcU.

The development of race consciousness in the American Negro is traced in his literature through changes in (1) milieu, (2) character, and (3) mood.

BROWN, WILLIAM O. "Emergence of Race Consciousness," *Sociology and Social Research,* XV (May, 1931), 428-36. NcD, NcU.

Race consciousness is the tendency of members of a race to identify their interests, status, and destiny with that of their race.

BROWN, WILLIAM O. "The Nature of Race Consciousness," *Social Forces,* X (October, 1931), 90-97. NcD, NcU, NcC.

The race-conscious person is acutely sensitive to the qualities, honor, and prestige of his race. His race to him becomes a social object to which he writes poetry and which evokes his devotion and loyalty.

BROWN, WILLIAM O. "Race Consciousness Among South African Natives," *American Journal of Sociology,* XL (March, 1935), 569-81. NcD, NcU.

Race consciousness among South African natives lacks maturity, form, and organization but is destined to grow as natives continue to penetrate into the white world.

CAYTON, HORACE R. "Negro Morale," *Opportunity,* XIX (December, 1941), 371-75. NcD, NcU, NcC.

"It has seeped through to the consciousness of the Negro that Hitler considers his Germans superior to all people—even American white people. This gives the American Negro what *Variety Magazine* would call a 'belly laugh.'"

CLARK, J. L. "The Effects of the World War upon the National Spirit of the Colored Peoples," *Southwestern Political and Social Science Quarterly,* IV (September, 1923), 123-37. NcD, NcU.

It was the First World War that intensified imperialism in Japan; started China on the road to national unity; emboldened the brown peoples of India to strike for independence; and raised the blacks of Africa and the Americas in their own estimation.

CLARK, KENNETH B., and CLARK, MAMIE K. "Development of Consciousness of Self and the Emergence of Racial Identification in Negro Pre-School Children," *Journal of Social Psychology,* X (November, 1939), 591-99. NcD, NcU.

Racial identification is assumed to be indicative of a phase in the development of consciousness of self.

CLARK, KENNETH B., and CLARK, MAMIE K. "Skin Color as a Factor in Racial Identification of Negro Pre-School Children," *Journal of Social Psychology,* XI (February, 1940), 159-69. NcD, NcU.

Consciousness of difference from others on the basis of skin color precedes any consciousness of self in terms of socially defined group differences.

DAYKIN, W. L. "Nationalism as Expressed in Negro History," *Social Forces,* XIII (December, 1934), 257-63. NcD, NcU, NcC.

The differentiation of Negro history from general American history "has been paralleled by racial pride, racial consciousness, racial unity and nationalism."

FERGUSON, E. A. "Race Consciousness Among American Negroes," *Journal of Negro Education,* VII (January, 1938), 32-40. NcD, NcU, NcC.

The nature of race consciousness and the agencies fostering it among American Negroes.

GOFFMAN, KIMBAL. "Black Pride," *Atlantic Monthly*, CLXIII (February, 1939), 235-41. NcD, NcU, NcC.
A Negro woman laments the absence of race pride in Negroes. "Black people," she says, "are more prejudiced in favor of the white race, than white people are themselves."

GORDON, EUGENE. "The Negro's Inhibitions," *American Mercury*, XIII (February, 1928), 159-65. NcD, NcU, NcC.
Illustrations of racial self-consciousness in the New Negro.

GUÉRARD, ALBERT. "Southern Memories: Sidelights on the Race Problem," *Scribner's Magazine*, LXXVII (May, 1925), 492-98. NcD, NcU.
Southern white race consciousness is based upon the struggle to "keep the Negro in his place."

JOHNSON, GUY B. "Negro Racial Movements and Leadership in the United States," *American Journal of Sociology*, XLIII (July, 1937), 57-71. NcD, NcU, NcC.
Two opposing Negro philosophies were personified in Booker T. Washington, who preached economic advancement, and in W. E. B. DuBois, who urged militant tactics to secure and enforce legal rights. At present Negro leadership is being realigned.

MENCKEN, HENRY L. "Designations for Colored Folk," *American Speech*, XIX (October, 1944), 161-74. NcD, NcU, NcC.
In their quest for status Negroes have devoted a good deal of effort to the search for a proper and respectable name for their race.

PARK, ROBERT E. "Negro Race Consciousness as Reflected in Race Literature," *American Review*, I (September, October, 1923), 505-16. NcU.
The Negro literary renaissance is not unlike the nationalist struggles in Europe and elsewhere since they too were at the same time linguistic and literary movements.

STANDING, T. G. "Nationalism in Negro Leadership," *American Journal of Sociology*, XL (September, 1934), 180-92. NcD, NcU.
A consideration of Negro leadership in connection with the social movements which produced them and which they led.

STANDING, T. G. "Race Consciousness as Reflected in the Negro Press," *Southwestern Social Science Quarterly*, XIX (December, 1938), 269-80. NcD, NcU.
The most significant feature of the Negro press since Emancipation is its increasingly militant tone and the complete shift of emphasis from a white to a Negro audience.

WINSTON, SANFORD. "Studies in Negro Leadership: Age and Occupational Distribution of 1608 Negro Leaders," *American Journal of Sociology*, XXXVII (January, 1932), 595-602. NcD, NcU, NcC.
Medicine and law are rising to compete with the time-honored occupations of teaching and preaching. The newer occupations require greater support directly from the Negro group.

WOODSON, CARTER G., ed. *The Mind of the Negro as Reflected in Letters Written During the Crisis, 1800-1860*. Washington: Association for the Study of Negro Life and History, 1926. Pp. xxxii, 672. NcD, NcU, NcC.
A mine of information yielding rich insights.

9. RACIAL IDEOLOGIES AND DOCTRINES

BACH, JULIAN S. "The Social Thought of the Old South," *American Journal of Sociology*, XLVI (September, 1940), 179-88. NcD, NcU, NcC.

The social thought of the ante-bellum South was an extension of the slavery argument.

BAILEY, THOMAS P. *Race Orthodoxy in the South.* New York: The Neale Publishing Co., 1914. Pp. vi, 386. NcD, NcU, NcC.
The racial creed of Southern whites.

BROWN, WILLIAM O. "Rationalization of Race Prejudice," *International Journal of Ethics,* XLIII (April, 1933), 294-306. NcD, NcU.
A discussion of the various ideologies—religious, ethical, "scientific," biological, sociological, and historical—that have grown up in support of the prejudices of race.

CALHOUN, JOHN C. *A Disquisition on Government.* Columbia, S. C.: A. S. Johnston, 1851. Pp. vii, 406. NcD, NcU.
Calhoun argued for slavery as a natural social consequence of individual and racial inequalities.

CALVIN, IRA. *The Lost White Race.* Brookline, Massachusetts: Countway-White, 1944. Pp. 192. NcD.
Negroes are ruining American civilization and endangering white supremacy with their demands for equal rights.

CAMPBELL, JOHN. *Negro-Mania.* Philadelphia: Campbell and Power, 1851. Pp. 549. NcD, NcU.
A document produced during the history of the great American debate on the query: "Can the colored races of men be made mentally, politically and socially equal with the white?" The author's lengthy answer is NO.

CLINCHY, EVERETT ROSS. *All in the Name of God.* New York: The John Day Co., 1934. Pp. 194. NcD, NcU.
Some of the more systematic ideologies which have been advanced to justify religious and racial persecution.

COPELAND, LEWIS C. "The Negro as a Contrast Conception." Chap. VI in Edgar T. Thompson, ed., *Race Relations and the Race Problem.* Durham, N. C.: Duke University Press, 1939. NcD, NcU, NcC.
A discussion of the polarization of values and beliefs which has developed in the relations between white and Negro in the South.

COX, EARNEST S. *White America.* Richmond, Va.: White America Society, 1923. Pp. 389. NcU.
A reaction against liberal tendencies in race relations. Argues that if America wants to remain white she must rid herself of her black population.

DEW, THOMAS R. *Reports of the Debates in the Virginia Convention, 1831-1833. Abolition of Slavery. Review of the Debate in the Virginia Legislature, 1831-32.* Included in *The Political Register,* Oct. 16, 1833. Bound with other pamphlets as Congressional Speeches. Pp. 133. NcD, NcU.
Just when the Virginia Constitution Convention of 1831 was considering abolishing slavery, Dew justified it as having always existed. The idea of equality is a vain one, he argued.

DODD, WILLIAM E. "The Social Philosophy of the Old South," *American Journal of Sociology,* XXIII (May, 1918), 735-46. NcD, NcU.
The social philosophers of the Old South examined slavery and found it good.

EATON, CLEMENT. *Freedom of Thought in the Old South.* Durham, N. C.: Duke University Press, 1940. Pp. xix, 343. NcD, NcU.
After the death of Jefferson, Southern thought tended in the direction of a defense of slavery. The turning point was the Nat Turner rebellion and the appearance of the *Liberator,* that is, about 1831. After this time the holder of

"dangerous thoughts" in the South had more to fear from the multitude than from the law.

FITZHUGH, GEORGE. *Sociology for the South: or, The Failure of Free Society*. Richmond, Virginia: A. Morris, 1854. Pp. vi, 310. NcD, NcU.

Fitzhugh went beyond T. R. Dew and John C. Calhoun in his defense of Negro slavery. His book is a curious mixture of contradictions. Political economy is identified with free society, competition, and *laissez faire*. Slavery, rather than socialism, is the best way to eliminate the evils of competition, and Fitzhugh calls this program Sociology.

FORD, JAMES W. *The Negro and the Democratic Front*. New York: International Publishers, 1938. Pp. viii, 222. NcD, NcU, NcC.

Speeches and articles of the Negro vice-presidential candidate of the Communist Party. His ideas on "a way out" for his people are in accord with the orthodox position of the Party.

GOBINEAU, JOSEPH ARTHUR DE. *The Moral and Intellectual Diversity of Races, with Particular Reference to Their Respective Influence in the Civil and Political History of Mankind*. To which is added an appendix containing a summary of the latest scientific facts bearing upon the question of unity or plurality of species by J. C. Nott. Philadelphia: Lippincott, 1856. Pp. xvi, 512. NcD, NcU.

It is quite possible that Gobineau was influenced in the formulation of his doctrines by Josiah Nott, G. R. Gliddon, and other Southern racial philosophers.

GOBINEAU, JOSEPH ARTHUR DE. *The Inequality of Human Races*. New York: G. P. Putnam's Sons, 1915. Pp. xiv, 217. NcD.

This translation by Adrian Collins is only the first book of Gobineau's famous *Essai sur l'inégalité des races humaines*, a polemic against upsurging democratic sentiment in Europe.

GRANT, MADISON. *The Passing of the Great Race: or, The Racial Basis of European History*. New York: Charles Scribner's Sons, 1918. Pp. ix, 441. NcD, NcU.

An American version of the Nordiculous theory.

GRAYSON, WILLIAM J. *The Hireling and the Slave: Chicora and Other Poems*. Charleston, South Carolina: McCarter and Co., 1856. Pp. xv, 190. NcD, NcU.

A Southern white poet's defense of slavery.

HILL, JOHN LOUIS. *Negro: National Asset or Liability?* New York: Literary Associates, Inc., 1930. Pp. xiii, 233. NcD, NcU.

The author, a Southern white man, having arrived at the point where he is willing to accept the Negro as a man like other men, is justly proud of his achievement and desires to tell the world about it.

JENKINS, WILLIAM SUMNER. *Pro-Slavery Thought of the Old South*. Chapel Hill: The University of North Carolina Press, 1935. Pp. xi, 381. NcD, NcU, NcC.

Pro-slavery thought from the mildly apologetic acceptance of colonial days to the militant justification of the period which preceded the Civil War.

LANDRY, STUART OMER. *The Cult of Equality: A Study of the Race Problem*. New Orleans: Pelican Publishing Co., 1945. Pp. xii, 359. NcD.

Hitler's body may lie moldering in his grave, but in this book some of his ideas go marching on.

McKINNEY, THOMAS T. *All White America: A Candid Discussion of Race Mixture and Race Prejudice in the United States.* Boston: Meador Publishing Co., 1937. Pp. 214. NcU.
The author argues that race fusion is inevitable.

MANNHEIM, KARL. *Ideology and Utopia.* New York: Harcourt, Brace and Co., 1936. Pp. xxx, 318. NcD, NcU, NcC.
To those who understand that most racial "knowledge" is ideology this book will have considerable significance.

MEANS, PHILIP A. *Racial Factors in Democracy.* Boston: Marshall Jones Co., 1918. Pp. 278. NcD, NcU.
Emphasizes the interdependence of all groups.

MYERS, HENRY ALONZO. *Are Men Equal? An Inquiry into the Meaning of American Democracy.* New York: G. P. Putnam's Sons, 1945. Pp. viii, 188. NcD.
The development of the idea of human equality in America is traced through six chapters.

MYRDAL, GUNNAR. *An American Dilemma.* 2 vols. (Vol. I, Chap. 4; Vol. II, Chap. 38; and pp. 956-66). New York: Harper and Brothers, 1944. NcD, NcU, NcC.
Popular theories of race are not necessarily logical or accurate but they are intended to serve a well-understood purpose.

ODUM, HOWARD W. *Race and Rumors of Race: Challenge to American Crisis.* Chapel Hill: The University of North Carolina Press, 1943. Pp. x, 245. NcD, NcU, NcC.
This collection of wartime rumors tells a great deal about the body of Southern racial beliefs.

OGBURN, WILLIAM F. "Ideologies of the South in Transition," *Social Forces,* XXIII (March, 1945), 334-42. NcD, NcU, NcC.
"The northern cities are centers of dispersal for the new conquering mores that are spreading over the land. But the missionaries show a narrowness of understanding and an intolerance of the ideologies of other regions. And in the South some of the sectional patriots are equally narrow."

PARK, ROBERT E. "Racial Ideologies," in William F. Ogburn, *American Society in Wartime.* Chicago: The University of Chicago Press, 1943. NcD, NcU, NcC.
"With the progress of the war, the issues involved are becoming clarified, and the points of view of the contending parties, the Axis and the Allies, are in process of redefinition. . . . The issues which were economic and political have become racial and cultural."

POWELL, ADAM CLAYTON. *Riots and Ruins.* New York: Richard B. Smith, 1945. Pp. xiv, 171. NcD, NcU, NcC.
An interesting and startling personal document.

POWELL, ADAM CLAYTON, JR. *Marching Blacks.* New York: The Dial Press, 1946. Pp. 218. NcD, NcU, NcC.
The racial program of a bitter man.

ROMAN, CHARLES VICTOR. *American Civilization and the Negro.* Philadelphia: F. A. Davis Co., 1916. Pp. xii, 434. NcD, NcU.
Myrdal calls this book by a Negro doctor "one of the most brilliant of the early discussions of the biological equality of whites and Negroes."

ROSENBERG, ALFRED. *Der Mythus des 20. Jahrhunderts:eine wertung der seelischgeistigen gestaltenkämpfe unserer zeit.* Munich: Hoheneichen—verlag, 1933. Pp. xxi, 712. NcD, NcU.
The doctrine of Nordic superiority by the high priest of national socialism in Germany.

SHUFELDT, ROBERT W. *America's Greatest Problem: the Negro.* Philadelphia: F. A. Davis Co., 1915. Pp. xii, 377. NcD.
This book, which argues the inferiority of the Negro, had for a time a considerable influence in America.

STODDARD, T. LOTHROP. *The Rising Tide of Color Against White World-Supremacy.* New York: Charles Scribner's Sons, 1922. Pp. xxxii, 320. NcD, NcC.
Much has happened in and to the world since this book was written, but much that has happened since has been the outgrowth of doctrines such as those presented in this and other books by the same author.

VAN EVRIE, JOHN H. *White Supremacy and Negro Subordination.* New York: Van Evrie, Horton and Co., 1868. Pp. xvi, 339. NcD, NcU.
A book written to prove that slavery was not slavery at all, "but a natural relation of the races."

WESLEY, CHARLES H. "The Concept of Negro Inferiority in American Thought," *Journal of Negro History,* XXV (October, 1940), 540-60. NcD, NcU, NcC.
Some interesting direct quotations from the literature are presented.

XVII. Mental Disorders Among Negroes

BENDER, LORETTA. "Behavior Problems in Negro Children," *Psychiatry*, II (May, 1939), 213-28. NcD.
A review of the psychiatric disorders of over 1,000 Negro children at the Bellevue Hospital in New York City directs attention to the connection between these disorders and family disorganization in lower class Negro life.

BEVIS, W. M. "Psychological Traits of the Southern Negro with Observations as to Some of His Psychoses," *American Journal of Psychiatry*, I (July, 1921), 69-78. NcD, NcU.
According to this author Negroes are very much less likely to develop general paresis and alcoholic psychoses than whites.

EVARTS, ARRAH B. "Dementia Praecox in the Colored Race," *Psychoanalytic Review*, I (October, 1913), 388-403. NcD, NcU.
The behavior of each of the three patients studied is clearly related to their special experiences.

EVARTS, ARRAH B. "The Ontogenetic against the Phylogenetic Elements in the Psychoses of the Colored Race," *Psychoanalytic Review*, II (July, 1916), 272-87. NcD. NcU.
The beliefs of mentally ill Negroes are, according to the author, traceable to their African background.

GREEN, E. M. "Manic-Depressive Psychosis in the Negro," *American Journal of Insanity*, LXXIII (April, 1917), 619-25. NcD.
An inadequate study based upon admissions to certain Georgia hospitals.

GREENE, J. E. "Analyses of Racial Differences Within Seven Clinical Categories of White and Negro Mental Patients in the Georgia State Hospital, 1923-32," *Social Forces*, XVII (December, 1938), 201-11. NcD, NcU, NcC.
The data presented "do not justify the assumption of an unquestioned constitutional inferiority among Negroes; nor do they prove conclusively that Negroes have been subjected to socio-economic discrimination prejudicial to mental health."

JACOB, JOSEPH SIMEON. *A Comparative Study of the Incidence of Insanity Among Negroes and Whites*. Bulletin of the University of Georgia, Vol. XXXVIII, No. 2a. Athens, Georgia: University of Georgia, 1938. Pp. 77. NcD.
A study of data from reports of certain state hospitals and U. S. Census summaries. Other data concerning environment, marital, economic, and educational status.

KLINEBERG, OTTO. *Race Differences* (Chap. XIII, "Mental Abnormalities in Race Differences"). New York: Harper and Brothers, 1935. NcD, NcU, NcC.
The author emphasizes the importance of the urbanization of the Negro in the Northern states in producing mental abnormalities.

LIND, JOHN E. "The Color Complex in the Negro," *Psychoanalytic Review*, I (October, 1914), 404-14. NcD, NcU.
The Negro has developed a racial inferiority complex.

LIND, JOHN E. "Phylogenetic Elements in the Psychoses of Negroes," *Psychoanalytic Review*, IV (July, 1917), 303-32. NcD.

[88]

This article reveals more about the author and his racial beliefs than it does about the psychoses of Negroes.

MALZBERG, BENJAMIN. "Mental Disease Among Negroes in New York State," *Human Biology*, VII (December, 1935), 471-513. NcD, NcU.

A study based upon all first admissions to all hospitals for mental disease in New York State during 1929-1931.

MALZBERG, BENJAMIN. "Migration and Mental Disease Among Negroes in New York State," *American Journal of Physical Anthropology*, XXI (January-March, 1936), 107-13. NcD, NcU.

"The author finds that admissions of Negroes to institutions for mental treatment in New York include a much higher proportion of migratory than of New York born persons and suggests that environmental influences are operative and that the supposed special tendency of Negroes to mental disturbance is very dubious."

MALZBERG, BENJAMIN. "Mental Health Among American Negroes: A Statistical Analysis," in Otto Klineberg, ed., *Characteristics of the American Negro*, New York: Harper and Brothers, 1944. NcD, NcU, NcC.

The author opposes the view that "race" is related to the prevalence of mental disease among Negroes.

MOORE, GEORGE S. "Introduction to a Study of Neuropsychiatric Problems Among Negroes," *United States Veterans' Medical Bulletin*, Vol. II, Part I (November, 1926), 1042-51; Vol. III, Part II (September, 1927), 887-97. NcD.

The lower social status of the Negro has a marked effect upon his mental abnormalities.

O'MALLEY, MARY. "Psychoses in the Colored Race," *American Journal of Insanity*, LXXI (October, 1914), 309-37. NcD.

A none-too-critical study of proportionate rates for whites and Negroes.

POWELL, T. O. "The Increase of Insanity and Tuberculosis in the Southern Negro since 1860, and Its Alliance and Some of the Supposed Causes," *Journal of the American Medical Association*, XXVII (December 5, 1896), 1185-88. NcU.

An increase in mental disease and tuberculosis accompanied emancipation and freedom.

ROSENTHAL, SOLOMON P. "Racial Differences in the Mental Diseases," *Journal of Abnormal and Social Psychology*, XXVIII (October-December, 1933), 301-18. NcD, NcU, NcC.

A criticism of available statistics and of the conclusions of others who have written on the subject.

ROSENTHAL, SOLOMON P. "Racial Differences in the Incidence of Mental Disease," *Journal of Negro Education*, III (July, 1934), 484-93. NcD, NcU, NcC.

An analysis of Negro and white mental disease rates. Faulty hospital statistics make it difficult if not impossible to decide the question of racial differences in susceptibility to mental disease.

SHERMAN, MANDEL, and SHERMAN, IRENE C. "Psychic Symptoms and Social Backgrounds." Chap. XVIII in I. M. Bentley and E. V. Cowdry, eds., *The Problem of Mental Disorder*. New York: McGraw-Hill Book Co., 1934. NcD, NcU.

Notes the similarity between the mental symptoms of Negro women patients and those of white men patients.

SWIFT, H. M. "Insanity and Race," *American Journal of Insanity*, LXX (July, 1913), 143-54. NcD.

Material bearing upon the frequency of insanity among various immigrant nationality or racial groups as shown by admissions to Massachusetts state hospitals for the insane.

WAGNER, P. S. "A Comparative Study of the Negro and White Admissions to the Psychiatric Pavilion of the Cincinnati General Hospital," *American Journal of Psychiatry*, XCV (July, 1938), 156-83. NcD, NcU.

This uncritical study concludes that Negroes had higher admission rates than whites.

WIGGINS, E. J., and LYMAN, RICHARD S. "Manic Psychosis in a Negro. With Special Reference to the Role of the Psychogenic and Sociogenic Factors," *American Journal of Psychiatry*, C (May, 1944), 781-87. NcD, NcU.

A case study emphasizing environmental factors in the psychosis of a Negro farmer.

XVIII. Negro Crime and Delinquency

BONGER, WILLIAM A. *Race and Crime.* Translated from the Dutch by
Margaret Mathews Hordyk. New York: Columbia University Press, 1943.
Pp. x, 130. NcD, NcU.

A study of the supposed influence of race in criminality. The author concludes that the theory of racial predisposition to crime has no scientific basis.

BREARLEY, H. C. *Homicide in the United States* (Chap. VI, "The Negro and
Homicide"). Chapel Hill: The University of North Carolina Press, 1932.
NcD, NcU.

The facts presented on the high homicide rate for Negroes are important,
but the explanation of the facts is inadequate.

BRINTON, HUGH P. "Negroes Who Run Afoul of the Law," *Social Forces,*
XI (October, 1932), 96-101. NcD, NcU, NcC.

A report on a study of Negro crime in Durham, North Carolina, from July
1, 1922 to July 1, 1927. The evidence shows that Durham Negroes are not
ordinarily arrested for crimes of a serious nature, but rather for causes indicating social disorganization such as fighting and drinking.

CANTOR, NATHANIEL. "Crime and the Negro," *Journal of Negro History,*
XVI (January, 1931), 61-66. NcD, NcU, NcC.

More crimes of a certain kind are committed by Negroes because of their
relations with whites.

GILMORE, HARLAN W. *Racial Disorganization in a Southern City.* Nashville,
Tenn.: The McQuiddy Press, 1931. Pp. vi, 70. NcU.

The distribution of white and Negro dependency and delinquency studied and
compared.

JOHNSON, GUY B. "The Negro and Crime," *Annals of the American Academy
of Political and Social Science,* CCXVII (September, 1941), 93-104. NcD,
NcU, NcC.

Not physiological or mental difference, not cultural difference, but the low
status of the Negro in American society is perhaps the most important factor
in Negro crime.

JOINT Committee on Negro Child Study in New York City. *A Study of Delinquent and Neglected Negro Children.* New York: Joint Committee on Negro
Child Study in New York City, 1927. Pp. 48. NcD.

Disorderly conduct and desertion of home are the most frequent charges
against Negro boys whereas stealing and burglary rank first among white boys.
This indicates the absence of a strong family tradition among Negroes.

LIGHTFOOT, ROBERT M. *Negro Crime in a Small Urban Community.* Publications of the University of Virginia. Phelps-Stokes Fellowship Papers
No. 12, 1934. Pp. 85. NcD, NcU.

When all the factors are considered the question changes from, "Why do
Negroes commit so many crimes?" to "Why do not Negroes commit more
crimes than they do?"

MOSES, EARL R. "Community Factors in Negro Delinquency," *Journal of
Negro Education,* V (April, 1936), 220-27. NcD, NcU, NcC.

The Negro delinquent in the city is to a great extent the product of settlement in disorganized areas where delinquent patterns of behavior prevail.

MYRDAL, GUNNAR. *An American Dilemma.* 2 vols. (Vol. II, pp. 966-79). New York: Harper and Brothers, 1944. NcD, NcU, NcC.

Negroes are not ordinarily in a position to commit respectable, white-collar crimes; "they commit the crimes which much more frequently result in apprehension and punishment."

SELLIN, THORSTEN. "The Negro Criminal: A Statistical Note," *Annals of the American Academy of Political and Social Science,* CXL (November, 1928), 52-64. NcD, NcU, NcC.

"It is the purpose of this article to indicate some of the ways by which the differential treatment to which the Negro is subjected by our agencies of criminal justice artificially increases his *apparent* criminality, while that of the white is, by virtue of the same treatment, so reduced that comparisons between the two become exceedingly hazardous unless this situation is properly evaluated and the rates corrected."

SPIRER, JESSE. *Negro Crime.* Comparative Psychological Monographs, Serial No. 81, Vol. XVI. Baltimore: The Johns Hopkins Press, 1940. Pp. 64. NcD, NcU, NcC.

A study of commitments in the Western State Penitentiary of Pennsylvania from 1906 through 1935.

STEINER, JESSE F., and BROWN, ROY M. *The North Carolina Chain Gang: A Study of County Convict Road Work.* Chapel Hill: The University of North Carolina Press, 1927. Pp. viii, 194. NcD, NcU, NcC.

An objective study of the chain gang existence of white and Negro convicts.

TULCHIN, SIMON H. *Intelligence and Crime: A Study of Penitentiary and Reformatory Offenders.* Chicago: The University of Chicago Press, 1939. Pp. xiii, 166. NcD, NcU, NcC.

The race factor in crime is considered along with other factors such as age, sex, etc.

VON HENTIG, HANS. "The Criminality of the Negro," *Journal of Criminal Law and Criminology,* XXX (January, 1940), 662-80. NcD, NcU.

Based on an incomplete knowledge of statistical intricacies and the use of misleading absolute figures, a real mythology of racial delinquency has sprung up. This article attempts a correction.

WILDER, FRANCIS S. "Crime in the Superior Courts of North Carolina," *Social Forces,* V (March, 1927), 423-27. NcD, NcU, NcC.

In the period 1922-25 there were reported 4.65 indictments per 1,000 whites and 8.71 indictments per 1,000 Negroes.

WORK, MONROE N. "Negro Criminality in the South," *Annals of the American Academy of Political and Social Science,* XLIX (September, 1913), 74-80. NcD, NcU.

It is significant that the number of lynchings reached its highest point about the same period that Negro crime reached its highest point, about 1892.

XIX. Racial Pride and Prejudice

ALEXANDER, CHESTER. "Antipathy and Social Behavior," *American Journal of Sociology*, LI (January, 1946), 288-92. NcD, NcU, NcC.
Although prejudice is dependent on antipathy there is a fundamental distinction between the two.

ALLPORT, GORDON W., ed. "Controlling Group Prejudice," *Annals of the American Academy of Political and Social Science*, CCXLIV (March, 1946). NcD, NcU, NcC.
Moralists, industrialists, educators, legislators, social scientists, and other specialists consider the problem of controlling prejudice against minority groups.

BARUCH, DOROTHY W. *The Glass House of Prejudice.* New York: William Morrow and Co., 1946. Pp. ix, 205. NcD, NcC.
"Minority problems," says the author, "are problems of the majority."

BAYTON, JAMES A. "The Racial Stereotypes of Negro College Students," *Journal of Abnormal and Social Psychology*, XXXVI (January, 1941), 97-102. NcD, NcU, NcC.
Here it is shown that Negro college students have a conception of the typical Negro which is highly similar to that held by white college students. The two groups agree that the Negro is superstitious, lazy, happy-go-lucky, very religious, loud, and musical.

BELFRAGE, CEDRIC. *A Faith to Free the People.* New York: Dryden Press, 1944. Pp. ix, 317. NcD.
The story of the conversion of Claude Williams, a Southern poor white, from prejudice to humanitarianism.

BLUMER, HERBERT. "The Nature of Race Prejudice," *Social Process in Hawaii*, V, 11-20. NcD.
Race relations occur in a situation where the dominant and subordinate ethnic groups are usually living together. This means that, to the dominant group, the threat of attack seems to come from an "inner enemy" which makes the resulting apprehension more abiding, more perplexing, more worrisome, and more unstable.

BOGARDUS, EMORY S. "Social Distance and Its Origins," *Journal of Applied Sociology*, IX (January-February, 1925), 216-26. NcD, NcU.
Thirty-nine racial and national groups were ranked in order of preference by a group in Los Angeles. The greatest opposition was expressed toward Turks, with Negroes, mulattoes, Japanese, and Hindus following in that order.

BOGARDUS, EMORY S. "Measuring Social Distance," *Journal of Applied Sociology*, IX (March-April, 1925), 299-308. NcD, NcU.
A report on an interesting and significant test of inter-racial and inter-nationality attitudes.

BROWN, FRED. "A Socio-Psychological Analysis of Race Prejudice," *Journal of Abnormal and Social Psychology*, XXVII (January-March, 1933), 364-74. NcD, NcU.
" . . . racial prejudice arises when we have on the one hand a dominant habitat controlling group and on the other an 'inferior' group making the superior group's habitat its own."

BROWN, WILLIAM O. "Race Prejudice as a Factor in the Status of the American Negro," *Journal of Negro Education,* VIII (July, 1939), 349-58. NcD, NcU, NcC.
"Any movement resulting in the economic, political or social collaboration of Negroes and whites is far more important in the mitigation of prejudice than all the grand gestures across race lines."

BRYANT, SOPHIE. "Antipathy and Sympathy," *Mind,* IV (July, 1895), 365-70. N.S. NcD, NcU.
An analysis of antipathy and its relation to sympathy.

CLARK, FRANCIS EDWARD. "Our Dearest Antipathies," *Atlantic Monthly,* CXXVII (February, 1921), 239-43. NcD, NcU.
Racial and national prejudices as well as our more obvious, every-day antipathies.

COX, OLIVER C. "Race Prejudice and Intolerance—A Distinction," *Social Forces,* XXIV (December, 1945), 216-19. NcD, NcU, NcC.
White American gentiles "are ordinarily intolerant of Jews but prejudiced against Negroes."

CURRIER, ISABEL. "Prejudice Among the Unprejudiced," *Common Ground,* V (Spring, 1945), 3-9. NcD, NcC.
It seems that almost everyone is prejudiced.

DAVIDSON, HENRY A. "The Anatomy of Prejudice," *Common Ground,* I (Winter, 1941), 3-12. NcD.
A summary of various theories that have been advanced to account for race prejudice.

EDWARDS, LYFORD P. "Religious Sectarianism and Race Prejudice," *American Journal of Sociology,* XLI (September, 1935), 167-79. NcD, NcU.
"Religious sectarianism may on occasion mitigate race prejudice, but among the vast majority of members of most sects race prejudice is dominant over sectarianism. In certain cases they are hardly distinguishable. That which gives sectarianism greater power over patriotism or race consciousness is mystical experience."

FARIS, ELLSWORTH. "Racial Attitudes and Sentiments," *Southwestern Political and Social Science Quarterly,* IX (March, 1929), 479-90. NcD, NcU. Also in Ellsworth Faris, *The Nature of Human Nature* (Chap. XXVIII). New York: McGraw-Hill Book Co., 1937. NcD, NcU, NcC.
"Race prejudice, being a collective phenomenon, is always localized in space, for groups are situated on the land. Race prejudice is thus attached to the soil. It should be studied with the assistance of the map. It would be highly profitable to have a world map of race prejudice."

FARIS, ELLSWORTH. "Remarks on Race Superiority," *Social Service Review,* I (March, 1927), 36-45. NcD, NcU. Also in Ellsworth Faris, *The Nature of Human Nature* (Chap. XXIX). New York: McGraw-Hill Book Co., 1937. NcD, NcU, NcC.
"In order to be superior, we must act inferior. We Nordics are in a dilemma."

FARIS, ELLSWORTH. "The Natural History of Race Prejudice," in Charles S. Johnson, ed., *Ebony and Topaz.* New York: National Urban League, Journal of Negro Life Press, 1927. NcU. Also in Ellsworth Faris, *The Nature of Human Nature* (Chap. XXXII). New York: McGraw-Hill Book Co., 1937. NcD, NcU, NcC.
"The reader is asked to regard the occurrence of race prejudice as a natural phenomenon, just as truly as a drought, an earthquake, or an epidemic of smallpox."

FINOT, JEAN. *Race Prejudice.* New York: E. P. Dutton and Co., 1921. Pp. xvi, 320. NcD, NcU, NcC.

Translated from the French by Florence Wade-Evans. The thesis of this book is that there are superior and inferior races, but that races vary because they are living within or without different spheres of cultural influence.

FRAZIER, E. FRANKLIN. "The Pathology of Race Prejudice," *Forum,* LXXVII (June, 1927), 856-62. Discussion, *Forum, LXXVIII* (September, 1927), 458-60. NcD, NcU.

This article begins with the statement by Walter Hines Page that "The Negro-in-America . . . is a form of insanity that overtakes white men," and concludes with Nietzsche's remark that "insanity in individuals is something rare—but in groups, parties, nations, and epochs it is the rule."

GIESEBRECHT, FRANZ. *Die Behandlung der Eingeborenen in den deutschen Kolonieen.* Berlin: S. Fischer, 1898. Pp. 194. NcD.

A collection of opinions concerning natives in the former German colonies in Africa from anthropologists, colonial officials, and missionaries.

HARTLEY, EUGENE L. *Problems in Prejudice.* New York: Columbia University Press, 1946. Pp. x, 124. NcD.

An experimental and quantitative study. Prejudice, the author concludes, is general, not specific. There is no such thing, basically, as anti-Semitism or Negro prejudice.

HELLENBACH VON PACZOLAY, LAZAR. *Die Vorurtheile der Menschheit.* 3rd ed. 3 vols. Leipzig: Oswald Muntze, 1893. NcD.

A comprehensive study of prejudice done with characteristic German thoroughness.

HIBBEN, JOHN GRIER. *A Defense of Prejudice and Other Essays.* New York: Charles Scribner's Sons, 1921. Pp. 183. NcD, NcC.

In the principal essay the former president of Princeton University argues that a man without prejudice is a man without conviction, and ultimately without character. Prejudice is a profoundly human phenomenon and as such deserves some defense against those who are prejudiced against it.

HOROWITZ, EUGENE L. "The Development of Attitudes Toward the Negro," *Archives of Psychology,* XXVIII, No. 194 (January, 1936). Pp. 47. NcD, NcU.

A study of the development of white children's attitudes toward the Negro.

HOROWITZ, EUGENE L. "'Race' Attitudes," in Otto Klineberg, ed., *Characteristics of the American Negro.* New York: Harper and Brothers, 1944. NcD, NcU, NcC.

A summary and evaluation of the literature with hypotheses for future research suggested by the author.

HUSSEY, L. M. "Aframerican, North and South," *American Mercury,* VII (February, 1926), 196-200. NcD, NcU, NcC.

In the South he is ignored. In the North he often is over-praised.

HUSZAR, GEORGE B. DE, comp. *Antatomy of Racial Intolerance.* New York: The H. W. Wilson Co., 1946. Pp. 283. NcD, NcU, NcC.

A wide variety of pronouncements on the subject of race prejudice by experts and laymen.

JACKSON, HOLBROOK. "The Advantage of Being Prejudiced," *The Living Age,* CCCII (September 27, 1919), 780-82. NcD, NcU.

96 RACE AND REGION

"We are only too ready to blame in another those weaknesses which we secretly cherish in ourselves. For instance, what we call meanness in others we call carefulness, economy, thrift, and other high-sounding names in ourselves. It has occurred to some, therefore, that the same fate may have happened to this maligned thing, prejudice."

JOHNSON, CHARLES S. "Measurement of Race Attitudes," *Publications of the American Sociological Society*, XXV (May, 1931), 150-57. NcD, NcU.

The writer "is concerned with the development of a method of studying racial attitudes quantitatively and in relating these attitudes to types of group contact and such factors as sex, age, education, religion, party affiliation and immediate ancestry."

LASKER, BRUNO. *Race Attitudes in Children*. New York: Henry Holt and Co., 1929. Pp. xvi, 394. NcD, NcU, NcC.

How acquired, how expressed, and how modified. A study of the role of institutionalized antagonism and absorption of adult attitudes in early childhood as a cause of race prejudice.

MAZYCK, WALTER H. *George Washington and the Negro*. Washington: Associated Publishers, Inc., 1932. Pp. vii, 180. NcD, NcU, NcC.

This book traces the gradual evolution of George Washington's "regard for human rights as unfolded by his changing attitude toward the Negro."

MORSE, JOSIAH. "The Psychology of Prejudice," *International Journal of Ethics*, XVII (July, 1907), 490-506. NcD, NcU.

"It is characteristic of those who are prejudiced the most that they not only lack high mental and moral development, but they have little desire to attain it."

MYERS, GUSTAVUS. *History of Bigotry in the United States*. New York: Random House, 1943. Pp. viii, 504. NcD, NcU, NcC.

The author believes bigotry and intolerance to be more of a threat to American security than an attack by an armed foe.

MYRDAL, GUNNAR. *An American Dilemma*. 2 vols. (Vol. II, Appendix 10). New York: Harper and Brothers, 1944. NcD, NcU, NcC.

Quantitative studies of race attitudes.

O'HARA, JOHN. *Pipe Night*. New York: Duell, Sloan and Pearce, 1945. Pp. xiv, 205. NcD.

These skillful little stories illustrate the fact that snobberies, points of social honor, and idiosyncracies of personal prestige are by no means confined to the relationships of race.

OLIVIER, SYDNEY HALDANE. "Colour Prejudice," *Contemporary Review*, CXXIV (October, 1923), 448-57. NcD, NcU.

Although closely related there is, nevertheless, an important distinction to be made between race prejudice and color prejudice. "Race prejudice is a much more ancient, widespread, and deeply-seated phenomenon, and in so far as skin and hair are an ensign and advertisement of race and are interpreted as a docket of the qualities inductively attributed to a race, colour prejudice is merely a reflex of race prejudice."

PARK, ROBERT E. "The Concept of Social Distance," *Journal of Applied Sociology*, VIII (July-August, 1924), 339-44. NcD, NcU.

In our personal relations with others we are conscious of degrees of intimacy. These grades and degrees measure "social distance." What we ordinarily call prejudice is a disposition to maintain social distance.

PARK, ROBERT E. "The Bases of Race Prejudice," *Annals of the American Academy of Political and Social Science*, CXL (November, 1928), 11-20. NcD, NcU, NcC.

Park distinguishes between antipathy and prejudice. Antipathy is more elemental and rooted in original nature. Prejudice, on the other hand, is "an elementary expression of conservatism."

PARTON, JAMES. "Antipathy to the Negro," *North American Review*, CXXVII (November-December, 1878), 476-91. NcD, NcU.

What we now call prejudice was earlier referred to as antipathy.

POWDERMAKER, HORTENSE. *Probing our Prejudices*. New York: Harper and Brothers, 1944. Pp. viii, 73. NcD, NcU, NcC.

"This small book is an attempt to help high school students become aware of their prejudices, to understand the nature, origin, and effect of prejudices, and to suggest activities which can help reduce them."

RACIAL Attitudes. Social Science Source Documents No. 3. Nashville: Social Science Institute, Fisk University, 1946. Pp. 270. NcD, NcU, NcC.

Interviews revealing attitudes of Northern and Southern whites toward Negroes. Mimeographed.

SCHUYLER, GEORGE S. "Our White Folks," *American Mercury*, XII (December, 1927), 385-92. NcD, NcU, NcC.

This journalistic account of white society reveals what Blumer calls counter-prejudice.

SHALER, NATHANIEL S. "Race Prejudices," *Atlantic Monthly*, LVIII (October, 1886), 510-18. NcD, NcU.

Whatever sets men apart creates a boundary to the extension of the sense of sympathy. Of all the circumstances which naturally limit the sympathies the most effective is physical difference.

SIMS, V. M., and PATRICK, J. R. "Attitude Toward the Negro of Northern and Southern College Students," *Journal of Social Psychology*, VII (May, 1936), 192-204. NcD, NcU.

Northern white college students on the average are apparently more favorable toward the Negro than are Southern white students, but Northern students in Southern institutions approach more nearly the attitude of Southern students.

SMITH, FRED TREDWELL. *An Experiment in Modifying Attitudes Toward the Negro*. New York: Teachers' College, Columbia University, 1943. Pp. x, 135. NcD, NcU, NcC.

Can planned and controlled new experiences change the attitudes of whites toward Negroes?

TENENBAUM, SAMUEL. *Why Men Hate*. New York: Beechhurst Press, 1947. Pp. 368. NcD.

Forty-five short essays on the pervasive elements in all sorts of prejudice.

THOMAS, WILLIAM I. "The Psychology of Race-Prejudice," *American Journal of Sociology*, IX (March, 1904), 593-611. NcD, NcU.

This article contains an excellent discussion of prejudice in relation to various physical traits and features.

THURSTON, L. L. "An Experimental Study of Nationality Preferences," *Journal of General Psychology*, I (July-October, 1928), 405-25. NcD, NcU.

In this first genuine effort to measure racial preference students at the University of Chicago ranked American whites first and Negroes last in a ranking of twenty-one ethnic and cultural groups. Turks ranked just above the Negroes.

WALLIS, W. D. "The Prejudices of Men," *American Journal of Sociology*, XXXIV, (March, 1929), 804-21. NcD, NcU.

Prejudice is kept alive by interests, ignorance, inertia of opinion, and isolation.

YOUNG, ERLE FISKE. "What Is Race Prejudice?" *Journal of Applied Sociology*, X (November, 1925), 135-40. NcD, NcU.

Although we are able to recognize our prejudices as such, we continue to entertain them and to be influenced by them. We can recognize them but we cannot reason them away.

YOUNG, ERLE FISKE. "Race and Religion," *Sociology and Social Research*, XIII (1928-1929), 459-64. NcD, NcU.

Race prejudice is often strongly reinforced by religious prejudice and one is not always certain which is operating in a given case.

XX. The Negro in His "Place"

I. SLAVERY

BALLAGH, JAMES C. "The Institutional Origin of Slavery," *Conservative Review*, II (August, 1899), 47-64. NcD.
Negro slavery in Virginia was a growth, not a transplantation.

BALLAGH, JAMES C. *A History of Slavery in Virginia.* Baltimore: The Johns Hopkins Press, 1902. Pp. viii, 160. NcD, NcU.
Ballagh was the first to call attention to the fact that Negro slavery in Virginia developed from white indentured servitude.

BASSETT, JOHN SPENCER. *Slavery and Servitude in the Colony of North Carolina,* Johns Hopkins University Studies in Historical and Political Science, Series XIV, IV-V (1896). Pp. 86. NcD, NcU.
On the introduction, legal status, religious and social life of Negro slaves. Other chapters deal with the free Negro, Indian slavery, and white servitude.

BASSETT, JOHN SPENCER. *Slavery in the State of North Carolina,* Johns Hopkins University Studies in Historical and Political Science, Series XVII, VII-VIII (1899). Pp. 111. NcD, NcU, NcC.
The standard work on the subject.

BOTKIN, B. A., ed. *Lay My Burden Down: A Folk History of Slavery.* Chicago: The University of Chicago Press, 1945. Pp. xxi, 285. NcD, NcC.
What was slavery like? How does it feel to be owned by someone? What is freedom like? Negro slaves tell their own story of slavery and emancipation.

EMERSON, FREDERICK V. "Geographical Influences in American Slavery," *Bulletin of the American Geographical Society,* XLIII (January-March, 1911), 13-26, 106-18, 170-81. NcD, NcU.
"The purpose of this paper is to trace from the geographic standpoint the development and extension of slavery."

HEDRICK, CHARLES EMBURY. *Social and Economic Aspects of Slavery in the Transmontane Prior to 1850.* Nashville, Tennessee: George Peabody College for Teachers, 1927. Pp. 143. NcD, NcU.
Slavery in the transmontane states of West Virginia, Kentucky, and Tennessee compared and contrasted with slavery in the older plantation states.

HURSTON, ZORA NEALE. "Cudjo's Own Story of the Last African Slaver," *Journal of Negro History,* XII (October, 1927), 648-63. NcD, NcU, NcC.
The story of Cudjo Lewis, the last survivor of the last slave cargo landed in America reported by a competent Negro anthropologist.

JERNEGAN, MARCUS W. "Slavery and Conversion in the American Colonies," *American Historical Review,* XXI (April, 1916), 504-27. NcD, NcU.
When religious difference became an insecure basis for slavery a new justification was found in the idea of race.

LORIA, A. "The Historical Origin of Slavery: A Fragment of the 'Analysis of the Theory of Capital,'" translated by W. Lloyd Bevan, *Sewanee Review,* VIII (October, 1900), 466-77. NcD, NcU.
Compares the situation in which slavery developed in America with the situation in the Roman Empire, in Russia, and with other historical situations characterized by slavery.

MATTHEWS, ESSIE COLLINS. *Aunt Phebe, Uncle Tom and Others: Character Studies Among the Old Slaves of the South. Fifty Years After.* Columbus, Ohio: The Champlin Press, 1915. Pp. 140. NcD, NcU.
Significant for its pictures.

MOORE, WILBERT E. "Slave Law and the Social Structure," *Journal of Negro History,* XXVI (April, 1941), 171-202. NcD, NcU, NcC.
This important article traces the transition from heathenism to racialism as the justification for Negro slavery in the American colonies.

MUNFORD, BEVERLY BLAND. *Virginia's Attitude Toward Slavery and Secession.* New York: Longmans, Green and Co., 1909. Pp. xiii, 329. NcD, NcU, NcC.
Here are shown, among many other matters, extremely interesting human documents in the form of deeds and wills emancipating slaves.

NIEBOER, H. J. *Slavery as an Industrial System.* The Hague: M. Nejhoff, 1910. Pp. xx, 474. NcD, NcU.
The most important study of slavery in print. The author accounts for it as a response to a situation of "open resources" as opposed to a situation of "closed resources" to which free labor is a response.

PHILLIPS, ULRICH B. *American Negro Slavery: A Survey of the Supply, Employment and Control of Negro Labor as Determined by the Plantation Régime.* New York: D. Appleton and Co., 1918. Pp. xi, 529. NcD, NcU, NcC.
A comprehensive study of the wide ramification of Negro slavery in the old South.

RAMSDELL, CHARLES W. "The Natural Limits of Slavery Expansion," *Mississippi Valley Historical Review,* XVI (September, 1929), 151-71. NcD, NcU.
In 1860 slavery was losing ground along the northern border of the South and was no longer moving westward. It had reached its limits in both profits and lands.

RUSSELL, JOHN HENDERSON. "Colored Freemen as Slave Owners in Virginia," *Journal of Negro History,* I (July, 1916), 233-42. NcD, NcU, NcC.
Until the Civil War some Negroes held other Negroes as slaves but the constant trend was to restrict slavery to Negroes and mastership to whites.

SETTLE, OPHELIA. "Social Attitudes During the Slave Regime: Household Servants versus Field Hands," *Publications of the American Sociological Society,* XXVIII (May, 1934), 95-96. NcD, NcU.
During slavery there was a marked disposition for household servants to regard themselves as superior to field hands.

SYDNOR, CHARLES S. *Slavery in Mississippi.* New York: D. Appleton-Century Co., 1933. Pp. xiii, 270. NcD, NcU, NcC.
A description and an analysis of Negro slavery in Mississippi including information on working conditions, provisions for food, clothes, shelter, and physical and social care as well as on the buying and selling of slaves.

SYDNOR, CHARLES S. "The Biography of a Slave," *South Atlantic Quarterly,* XXXVI (January, 1937), 59-73. NcD, NcU, NcC.
The authentic and dramatic story of a Negro enslaved in Africa, brought to America, and finally returned to his homeland.

TAYLOR, ROSSER H. "Slaveholding in North Carolina: An Economic View," *James Sprunt Historical Publications,* Vol. XVIII, Nos. 1-2 (1926). NcD, NcU, NcC.
A close reading of this factual study suggests why the relations between the races in North Carolina are even today different from what they are in the other Southern states. North Carolina was never a great plantation state.

TODD, T. WINGATE. "Anthropology and Negro Slavery," *Medical Life,* XXXVI (March, 1929), 157-67. NcD.
A brief but significant survey of the rise of anthropology in connection with the slave trade and its abolition.

UNWRITTEN History of Slavery. Social Science Source Documents No. 1. Nashville: Social Science Institute, Fisk University, 1946. Pp. 322. NcD, NcU, NcC.
Autobiographical accounts of Negro ex-slaves. Mimeographed.

VASSA, GUSTAVUS. *The Interesting Narrative of the Life of Olaudah Equiano, or Gustavus Vassa, the African.* Boston: Isaac Knapp, 1837. Pp. vi, 294. NcD, NcU, NcC.
A description of colonial America seen through the eyes of an African slave.

WILKINSON, (MRS.) ELIZA. *Letters of Eliza Wilkinson.* Arranged from the Original Manuscripts by Caroline Gilman. New York: S. Colman, 1839. Pp. viii, 108. NcD, NcU.
To Mrs. Wilkinson, a naïve person of buoyant spirit, the presence of Negro slaves around her on her South Carolina plantation was as natural as the air she breathed or the food she ate.

WILLIAMS, ERIC. *Capitalism and Slavery.* Chapel Hill: The University of North Carolina Press, 1944. Pp. ix, 285. NcD, NcU, NcC.
A study of the role of Negro slavery in the development of industrial capitalism.

WILSON, CALVIN D. "Black Masters: A Side-Light on Slavery," *North American Review,* CLXXXI (November, 1905), 685-98. NcD, NcU.
A singular and dramatic aspect of slavery in the United States was the occasional ownership of bondsmen by free blacks.

WILSON, CALVIN D. "Negroes Who Owned Slaves," *Popular Science Monthly,* LXXXI (November, 1912), 483-94. NcD, NcU.
This article presents material, much of it gathered by A. H. Stone, on Negro and mulatto masters of from one to a hundred slaves.

WOODSON, CARTER G., ed. *Free Negro Owners of Slaves in the United States in 1830: Together with Absentee Ownership of Slaves in the United States in 1830.* Washington: The Association for the Study of Negro Life and History, 1924. Pp. viii, 78. NcD, NcU, NcC.
The majority of Negro owners of slaves were such because of the purchase of a wife, husband, or relative through motives of natural affection. Most lived in urban communities. Names of specific slave holders and their holdings are given by states.

2. THE FREE NEGRO

DODGE, DAVID (pseud.). "The Free Negroes of North Carolina," *Atlantic Monthly,* LVII (January, 1886), 20-30. NcD, NcU.
One of the earliest articles dealing with the free Negroes of the South. Explains the origin of the distinction between the "Old Issue" and the "New Issue."

FITCHETT, E. HORACE. "The Traditions of the Free Negro in Charleston, South Carolina," *Journal of Negro History,* XXV (April, 1940), 139-52. NcD, NcU, NcC.
A study of free Negroes who were, however, not entirely free men.

FLANDERS, RALPH B. "The Free Negro in Ante-Bellum Georgia," *North Carolina Historical Review,* IX (July, 1932), 250-72. NcD, NcU, NcC.
"It is the purpose of this essay to investigate the legal status of this unenviable class, to describe the hardships and mitigations of the system of society under which they lived and moved, and explain the sentiment of Georgia with respect to them."

FRANKLIN, JOHN HOPE. *The Free Negro in North Carolina, 1790-1860.* Chapel Hill: The University of North Carolina Press, 1943. Pp. x, 271. NcD, NcU, NcC.

Numbers, distribution, manumission, runaway slaves, immigrant free Negroes, and their occupations, are aspects of Negro population treated by the author. The book has the dramatic force of a study in mass frustration.

FRANKLIN, JOHN HOPE. "The Enslavement of Free Negroes in North Carolina," *Journal of Negro History,* XXIX (October, 1944), 401-28. NcD, NcU, NcC.

An account of those free Negroes who sought enslavement to white masters and also of the unsuccessful movement for the re-enslavement of free Negroes generally.

FRANKLIN, JOHN HOPE. "James Boon, Free Negro Artisan," *Journal of Negro History,* XXX (April, 1945), 150-80. NcD, NcU, NcC.

The story of one free Negro gives insight into the status and role of the free Negro generally.

FRAZIER, E. FRANKLIN. *The Free Negro Family: A Study of Family Origins Before the Civil War.* Nashville, Tennessee: Fisk University Press, 1932. Pp. 75. NcD, NcU, NcC.

A short study of the families that became the vanguard in the cultural and economic progress of the race.

IMES, WILLIAM LLOYD. "The Legal Status of Free Negroes and Slaves in Tennessee," *Journal of Negro History,* IV (July, 1919), 254-72. NcD, NcU, NcC.

A historical survey of laws in Tennessee from 1834 to 1865 showing the tendency to increase the restrictions on the slave and to eliminate the free Negro.

JACKSON, LUTHER P. "Free Negroes of Petersburg, Va.," *Journal of Negro History,* XII (July, 1927), 365-88. NcD, NcU, NcC.

A valuable article containing biographical narratives of several free Negroes.

JACKSON, LUTHER P. *Free Negro Labor and Property Holding in Virginia, 1830-1860.* New York: D. Appleton-Century Co., 1942. Pp. xix, 270. NcD, NcU, NcC.

"The advancement made by the free Negro, in spite of the law, is the theme of this study."

RUSSELL, JOHN HENDERSON. *The Free Negro in Virginia, 1619-1865.* Baltimore: The Johns Hopkins Press, 1913. Pp. viii, 194. NcD, NcU.

The position of the free Negro in the ante-bellum South is evidence of the fact that the artificial restrictions of a slave system tend to give way before the demands of a common daily life, as a result of which a new order of society appears in which personal ability plays a greater part in determining status. Even in such a case, however, a single mark of difference may preserve a narrow but unbridgeable chasm between the two races.

SYDNOR, CHARLES S. "The Free Negro in Mississippi before the Civil War," *American Historical Review,* XXXII (July, 1927), 769-88. NcD, NcU, NcC.

In Mississippi, as elsewhere in the ante-bellum South, the free Negro was a free man in name only.

THOMAS, DAVID Y. "The Free Negro in Florida before 1865," *South Atlantic Quarterly,* X (January-October, 1911), 335-45. NcD, NcU.

The free Negroes of Florida were of American-African, Spanish-African, French-African, and Indian-African origin. Their status seems to have differed in many respects from that of free Negroes in other Southern states.

WOODSON, CARTER G. *Free Negro Heads of Families in the United States in 1830, Together with a Brief Treatment of the Free Negro.* Washington: Association for the Study of Negro Life and History, 1925. Pp. lviii, 296. NcD, NcU, NcC.

A study made to facilitate further study of those Negroes who have a family tradition going back into the period before the Civil War.

WRIGHT, JAMES M. *The Free Negro in Maryland, 1634-1860.* Columbia University Studies in History, Economics and Public Law, Vol. XCVII, No. 3, 1921. Pp. 362. NcD, NcU.

There were important features connected with the rise of free Negroes in Maryland not found in other colonies and states.

3. Caste and Segregation

BAKER, RAY STANNARD. *Following the Color Line: An Account of Negro Citizenship in the American Democracy.* New York: Doubleday, Page and Co., 1908. Pp. xii, 314. NcD, NcU, NcC.

The chapters of this very important old book, originally published in the *American Magazine,* grew out of an investigation of the Atlanta race riot of September, 1906. Baker sought to go behind the newspaper reports and investigate the events that led up to the riot. "But he did more: he sought to discover what were the conditions which made such an outbreak of elemental passions possible. His report is not merely the first authentic account of a race riot, but the first disinterested study of the peculiar character of the racial relations under which these social eruptions arise."

Baker develops the thesis that the "color line" in the South is a function of interracial competition. It shifts with changes in the competitive situation. This fact largely accounts for the significant differences in race relations between the upper and lower South, the rural and the urban South, the tidewater and the piedmont South, and the trade towns and the industrial towns of the South.

BRUCE, PHILIP A. "Race Segregation in the United States," *Hibbert Journal,* XIII (July, 1915), 867-86. NcD, NcU.

Bruce thinks that the operation of both the written and the unwritten laws of segregation is promoting the homogeneity of American Negroes in the direction of the general type of their African ancestors.

CONRAD, EARL. *Jim Crow America.* New York: Duell, Sloan and Pearce, 1947. Pp. 237. NcD.

A white newspaper reporter scoops the inside story on the Jim Crow situation.

COX, OLIVER C. "The Modern Caste School of Race Relations," *Social Forces,* XXI (December, 1942), 218-26. NcD, NcU, NcC.

An attack leveled against the view that race relations in the South are caste relations.

COX, OLIVER C. "Race and Caste: A Distinction," *American Journal of Sociology,* L (March, 1945), 360-68. NcD, NcU, NcC.

"Race relations can be studied as a form of class exploitation; the assumption that they are caste relations is confusing and misleading."

COX, OLIVER C. *Caste, Class and Race: A Study in Social Dynamics.* Garden City, New York: Doubleday and Co., 1948. Pp. xxvi, 624. NcD, NcU, NcC.

Race, class, and caste are compared and contrasted with respect to their theoretical and doctrinal implications by a writer in the Marxian tradition.

CRISWELL, JOAN HENNING. "A Sociometric Study of Race Cleavage in the Classroom," *Archives of Psychology,* Vol. XXX, No. 235 (January, 1939). NcD, NcU.

In the mixed grammar school classes in Northern schools attitudes leading to race cleavage are initiated by the community and assimilated much more fully by white than by Negro children.

DOLLARD, JOHN. *Caste and Class in a Southern Town.* New Haven: Yale University Press, 1937. Pp. 502. NcD, NcU, NcC.

The psychoanalytic method is used to study Negroes and race relations in a Southern community described as Democratic, dry, Protestant, and agrarian. The rewards for belonging to the white caste are described as economic, sexual, and prestige gains.

DOYLE, BERTRAM W. *The Etiquette of Race Relations in the South: A Study in Social Control.* Chicago: The University of Chicago Press, 1937. Pp. xxv, 249. NcD, NcU, NcC.

A study in social control which analyzes the phenomena of relations between Negroes and whites in terms of the external forms in which the relations are symbolized. These forms were crystallized into a code of expected and accepted behavior. In the code there are provisions for terms of address, salutation, and conversation; observances proper to association in churches, on the streets, and in public conveyances; ceremonial acts necessary for the intimate contacts of the household and plantation; and, in short, for all the situations in which blacks and whites meet.

DUBOIS, W. E. B. "A Negro Nation Within the Nation," *Current History,* XLII (June, 1935), 265-70. NcD, NcU, NcC.

"It becomes clearer to more and more American Negroes that, through voluntary and increased segregation, by careful autonomy and planned economic organization, they may build so strong and efficient a unit that 12,000,000 men can no longer be refused fellowship and equality in the United States."

HURSTON, ZORA NEALE. "The 'Pet Negro' System," *American Mercury,* LVI (May, 1943), 593-600. NcD, NcU, NcC.

There are avenues of communication and inter-personal relations between whites and Negroes in the South which operate "to stabilize relations and give something to work from in adjustments."

JOHNSON, CHARLES S. *Patterns of Negro Segregation.* New York: Harper and Brothers, 1943. Pp. xxii, 332. NcD, NcU, NcC.

The variation of patterns of Negro segregation in various parts of the United States and in various areas of American life.

LOBB, JOHN. "Caste and Class in Haiti," *American Journal of Sociology,* XLVI (July, 1940), 23-34. NcD, NcU, NcC.

". . . Haiti is a nation of Negroes similar in African origin to those of the United States, whose solution of their national and social problems is of first-rate importance to Negroes and to students of their status and future."

LOESCHER, FRANK. *The Protestant Church and the Negro: A Pattern of Segregation.* New York: Association Press, 1948. Pp. 159. NcD, NcU.

An account of the interracial practices, principles, and policies of the Protestant church in America.

MILLER, Herbert A. "Race and Class Parallelism," *Annals of the American Academy of Political and Social Science,* CXL (November, 1928), 1-5. NcD, NcU, NcC.

Race theories are a special application of class rationalizations to groups identified as racial. The distinctive feature of the race-class is that color is a label which makes passing to another class difficult or impossible.

MOON, BUCKLIN. *The High Cost of Prejudice.* New York: Julian Messner, Inc., 1947. Pp. 168. NcD, NcU.

Segregation is expensive.

MYRDAL, GUNNAR. *An American Dilemma.* 2 vols. (Vol. I, Part VII, "Social Inequality"; Part VIII, "Social Stratification"; and Appendix 8). New York: Harper and Brothers, 1944. NcD, NcU, NcC.

The various forms of adjustment to social inequality have effected an extreme isolation of whites and Negroes into separate social worlds.

POWDERMAKER, HORTENSE. *After Freedom: A Cultural Study in the Deep South.* New York: The Viking Press, 1939. Pp. xx, 408. NcD, NcU, NcC.

A study of race relations in a rural community in Mississippi by a well-known anthropologist. Her "Cottonville" is the same community studied by Dollard in *Caste and Class in a Southern Town.*

SCHULER, EDGAR A. "Attitudes Toward Racial Segregation in Baton Rouge, Louisiana," *Journal of Social Psychology,* XVIII (August, 1943), 33-53. NcD, NcU.

Both whites and Negroes in Baton Rouge accept segregation as the desirable pattern of co-existence.

SEGREGATION—Color Pattern of the Past—Our Struggle to Wipe it Out, Survey Graphic, Vol. XXXVI, No. 1 (January, 1947). NcD, NcU, NcC.

A symposium on segregation.

WARNER, W. LLOYD. "American Caste and Class," *American Journal of Sociology,* XLII (September, 1936), 234-37. NcD, NcU.

This short article presents a scheme for viewing two different kinds of social stratification in the South, i.e., the relation between the caste (race) system and the class structure within each caste.

WARNER, W. LLOYD, and DAVIS, ALLISON. "A Comparative Study of American Caste." Chap. VIII in Edgar T. Thompson, ed., *Race Relations and the Race Problem.* Durham: Duke University Press, 1939. NcD, NcU, NcC.

Caste is defined and the East Indian and Southern caste orders analyzed.

WIRTH, LOUIS. "Segregation," *Encyclopaedia of the Social Sciences,* XIII, 643-47. NcD, NcU.

A definition of segregation as a process and some of its expressions.

XXI. Race Mixture and the Mulatto

BARRON, MILTON L. *People Who Intermarry: Intermarriage in a New England Industrial Community.* Syracuse, New York: Syracuse University Press, 1946. Pp. 389. NcD.
"Intermarriage as deviation from the mores of mate selection generally occurs most often between ethnic groups, less often between religious groups and least between racial groups."

BURMA, JOHN H., "The Measurement of Negro 'Passing,'" *American Journal of Sociology,* LII (July, 1946), 18-22. NcD, NcU, NcC.
It is probable that the amount of "passing" is not nearly as great as popularly supposed.

DAVIS, KINGSLEY. "Intermarriage in Caste Societies," *American Anthropologist,* XLIII (July-September, 1941), 376-95. NcD, NcU.
A discussion of the interrelation between marriage and caste.

DAY, (MRS.) CAROLINE BOND. *A Study of Some Negro-White Families in the United States.* Cambridge, Massachusetts: Peabody Museum of Harvard University, 1932. Pp. ix, 126. NcD, NcU, NcC.
Anthropological, sociological, genealogical, and photographic aspects of 346 Negro-white families.

DUNBAR-NELSON, ALICE. "People of Color in Louisiana," *Journal of Negro History,* Vol. I, Part I (October, 1916), 361-76; Vol. II, Part II (January, 1917), 51-78. NcD, NcU.
A review of the history of the *gens de couleur,* a class apart from both whites and Negroes, in Louisiana.

EMBREE, EDWIN R. *Brown Americans.* New York: The Viking Press, 1943. Pp. vi, 248. NcD, NcU, NcC.
A study of the Negro's share in American life. This book brings up to date the author's earlier *Brown America.*

GOUMAY, P. F. DE. "The F.M.C.'s of Louisiana," *Lippincott's Monthly Magazine,* LIII (April, 1894), 511-17. NcD.
The Free Men of Color of the Old South occupied an anomalous position between the free whites and the enslaved blacks.

HERSKOVITS, MELVILLE J. *The American Negro: A Study in Racial Crossing.* New York: A. A. Knopf Co., 1928. Pp. xiv, 92. NcD, NcU, NcC.
The American Negro is evolving into a new homogeneous race whose physical traits stand between those of the whites and the African. The mechanism which is creating this new type is the selection by dark men of lighter wives.

HERSKOVITS, MELVILLE J. "Race Mixture," *Encyclopaedia of the Social Sciences,* XIII, 41-43. NcD, NcU.
Whether race mixture weakens or strengthens the hybrid is a moot question concerning which there are many claims but no proof.

JOHNSON, J. H. "Documentary Evidence of the Relations of Negroes and Indians," *Journal of Negro History,* XIV (January, 1929), 21-43. NcD, NcU, NcC.
"The Indian has not disappeared from the land, but is now a part of the Negro population of the United States."

LINTON, RALPH. "An Anthropological View of Race Mixture," *Publications of the American Sociological Society*, XIX (1925), 69-77. NcD, NcU.
The absorption into the white population of the United States of our present Indian, Mongol, and Negro minorities is not likely to influence our culture unfavorably.

MILLER, KELLY. "Is the American Negro to Remain Black or Become Bleached?" *South Atlantic Quarterly*, XXV (July, 1926), 240-52. NcD, NcU.
"Within the next three or four generations it will be hard to find a pure blooded Negro outside the remote black belts of the rural South . . . a new Negroid race will have arisen."

MISCEGENATION: The Theory of the Blending of the Races Applied to the American White Man and Negro. New York: H. Dexter, Hamilton and Co., 1864. Pp. ii, 72. NcD, NcU.
Authorship is attributed to D. G. Croly, George Wakeman, and E. C. Howell. They advocated "blending."

MOLLER, HERBERT. "Sex Composition and Correlated Culture Patterns of Colonial America," *The William and Mary College Quarterly*, II (April, 1945), 113-53. NcD, NcU.
"The development of aversion to racial miscegenation in the thirteen colonies can be traced to the invasion of feminine sentiments into colonial society."

PARK, ROBERT E. "Mentality of Racial Hybrids," *American Journal of Sociology*, XXXVI (January, 1931), 534-51. NcD, NcU, NcC.
The peculiar "mentality," or forms of thought and action, which the mixed-blood almost everywhere exhibits, his restlessness, and instability originate in the fact that he is a cultural as well as a biological hybrid.

PORTER, KENNETH W. "Relations Between Negroes and Indians Within the Present Limits of the United States," *Journal of Negro History*, XVII (July, 1932), 287-367; XVIII (July, 1933), 282-321. NcD, NcU, NcC.
Relations between Negroes and Indians have been of greater significance historically than we have ordinarily supposed.

REUTER, EDWARD B. *The Mulatto in the United States: Including a Study of the Role of Mixed-Blood Races Throughout the World*. Boston: R. G. Badger, 1918. Pp. 417. NcD, NcU.
"An attempt to state one sociological problem arising when two races, divergent as to culture and distinct as to physical appearance, are brought into contact under the conditions of modern life and produce a hybrid offspring whose characteristic physical appearance prevents them from passing as either the one or the other."

REUTER, EDWARD B. *Race Mixture: Studies in Intermarriage and Miscegenation*. New York: McGraw-Hill Book Co., 1931. Pp. vii, 224. NcD, NcU, NcC.
A collection of twelve papers, most of them previously published in scientific journals.

ROGERS, JOEL A. *Sex and Race*. 3 vols. (Vol. I, "Negro-Caucasian Mixing in All Ages and All Lands"; Vol. II, "A History of White, Negro, and Indian Miscegenation in the Two Americas"; Vol. III, "Why White and Black Mix in Spite of Opposition.") New York: J. A. Rogers Publications, 1940, 1942, 1944. NcD, NcU.
A rich assemblage of historical material on race crossing. Copiously illustrated.

STERN, BERNHARD J. "Intermarriage," *Encyclopaedia of the Social Sciences*, VIII, 151-54. NcD, NcU.

Prevailing attitudes toward intermarriage is one way of classifying inter-racial societies.

STONEQUIST, EVERETT V. *The Marginal Man: A Study in Personality and Culture Conflicts.* New York: Charles Scribner's Sons, 1937. Pp. xviii, 228. NcD, NcU, NcC.

"Native alien," "differently born," "cultural illegitimate" are synonymous expressions for what Stonequist, Park, and others term the "marginal man." Under whatever general or local name he may be called, the marginal man is one who cannot take either himself or his world for granted.

STONEQUIST, EVERETT V. "Race Mixture and the Mulatto." Chap. IX in Edgar T. Thompson, ed., *Race Relations and the Race Problem.* Durham: Duke University Press, 1939. NcD, NcU, NcC.

"The form, the extent, and the rate of mixture, like the status and role of the racial hybrids, are indexes of the kind of problem or lack of problem which exists, and they are also evidence of the direction in which race relations are moving."

WIRTH, LOUIS, and GOLDHAMER, HERBERT. "The Hybrid and the Problem of Miscegenation," in Otto Klineberg, ed., *Characteristics of the American Negro.* New York: Harper and Brothers, 1944. NcD, NcU, NcC.

A discussion of the extent of race mixture, its prospects and its implications, together with beliefs about the effects of race mixture.

WITTENBERG, PHILIP. "Miscegenation," *Encyclopaedia of the Social Sciences*, X, 531-34. NcD, NcU.

Some aspects of the history and present status of intermarriage and illicit intercourse between members of different races in various parts of the world including the United States.

WOODSON, CARTER G. "The Beginnings of the Miscegenation of the Whites and Blacks," *Journal of Negro History*, III (October, 1918), 335-53. NcD, NcU, NcC.

Some aspects of race mixing in America and elsewhere.

XXII. Isolated Racial Islands

BERRY, BREWTON. "The Mestizos of South Carolina," *American Journal of Sociology*, LI (July, 1945), 34-41. NcD, NcU, NcC.
The "mestizos" of South Carolina are known by such various terms as "Redbones," "Red Legs," "Brass Ankles," "Turks," "Buckheads," "Croatans," "Marlboro Blues," "Yellow Hammers," etc.

BOND, HORACE M. "Two Racial Islands in Alabama: Creoles and Cajuns," *American Journal of Sociology*, XXXVI (January, 1931), 552-67. NcD, NcU, NcC.
An account of (1) the Creoles and (2) the Cajuns of Alabama. Each group is disclaimed by the white-parent stock and each disclaims the Negro-parent stock.

BURNETT, SWAN M. "A Note on the Melungeons," *American Anthropologist*, II (October, 1889), 342-49. NcD, NcU.
These people of eastern Tennessee are believed by local whites to be a mixture of whites, Indians, and Negroes, but the Melungeons proudly call themselves Portuguese.

CHANLER, DAVID. "The Jackson Whites: An American Episode," *Crisis*, XLVI (May, 1939), 138. NcD, NcU, NcC.
Several thousand of these mixed Indian, Negro, German, English, and Italian people live in an isolated community in the Ramapo Mountains near New York City. They are concentrated at Ringwood, New Jersey, a company town unconnected with any other place by either railway or bus line.

DROMGOOLE, WILLIAM ALLEN. "The Malungeons," *The Arena*, III (March, 1891), 470-79; "The Malungeon Tree and Its Four Branches," *The Arena*, III (May, 1891), 745-51. NcD, NcU.
An account of the Malungeons of Newman's Ridge, Hancock County, Tennessee. They believe themselves to be of Cherokee and Portuguese extraction but they cannot account for the Portuguese blood.

ESTABROOK, ARTHUR H., and McDOUGLE, IVAN E. *Mongrel Virginians: The Win Tribe*. Baltimore, Md.: The Williams and Wilkins Co., 1926. Pp. 205. NcD, NcU.
A genealogical and sociological study of a small group of Indian-Negro-white crosses who have lived in the same locality in Virginia for over a hundred years. There is practically no music among them and no preacher has ever been produced by them.

FARRIS, JAMES J. "The Lowrie Gang: An Episode in the History of Robeson County, North Carolina, 1864-1874," *Historical Papers Published by the Trinity College Historical Society*. Series XV, pp. 55-93. Durham: Duke University Press, 1925. NcD, NcU.
An account of the outlaw gang led by a member of the Croatan community.

FISHER, GEORGE PURNELL. *The So-Called Moors of Delaware*. Reprinted by the Public Archives Commission of Delaware, 1929. Pp. 5. NcD.
An account of a small group now scattered throughout Delaware and southern New Jersey. Industrious, frugal, and law-abiding they mingle little with black or white.

GILBERT, WILLIAM H., JR. "The Wesorts of Southern Maryland; an Outcaste Group," *Journal of the Washington Academy of Sciences*, XXXV
(July 15, 1945), 237-46. NcU.

The Wesorts are mainly of white and Indian blood with an occasional strong
infusion of Negro blood.

GILBERT, WILLIAM H., Jr. "Mixed Bloods of the Upper Monongahela Valley, West Virginia," *Journal of the Washington Academy of Sciences*,
XXXVI, (January 15, 1946), 1-13. NcD, NcU.

The "Guineas," as they are locally known, number several thousand persons.

GILBERT, WILLIAM H., JR. "Memorandum Concerning the Characteristics
of the Larger Mixed-Blood Racial Islands of the Eastern United States,"
Social Forces, XXIV (May, 1946), 438-47. NcD, NcU, NcC.

An outline with bibliography of ten of these "racial islands."

HANCOCK, EARNEST. *A Sociological Study of the Tri-Racial Community in
Robeson County, North Carolina*. M.A. thesis, University of North Carolina,
1935. Pp. 129. NcU.

A study of the relations between the whites, Negroes, and "Indians" of the
county.

HARPER, ROLAND M. "A Statistical Study of the Croatans," *Rural Sociology*,
II (December, 1937), 444-56. NcD, NcU.

"The Croatans seem to be the most prolific people in the United States at
present; and if their birth rate continues high, while that of the whites and
Negroes continues to decrease as it has been doing lately, some interesting if not
disquieting situations should develop in the next few decades."

JOHNSON, GUY B. "Personality in a White-Indian-Negro Community," *American Sociological Review*, IV (August, 1939), 516-23. NcD, NcU.

The community studied is the so-called Croatan community of Robeson
County, North Carolina. A member of this group "feels that there is always a
question mark hanging over him. His wish to escape the stigma of Negro kinship, and thus be identified with the white man is uppermost in his mind. It is
this wish which dominates his behavior and determines his modes of personal
adjustment to the other races."

PARSONS, ELSIE CLEWS. "Folklore of the Cherokee of Robeson County,
North Carolina," *Journal of American Folklore*, XXXII (July-September,
1919), 384-93. NcD, NcU.
Some riddles, tales, and folk expressions.

STEWARD, WILLIAM, and STEWARD, THEOPHILUS G. *Gouldtown, a
Very Remarkable Settlement of Ancient Date; Studies of Some Sturdy Ex-
amples of Simple Life, Together with Sketches of Early Colonial History of
Cumberland County and Southern New Jersey and Some Early Genealogical
Records*. Philadelphia: J. B. Lippincott Co., 1913. Pp. 237. NcD.

The village of Gouldtown, Fairfax Township, New Jersey, is a settlement of
mulattoes almost all of whom bear the name of Gould or Pierce.

WESLAGER, C. A. *Delaware's Forgotten Folk: The Story of the Moors and
Nanticokes*. Philadelphia: University of Pennsylvania Press, 1943. Pp. ix,
215. NcD.

These two obscure groups of mixed Indian, white, and Negro ancestry live in
a world apart.

XXIII. The Negro in the American Melting Pot

BASCOM, WILLIAM R. "Acculturation Among the Gullah Negroes," *American Anthropologist*, XXXXIII (January-March, 1941), 43-50. NcD, NcU.
A study based upon field work in South Carolina and Georgia in 1939.

DUNCAN, OTIS DURANT. "The Fusion of White, Negro, and Indian Cultures at the Converging of the New South and the West," *Southwestern Social Science Quarterly*, XIV (March, 1934), 357-69. NcD, NcU.
A discussion of the role played by each racial group in the evolution of a common culture.

FRAZIER, E. FRANKLIN. "A Folk Culture in the Making," *Southern Workman*, LVII (June, 1928), 195-99. NcD, NcU, NcC.
Suggests the creation of artistic forms out of the daily lives of Negro people.

GOMILLION, CHARLES G. "The Influence of the Negro on the Culture of the South," *Social Forces*, XX (March, 1942), 386-90. NcD, NcU, NcC.
Negroes "have influenced the course of American life directly by their individual contributions and indirectly by their presence."

HERSKOVITS, MELVILLE J. "Acculturation and the American Negro," *Southwestern Political and Social Science Quarterly*, VIII (December, 1927), 211-24. NcD, NcU.
A point of view on the process whereby persons of Negro descent have absorbed the American culture to which they have been exposed.

HERSKOVITS, MELVILLE J. "The Negro in the New World: The Statement of a Problem," *American Anthropologist*, XXXII (January, 1930), 145-55. NcD, NcU.
The problems of the Negro in the New World center around two main foci: namely, his physical form and his language and culture. The Bush Negroes of Surinam and British Guiana have kept their African culture almost entirely intact.

HERSKOVITS, MELVILLE J. "On the Provenience of New World Negroes," *Social Forces*, XII (December, 1933), 247-62. NcD, NcU, NcC.
A consideration of the cultural equipment with which Negroes entered upon their lives in different areas in the western hemisphere.

HERSKOVITS, MELVILLE J. "What has Africa Given America?" *New Republic*, LXXXIV (September 4, 1935), 92-94. NcD, NcU, NcC.
There are many more Africanisms in America than is commonly supposed. Important African influences are present in American Negro music, speech, manners, and cuisine. These influences have extended over into white, and especially Southern white, society.

JOHNSON, GUY B. "The Negro Spiritual: A Problem in Anthropology," *American Anthropologist*, XXXIII (April-June, 1931), 157-71. NcD, NcU.
"Negro spirituals are derived from or are simply variants of the hymns written by white persons; even those sentiments which have been interpreted as originating in the yearnings and aspirations of Negroes have such origins. Structurally, spirituals and a certain type of white religious song cannot be differentiated."

JOHNSON, GUY B. "Some Factors in the Development of Negro Social Institutions in the United States," *American Journal of Sociology*, XL (November, 1934), 329-37. NcD, NcU.
American Negroes have almost completely adopted the culture of white
America. But there has been a lag. Much of present Negro superstition, speech,
manners, religious practice, and oratory characterized the Southern whites of
yesterday.

JOHNSON, JAMES WELDON. "Contributions of the Negro to American Culture," *Southern Workman*, LXVII (February, 1938), 57-60. NcD, NcU, NcC.
Negroes, like other groups in America, are bearers of gifts. But the conception
of the Negro as a contributor comes to many Americans almost as a shock.

JUNG, CARL GUSTAV. "Your Negroid and Indian Behavior," *Forum*,
LXXXIII (April, 1930), 193-99. NcD, NcU.
"The Negro, by his mere presence in America, is a source of temperamental
and mimetic infection which the European can't help noticing. . . ."

KLINGBERG, FRANK J. *An Appraisal of the Negro in Colonial South Carolina*. Washington: Associated Publishers, 1942. Pp. xii, 180. NcD, NcU, NcC.
A study of the early assimilation of the American Negro.

LOCKE, ALAIN. "The Negro's Contribution to American Culture," *Journal of
Negro Education*, VIII (July, 1939), 521-29. NcD, NcU, NcC.
"What is 'racial' for the American Negro resides merely in the overtones to
certain fundamental elements of culture common to white and black."

MYRDAL, GUNNAR. *An American Dilemma*. 2 vols. (Vol. II, Chap. 43, "Institutions"). New York: Harper and Brothers, 1944. NcD, NcU, NcC.
American Negro institutions are not independent of the general American
culture but represent distorted developments within that culture.

PARK, ROBERT E. "Racial Assimilation in Secondary Groups; With Particular Reference to the Negro," *Publications of the American Sociological Society*, VIII (1913), 66-83. NcD, NcU. Also in *American Journal of Sociology*, XIX (March, 1914), 606-23. NcD, NcU.
The race problem has been described as a problem in assimilation, and assimilation rarely becomes a problem except in groups characterized by impersonal
relations.

PARK, ROBERT E. "Education in its Relations to the Conflict and Fusion of
Cultures," *Publications of the American Sociological Society*, XIII (1918),
38-63. NcD, NcU.
There exists in each race, Park argues, a more or less distinct racial tempera-
ment. The "Negro is, by natural disposition, neither an intellectual nor an
idealist, like the Jew; nor a brooding introspective, like the East Indian; nor a
pioneer and frontiersman, like the Anglo-Saxon. He is primarily an artist, loving
life for its own sake. He is, so to speak, the lady among the races."

REUTER, EDWARD B. "The Possibility of a Distinctive Culture Contribution from the American Negro." Chap. XIV in Kimball Young, ed., *Social
Attitudes*. New York: Henry Holt and Co., 1931. NcD, NcU.
Whatever contribution Negroes may make to American culture will come from
their isolated life and their peculiar social status. There will be no reason whatever for treating any such contribution as a biological expression of race. It
will be Negro only in the sense that the excluded group is composed of Negroes.

SMITH, T. LYNN, and PARENTON, VERNON J. "Acculturation Among the
Louisiana French," *American Journal of Sociology*, XLIV (November, 1938),
355-64. NcD, NcU.

Of special interest is the extent to which original German, Irish, Spanish, and Anglo-Saxon elements have been absorbed into the French culture of Louisiana.

STANDING, T. G. "The Possibility of a Distinctive Culture Contribution from the American Negro," *Social Forces*, XVII (October, 1938), 99-106. NcD, NcU, NcC.

If the trend toward racial self-sufficiency continues there will be a further development of Negro literature and art and an increasing tendency to exploit more fully their folk music, but Negroes will continue to seek recognition for achievement in the larger American society.

WINSTON, SANFORD. "Cultural Participation and the Negro," *American Journal of Sociology*, XL (March, 1935), 593-601. NcD, NcU.

The degrees of Negro participation in American culture are quantitatively described in the economic, educational, and health fields.

XXIV. The Language and Dialect of the American Negro

BENNETT, JOHN. "Gullah: A Negro Patois," *South Atlantic Quarterly*, Vol. VII, Part I (October, 1908), 332-47; Vol. VIII, Part II (January, 1909), 39-52. NcD, NcU.
One of the earliest discussions of Gullah. The author concludes: "It is the oddest Negro patios in America; the most African; unaltered it is one of the oldest; if not the oldest, certainly it is the most archaic."

BURLEY, DAN. *Dan Burley's Original Handbook of Harlem Jive*. New York: The author, 1944. Pp. 158. NcD.
For those who would like to know what this double-talk is all about.

CONRAD, EARL. "The Philology of Negro Dialect," *Journal of Negro Education*, XIII (Spring, 1944), 150-54. NcD, NcU, NcC.
What is the Negro dialect? What is it to the white reader or listener? to the Northerner and to the Southerner?

GREET, WILLIAM CABELL. "Southern Speech." Chap. XXVII in W. T. Couch, ed., *Culture in the South*. Chapel Hill: The University of North Carolina Press, 1935. NcD, NcU.
"The real influence of the Negro has been like that of the illiterate whites in the South."

HARRISON, JAMES A. "Negro English," *Anglia*, VII (1884), 232-79. NcD, NcU.
"Negro English is an ear-language . . . an error of ear, a mishearing . . ."

JOHNSON, GUY B. *Folk Culture on St. Helena Island, South Carolina* (Chapter I, pp. 3-62, "Gullah: The Dialect of the Negroes of St. Helena Island"). Chapel Hill: The University of North Carolina Press, 1930. NcD, NcU.
Gullah "is as different from what is generally thought of as Negro dialect as the speech of the white Georgian is from that of the Chicagoan."

KRAPP, GEORGE PHILIP. "The English of the Negro," *American Mercury*, II (June, 1924), 190-95. NcD, NcU.
In one important respect, at least, the Negro is not a foreigner and an outcaste: his language is finally and completely English with only negligible exceptions.

READ, ALLEN WALKER. "Bilingualism in the Middle Colonies, 1725-1775," *American Speech*, XII (April, 1937), 93-99. NcD, NcU, NcC.
Bilingualism among Negro slaves and white servants in the colonial period.

READ, ALLEN WALKER. "The Speech of Negroes in Colonial America," *Journal of Negro History*, XXIV (July, 1939), 247-58. NcD, NcU, NcC.
The Negro in the New World was faced with the huge problem of learning and adopting a new language. In the light of his opportunities, his success has been equal to that of any other immigrant.

SMITH, REED. *Gullah*. Columbia: University of South Carolina, Bureau of Publications, 1926. Pp. 45. NcD, NcU.
On the language of the Negroes of the South Carolina-Georgia Coast.

STANLEY, ORNA. "Negro Speech in East Texas," *American Speech*, XVI (February, 1941), 3-16. NcD, NcU, NcC.
". . . innocent of any need for a standard of pronunciation."

THOMAS, J. J. *The Theory and Practice of Creole Grammar*. Port-of-Spain, Trinidad, B. W. I.: The Chronicle Publishing Office, 1869. Pp. viii, 134. NcD.
   This Creole dialect, developed by Negro slaves in the French West Indies and in Louisiana, is said to differ so radically from its parent tongue that philologists have classed it as a new language—the only one born on this continent since Columbus discovered it.

TINKER, EDWARD L. "Louisiana Gombo," *Yale Review*, N. S., XXI (March, 1932), 566-79. NcD, NcU.
   On the Creole dialect of Louisiana—"called by the white Americans 'Gombo,' and by the Negroes of the brash younger generation 'Congo.'"

TINKER, EDWARD L. *Gombo, the Creole Dialect of Louisiana, Together with a Bibliography*. New York: The author, 1936. Pp. 46. NcD.
   Reprinted from the Proceedings of the American Antiquarian Society.

TURNER, LORENZO. "Linguistic Research and African Survivals," *American Council of Learned Societies Bulletin*, No. 32 (September, 1941), pp. 68-78. NcD, NcU, NcC.
   The author takes exception to the view that only a few African linguistic survivals are to be found among New World Negroes. His list of African words used by the Gullah Negroes of South Carolina and Georgia number approximately five thousand.

WHITNEY, ANNIE WESTON. "Negro American Dialects," *The Independent*, Vol. LIII, Part I (August 22, 1901), 1979-81; Vol. LIII, Part II (August 29, 1901), 2039-42. NcD, NcU.
   ". . . it is not generally known that in some parts of the South, 'befo' de wah,' every large plantation had its own individual dialect."

WISE, C. M. "Negro Dialect," *The Quarterly Journal of Speech*, XIX (November, 1933), 522-28. NcD, NcU.
   ". . . the Negro speech is of all dialects the most strikingly different from cultivated English. . . . But the average Southern Negro is entirely unconscious of his variant speech, and does not know that improving it would improve his social standing."

XXV. The Negro Folk

ADAMS, E. C. L. *Congaree Sketches.* Chapel Hill: The University of North Carolina Press, 1927. Pp. xvii, 116. NcD, NcU.

Negro characters "down in de big swamps, down on the Congaree" speak for themselves in a series of short sketches, folk-tales, sermons, and prayers.

ADAMS, E. C. L. *Nigger to Nigger.* New York: Charles Scribner's Sons, 1928. Pp. xii, 270. NcD, NcU.

Negroes talk to themselves and to each other without self-consciousness, sentimentality, or clowning.

BALLOWE, HEWITT LEONARD. *The Lawd Sayin' the Same: Negro Folk Tales of the Creole Country.* Baton Rouge, La.: Louisiana State University Press, 1947. Pp. xvi, 254. NcD.

Folk stories from the Louisiana sugar cane country.

BECKWICK, MARTHA W. *Black Roadways: A Study of Jamaican Folk Life.* Chapel Hill: The University of North Carolina Press, 1929. Pp. xvii, 243. NcD, NcU.

A study of a folk culture which goes beyond a mere collection of songs, stories, games, and riddles.

BOYLE, VIRGINIA FRAZER. *Devil Tales.* New York: Harper and Brothers, 1900. Pp. xi, 210. NcU.

A collection of Negro folk tales.

BRADFORD, ROARK. *Ol' Man Adam an' His Chillun: Being the Tales They Tell About the Time When the Lord Walked the Earth Like a Natural Man.* New York: Harper and Brothers, 1928. Pp. xxiv, 264. NcD, NcU.

Highly entertaining stories portraying the religious ideology of rural Negro folk.

CAMPBELL, MARIE. *Folks Do Get Born.* New York: Rinehart and Co., 1946. Pp. x, 245. NcD, NcU.

The record of "granny midwifes"—their folk tales, their customs, and their discovery of the miracle of science.

COBB, LUCY M., and HICKS, MARY A. *Animal Tales from the Old North State.* New York: E. P. Dutton and Co., 1938. Pp. 200. NcD, NcU, NcC.

Here is a compilation of old Negro stories, handed down through generations and presented for children from six to sixty.

CRUM, MASON. *Gullah.* Durham, N. C.: Duke University Press, 1940. Pp. xv, 351. NcD, NcU, NcC.

A discussion of the Sea Islands and coastal region of South Carolina where, in cultural isolation, the Gullah Negroes have preserved a great many of the habits and attitudes of slavery.

DICKENS, DOROTHY. *Traditional Food Preparation Rules.* Bulletin 418 of the Agricultural Experiment Station of Mississippi State College. June, 1945. Pp. 60. NcD.

An interesting study of traditional food preparation practices now prevalent in white and Negro rural families in Mississippi.

EMERSON, WILLIAM C. *Stories and Spirituals of the Negro Slave.* Boston: R. G. Badger, 1930. Pp. 79. NcU.

A collection of stories and folk songs which preserves the biographies and pictures of the Old South.

FORTIER, ALCÉE, collector and editor. *Louisiana Folk Tales in French Dialect and English Translation.* Boston: Published for the American Folklore Society, 1895. Pp. xi, 122. NcD, NcU.
The only important collection of Louisiana Negro folk tales.

GEORGIA Writers' Program. *Drums and Shadows.* Athens: The University of Georgia Press, 1940. Pp. xx, 274. NcD, NcU, NcC.
Foreword by Guy B. Johnson. A series of anthropological field studies on survival customs and beliefs among Georgia coastal Negroes.

GONZALES, AMBROSE E. *The Black Border: Gullah Stories of the Carolina Coast.* Columbia, S. C.: The State Co., 1922. Pp. 348. NcD, NcU.
Folk tales of the Gullah Negroes along the sea islands of the South Carolina coast.

HARRIS, JOEL CHANDLER. *Nights with Uncle Remus: Myths and Legends of the Old Plantation.* Boston: Houghton Mifflin Co., 1911. Pp. xlii, 404. NcD, NcU.
In September, 1866, a writer in *Scott's Monthly Magazine* (Atlanta) expressed the opinion that the Brer Rabbit stories, although he was fond of them, could not be successfully put into print. But here are seventy-one of them which have become classic.

HARRIS, JOEL CHANDLER. *Uncle Remus: His Songs and His Sayings.* New and rev. ed. New York: D. Appleton and Co., 1934. Pp. xxi, 265. NcD, NcU.
Among other animals there is the well-known Brer Rabbit who through craft, trickery, and flattery was always able to get the better of a master race of animals bigger and stronger than himself.

HIGGINSON, T. W. *Army Life in a Black Regiment* (Chap. IX). Boston: Fields, Osgood and Co., 1870. Pp. iv, 296. NcD, NcU.
Colonel Higginson, a Union officer who saw service in the South during the Civil War, was perhaps the first to make a serious study of Negro spirituals. He compared them to the Scottish ballads.

HURSTON, ZORA NEALE. *Mules and Men.* Philadelphia: J. B. Lippincott Co., 1935. Pp. 342. NcD, NcU, NcC.
A collection of Negro folk tales, tall tales, and tall sermons. This is the first important collection to be made by a Negro scholar.

JOHNSON, GUY B. *John Henry: Tracking Down a Negro Legend.* Chapel Hill: The University of North Carolina Press, 1929. Pp. 155. NcD, NcU, NcC.
"Ask almost any Negro workingman who John Henry was, and he will reply with, 'He's man beat the steam drill!', or 'He's best steel driver the world ever afforded!' "

JOHNSON, GUY B. "Folk Values in Recent Literature on the Negro," in B.A. Botkin, ed., *Folk-Say.* Norman: University of Oklahoma Press, 1930. NcD, NcU.
The use made by certain white authors of Negro dialect, songs, superstitions and beliefs, tales, and humor.

JONES, CHARLES COLCOCK. *Negro Myths From the Georgia Coast Told in the Vernacular.* Boston: Houghton Mifflin & Co., 1888. Pp. x, 171. NcD.
A collection of Negro folk lore interesting to the general reader.

KUPS OF KAUPHY: A Georgia Book, in Warp and Woof. Containing Tales, Incidents, etc., of the "Empire State of the South," with a Slight Sketch of the Well-known and Eccentric "Colored Gemman," Old Jack C. . . . . . . By "K of K." Athens, Georgia: Christie and Kelsea, 1853. Pp. 107. NcD.
One of the earliest ventures in the field of Negro humor.

OWENS, WILLIAM. "Folk-Lore of the Southern Negroes," *Lippincott's Maga-zine*, XX (December, 1877), 748-55. NcD, NcU.
One of the first reports on Southern Negro folklore. "This article gave me my cue," said Joel Chandler Harris.

PARSONS, ELSIE CLEWS. *Folk-Lore of the Sea Islands, South Carolina.* Cambridge, Mass.: The American Folk-Lore Society, 1923. Pp. xxx, 219. NcD, NcU.
Tales, riddles, unsophisticated beliefs, odds and ends of folk-lore collected in 1919.

PIPES, JAMES. *Ziba.* Norman: University of Oklahoma Press, 1943. Pp. 188. NcD, NcU, NcC.
A collection of Negro folklore and folk poetry gathered by a white clerk in a Louisiana crossroads store.

PUCKETT, NEWBELL N. *Folk Beliefs of the Southern Negro.* Chapel Hill: The University of North Carolina Press, 1926. Pp. xiv, 644. NcD, NcU, NcC.
African and Christian elements in the folk beliefs of the American Negro. Voo-dooism, omens, signs, and superstitions are traced to their origin, and examples given.

PUCKETT, NEWBELL N. "Negro Character as Revealed in Folk Lore," *Pub-lications of the American Sociological Society*, XXVIII (May, 1934), 12-23. NcD, NcU.
The masses are the real bearers of the mores of society. Here are some beliefs of the Negro masses.

SALE, JOHN B. *The Tree Named John.* Chapel Hill: The University of North Carolina Press, 1929. Pp. xii, 191. NcD, NcU.
Delightful stories of the Uncle Remus type heard on a Mississippi plantation.

STONEY, SAMUEL G., and SHELBY, GERTRUDE. *Black Genesis.* New York: The Macmillan Company, 1930. Pp. xxix, 192. NcD, NcU.
A collection of biblical folk tales of the Gullah Negroes of South Carolina, told in dialect.

WOOFTER, THOMAS J., JR. *Black Yeomanry: Life on St. Helena Island.* New York: Henry Holt and Co., 1930. Pp. x, 391. NcD, NcU, NcC.
St. Helena is an island off the coast of South Carolina inhabited largely by Negroes. This study presents a picture of the community as a whole.

XXVI. Institutions

1. The Negro Family

BARKER, HOWARD F. "The Family Names of American Negroes," *American Speech*, XIV (October, 1939), 163-74. NcD, NcU, NcC.
"In 1860, the American Negro families were as inadequately named as were the English in the year 1200; by 1880, their naming had moved up to parallelism with that of the English in 1600; now it is nearly up-to-date by English standards."

BASS, RUTH. "The Little Man: Death Among the Negroes in Mississippi," *Scribner's Magazine*, XCVII (February, 1935), 120-23. NcD, NcU.
"Death ain' nothin' but a robber, an' he comes to de big house same as de cabin."

CANSLER, CHARLES W. *Three Generations*. Kingsport, Tennessee: Kingsport Press, 1940. Pp. viii, 173. NcD, NcU.
A Negro family in eastern Tennessee over the past century.

DICKENS, DOROTHY. "Negro Food Habits in the Yazoo Mississippi Delta," *Journal of Home Economics*, XVIII (September, 1926), 523-25. NcD, NcU, NcC.
The diet of these Negroes has changed from one of meat, meal, and molasses to one of a much wider variety. This is due to a change from the system of commissaries to one where the planters advance their tenants a certain amount of cash. The food selection is unwise and the preparation is poor, however, and the Negroes need a program of education in food.

DICKENS, DOROTHY. "Living Rooms of Low-Income Farm Families of Mississippi," *Journal of Home Economics*, XXIX (December, 1937), 702-9. NcD, NcU, NcC.
Standards of living as reflected in the living rooms of 281 Negro and white families.

EGGLESTON, CECELIA. "What a Negro Mother Faces," *The Forum and Century*, C (August, 1938), 59-62. NcD, NcU.
"Will my child rise up to call me blessed or curse the day that he was born?"

FRAZIER, E. FRANKLIN. "Certain Aspects of Conflict in the Negro Family," *Social Forces*, X (October, 1931), 76-84. NcD, NcU, NcC.
The role of cultural factors, such as rapid change in social and economic status, the relative absence of class traditions, and differences in color in the same family, are important sources of conflict in the Negro family.

FRAZIER, E. FRANKLIN. *The Negro Family in Chicago*. Chicago: The University of Chicago Press, 1932. Pp. xxv, 294. NcD, NcU, NcC.
Chicago provides the sample laboratory for a study of the effects of migration, segregation, and urbanization on Negro family life.

FRAZIER, E. FRANKLIN. "Analysis of Statistics on Negro Illegitimacy in the United States," *Social Forces*, XI (December, 1932), 249-57. NcD, NcU, NcC.
The rate of Negro illegitimacy, estimated at 25 per cent in 1908, had dropped to about 15 per cent in 1932.

FRAZIER, E. FRANKLIN. "Children in Black and Mulatto Families," *American Journal of Sociology*, XXXIX (July, 1933), 12-29. NcD, NcU, NcC.
A census study of the supposed hereditary inferiority of the mulatto.

FRAZIER, E. FRANKLIN. "Traditions and Patterns of Negro Family Life in the United States." Chap. XII in E. B. Reuter, ed., *Race and Culture Contacts*. New York: McGraw-Hill Book Co., 1934. NcD, NcU, NcC.
The traditions and patterns of the American Negro family are not vestiges of African culture.

FRAZIER, E. FRANKLIN. "The Present Status of the Negro Family in the United States," *Journal of Negro Education*, VIII (July, 1939), 376-82. NcD, NcU, NcC.
A summary statement of points discussed in detail in the author's *The Negro Family in the United States*.

FRAZIER, E. FRANKLIN. *The Negro Family in the United States*. Chicago: The University of Chicago Press, 1939. Pp. xxxii, 686. NcD, NcU, NcC.
Ernest W. Burgess in the Preface describes this book as ". . . the most valuable contribution to the literature on the family since the publication twenty years ago of *The Polish Peasant in Europe and America* by W. I. Thomas and Florian Znaniecki. For, it is a basic study of the family in its two chief aspects—as a natural *human* association and as a social institution subjected to the severest stresses and strains of social change." A revised and enlarged edition of this work was published by The Dryden Press in 1948. NcD, NcU.

HERTZ, HILDA. *Negro Illegitimacy in Durham, North Carolina*. M.A. thesis, Duke University, 1944. Pp. iv, 110. NcD.
Case material presented against a background of traditional views of Negro morality held by white Southerners.

JOHNSON, CHARLES S. "Negro Personality Changes in a Southern Community." Chap. XIII in E. B. Reuter, ed., *Race and Culture Contacts*. New York: McGraw-Hill Book Co., Inc., 1934. NcD, NcU, NcC.
When marriage, the relation of parents to children, divorce, extra-marital relations, illegitimacy, etc., among Negroes are viewed from the point of view of adjustment to life conditions, they take on an altogether new significance.

JOHNSON, CHARLES S. "Present Status and Trends of the Negro Family," *Social Forces*, XVI (December, 1937), 247-57. NcD, NcU, NcC.
"This paper attempts to provide a basis for interpreting changes noted statistically in the Negro family. It is suggested that directions of change are both *horizontal* and *vertical*, the first being marked by migration and the second by education."

KING, CHARLES E. "The Negro Maternal Family: A Product of an Economic and a Culture System," *Social Forces*, XXIV (October, 1945), 100-4. NcD, NcU, NcC.
There has been a good deal of interest in the Negro maternal family in the United States since Frazier and Johnson noted that this type of family is more prevalent among Negroes than among other racial groups in our population.

McDOUGALD, ELSIE JOHNSON. "The Double Task: The Struggle of Negro Women for Sex and Race Emancipation," *Survey*, LIII (March 1, 1925), 689-91. NcD, NcU.
"In the matter of sex equality, Negro women have contributed few outstanding militants. Their feminist efforts are directed chiefly toward the realization of the equality of the races, the sex struggle assuming a subordinate place."

PARK, ROBERT E. "Negro Home Life and Standards of Living," *Annals of the American Academy of Political and Social Science*, XLIX (September, 1913), 147-63. NcD, NcU.
It is in the standards of Negro home life that the results of education show up to best advantage.

REED, RUTH. "Illegitimacy Among Negroes," *Journal of Social Hygiene*, XI (February, 1925), 73-91. NcD, NcU.
The relative economic independence of Negro women makes them less dependent for support on undesirable husbands. The high proportion of these women who work in domestic service contributes greatly to the group of unmarried mothers.

REED, RUTH. *Negro Illegitimacy in New York City*. New York: Columbia University Press, 1926. Pp. 136. NcD, NcU.
A study of five hundred Negro mothers caught in problems which are theirs both as mothers and as Negroes.

SANDERS, WILEY B. (Director). *Negro Child Welfare in North Carolina*. Chapel Hill: The University of North Carolina Press, 1933. Pp. xiv, 326. NcD, NcU, NcC.
A Rosenwald study of the institutions caring for neglected, delinquent, and dependent Negro children in North Carolina.

WATKINS, ELIZABETH GRANT. "Cultural Backgrounds and Attitudes Among Negroes," *The Family*, XVII (April, May, June, 1936), 52-58, 86-89, 118-22. NcD, NcU.
Case studies of three Negro families analyzed from the point of view of a social worker.

WHITE, WILLIAM L. *Lost Boundaries*. New York: Harcourt, Brace and Co., 1948. Pp. 91. NcD.
An actual Negro family sympathetically portrayed.

2. The Negro Church and Religion

ACKISS, THELMA D. "Changing Patterns of Religious Thought Among Negroes," *Social Forces*, XXIII (December, 1944), 212-15. NcD, NcU, NcC.
There is an increasing tendency among Negroes to move toward the church and away from religion.

ADAMS, ELIZABETH LAURA. *Dark Symphony*. New York: Sheed & Ward, 1942. Pp. 194. NcD, NcU, NcC.
A Negro woman's account of her conversion to Roman Catholicism.

ARTHUR, GEORGE R. *Life on the Negro Frontier*. New York: Associated Press, 1934. Pp. viii, 259. NcU.
A study of the objectives and the success of the activities promoted in Young Men's Christian Associations operated in Rosenwald buildings.

BERRY, LEWELLYN L. *A Century of Missions of the African Methodist Episcopal Church, 1840-1940*. New York: Gutenberg Printing Co., 1942. Pp. xx, 333. NcD.
A historical survey.

BEYNON, ERDMANN D. "Voodoo Cult among Negro Migrants in Detroit," *American Journal of Sociology*, XLIII (May, 1938), 894-907. NcD, NcU, NcC.
"The 'Nation of Islam,' usually known as the 'Voodoo Cult' belongs to a chain of movements arising out of the growing disillusionment and race consciousness of recent Negro migrants to Northern industrial cities. . . . As a result of the teachings of this cult they have gained a new conception of themselves and regard themselves as superior, rather than inferior, to other people."

BILLINGS, R. A. "The Negro and His Church: A Psychogenetic Study," *Psychoanalytic Review*, XXI (October, 1934), 425-41. NcD, NcU.
The different ways in which the church functions in Negro lower, middle, and upper classes.

BOWEN, TREVOR. *Divine White Right: A Study of Race Segregation and Interracial Cooperation in Religious Organizations and Institutions in the United States.* With a section on "The Church and Education for Negroes," by Ira de A. Reid. Published for the Institute of Social and Religious Research. New York: Harper and Brothers, 1934. Pp. xv, 310. NcD, NcU.
This mis-named book is an inquiry into the racial attitudes of the Christian Church in America. It contributes little that is new.

BRAGG, GEORGE FREEMAN, JR. *History of the Afro-American Group of the Episcopal Church.* Baltimore: Church Advocate Press, 1922. Pp. 319. NcD, NcU.
The association of the Negro with the Episcopal Church is older than his connection with any other denomination in the United States.

CABLE, GEORGE W. "Creole Slave Songs," *Century Magazine*, XXXI (April, 1886), 807-28. NcD, NcU, NcC.
This article is one of the few authentic accounts of Negro native worship in the United States.

CANTRIL, HADLEY, and SHERIF, MUZAFER. "The Kingdom of Father Divine," *Journal of Abnormal and Social Psychology*, XXXIII (April, 1938), 147-67. NcD, NcU. Also in Hadley Cantril, *The Psychology of Social Movements* (Chap. V). New York: John Wiley and Sons, 1941. NcD, NcU, NcC.
An account and an explanation of the famous Negro preacher and his cult.

DANIEL, VATTEL E. "Ritual and Stratification in Chicago Negro Churches," *American Sociological Review*, VII (June, 1942), 352-61. NcD, NcU.
Not only do Negro churches "enable the communicants to express their religious life, but they also enhance the morale of members of a subordinate racial class, and through differentiation in ritual, minister to various classes within the Negro population."

DANIEL, VATTEL E. "Negro Classes and Life in the Church," *Journal of Negro Education*, XIII (Winter, 1944), 19-29. NcD, NcU, NcC.
A discussion of (1) the ecstatic cult, (2) the semi-demonstrative group, (3) the deliberative congregation, and (4) the church with formal liturgy.

DANIEL, WILLIAM ANDREW. *Education of Negro Ministers.* New York: George H. Doran Co., 1925. Pp. vii, 187. NcD, NcU.
A study of 52 institutions offering theological courses in 1923-24. The author finds that the Negro ministry has suffered a lowering of status and that educational offerings are not adequate. There is a significant chapter on "The Student Factor."

DAVIS, JOHN W. "George Liele and Andrew Bryan, Pioneer Negro Baptist Preachers," *Journal of Negro History*, III (April, 1918), 119-27. NcD, NcU, NcC.
Liele and Bryan lived during the period of the American Revolution. They were important figures in the establishment of the Baptist Church among Negroes.

DUBOIS, W. E. B. "The Negro Church," Atlanta University *Publications*, No. 8 (1903). Pp. viii, 212. NcD, NcU.
This study is, if not the first, at least the first important sociological study of Negro religion in the United States.

FAUSET, ARTHUR HUFF. *Black Gods of the Metropolis.* Philadelphia: University of Pennsylvania Press, 1944. Pp. x, 126. NcD, NcU, NcC.
A study of Negro religious cults in the urban North.

FULLER, THOMAS OSCAR. *History of the Negro Baptists of Tennessee.* Memphis: Haskins Print, 1936. Pp. 346. NcD.
An account of the activities of Negro Baptists in Tennessee.

GILLARD, JOHN T. *The Catholic Church and the American Negro.* Baltimore, Md.: St. Joseph's Society Press, 1929. Pp. xv, 324. NcD, NcU.
A survey of Catholic missionary activity in behalf of Negroes in the United States, presenting the problem of the Negro as it relates to the Catholic Church.

GILLARD, JOHN T. *Colored Catholics in the United States.* Baltimore: The Josephite Press, 1941. Pp. x, 298. NcD, NcU, NcC.
This book is an account of the 296,998 colored Catholics in the United States in 1941. Why so few colored Catholics in the United States? One factor among others in the answer was Negro and Irish labor competition. Irish and Catholic became one to the Negro.

GOD Struck Me Dead. Social Science Source Document No. 2. Nashville: Social Science Institute, Fisk University, 1946. Pp. 218. NcD, NcU, NcC.
Religious conversion experiences and autobiographies of Negro ex-slaves.

HAMILTON, C. HORACE, and ELLISON, JOHN M. *The Negro Church in Rural Virginia.* Blacksburg, Va.: Virginia Agricultural Experiment Station, Bulletin 273, June, 1930. Pp. 40. NcD, NcU.
In recent years the rural Negro church, like the rural white church, has steadily lost ground in prestige and influence.

HATCHER, WILLIAM E. *John Jasper, the Unmatched Negro Philosopher and Preacher.* New York: Revell Co., 1908. Pp. 183. NcD, NcU.
This volume, containing Jasper's famous sermon, "The Sun Do Move," was written by a Virginian of the planter tradition who had not intended to write in praise of a black man, but did so.

HERSKOVITS, MELVILLE J. "African Gods and Catholic Saints in New World Negro Belief," *American Anthropologist,* XXXVIII (October-December, 1937), 635-43. NcD, NcU.
"The tendency of native peoples who have had long contact with Catholicism to achieve a syncretism between their aboriginal religious beliefs and the doctrines and rituals of the Church has received notice in the case of various folk— but the somewhat more thorough assimilation of Christian and pagan beliefs which has taken place among New World Negroes has, however, gone in large measure unrecognized."

HOSHOR, JOHN. *God in a Rolls Royce.* New York: Hillman-Curl, Inc., 1936. Pp. xii, 272. NcD, NcU, NcC.
A biography of Harlem's self-styled "God."

JORDAN, LEWIS G. *Negro Baptist History, U. S. A., 1750, 1930.* Nashville, Tennessee: Sunday School Publishing Board, N.B.C., 1930. Pp. 394. NcD, NcU.
A history of the Negro Baptist Church from 1750 to 1930. Contains minutes of the Baptist Foreign Mission Conventions, 1880 and 1883.

McKINNEY, RICHARD I. *Religion in Higher Education Among Negroes.* New Haven: Yale University Press, 1945. Pp. xvi, 165. NcD, NcU, NcC.
The Negro college is largely the product of missionary enterprise.

MAYS, BENJAMIN E. *The Negro's God As Reflected in His Literature.* Boston: Chapman and Grimes, 1938. Pp. viii, 269. NcD, NcU, NcC.

"The Negro's ideas of God grow out of the social situation in which he finds himself."

MAYS, BENJAMIN E., and NICHOLSON, JOSEPH WILLIAM. *The Negro's Church*. New York: Institute of Social and Religious Research, 1933. Pp. xiii, 321. NcD, NcU, NcC.

A description of the Negro church in the United States today based upon a first-hand study of 609 urban and 185 rural churches distributed in twelve cities and four country areas.

MYRDAL, GUNNAR. *An American Dilemma*. 2 vols. (Vol. II, Chap. 40, "The Negro Church"). New York: Harper and Brothers, 1944. NcD, NcU, NcC.

"Americans generally are a religious people; Southerners are more religious than the rest of the nation, and the Negroes, perhaps, still a little more religious than the white Southerners."

"NEGRO Preachers Serving Whites," *The Negro History Bulletin*, III (October, 1939), 8 ff. NcD.

In the eighteenth century it was not uncommon to find Negro pastors with white congregations, especially among the Baptists and Methodists.

PARKER, ROBERT A. *The Incredible Messiah: The Deification of Father Divine*. Boston: Little, Brown and Co., 1937. Pp. xiii, 323. NcD, NcU.

The story and the social significance of the rise of the evangelist.

PUCKETT, NEWBELL N. "The Negro Church in the United States," *Journal of Social Forces*, IV (March, 1926), 581-87. NcD, NcU, NcC.

Some points in its history.

REED, JOHN H. *Racial Adjustments in the Methodist Episcopal Church*. New York: The Neale Publishing Company, 1914. Pp. 193. NcD, NcU.

A former president of the College of West Africa in Liberia opposes the effort to "write caste into the Constitution of Methodism" at home and in the mission field.

RICHARDSON, HARRY V. *Dark Glory: A Picture of the Church Among Negroes in the Rural South*. New York: Friendship Press, 1947. Pp. 223. NcD.

A study sponsored by the Home Missions Council of North America and the Phelps-Stokes Fund.

SHERWOOD, GRACE H. *The Oblates' Hundred and One Years*. New York: The Macmillan Company, 1931. Pp. xi, 288. NcD, NcU.

The story of the founding in 1829 in Baltimore, Maryland, of the colored order of the Oblate Sisters of Providence and of its achievements in the religious education of Catholic Negro children.

TALLANT, ROBERT. *Voodoo in New Orleans*. New York: The Macmillan Company, 1946. Pp. viii, 247. NcD, NcU.

Voodoo seems to have evolved from religion through magic to racket.

THOONEN, J. P. *Black Martyrs*. London: Sheed and Ward, 1941. Pp. xviii, 302. NcD.

The story of the conversion and martyrdom of native African Christians.

WHITE, HORACE A. "Who Owns the Negro Churches?" *Christian Century*, LV (February 9, 1938), 176-77. NcD, NcU, NcC.

"It is common knowledge that politicians have learned how to exploit the Negro politically through the use of the Negro church. We are finding out in Detroit that industrialists have learned the same thing."

WHITE, WILLIAM S. *The African Preacher*. Philadelphia: Presbyterian Board of Publication, *c*. 1849. Pp. 139. NcD.

An account of Jack of Virginia, a Negro slave preacher of African birth, who held a place of importance in connection with the establishment of the Presbyterian Church among Negroes.

WOODSON, CARTER G. *The History of the Negro Church.* 2nd ed. Washington: Associated Publishers, 1921. Pp. x, 330. NcD, NcU, NcC.

A history of the first Afro-American institution to grow up under the slave regime.

WOOLRIDGE, NANCY BULLOCK. "The Slave Preacher—Portrait of a Leader," *Journal of Negro Education,* XIV (Winter, 1945), 28-37. NcD, NcU, NcC.

"The story of the Negro preacher in America has been the history of an expanding leadership."

3. Negro Educational Institutions and Problems

ADAMS, MYRON W. *A History of Atlanta University.* Atlanta, Georgia: Atlanta University Press, 1930. Pp. 120. NcD.

A history of the largest university for Negroes in the South.

ALEXANDER, FREDERICK MILTON. *Education for the Needs of the Negro in Virginia.* Washington: The Southern Education Foundation, 1943. Pp. xvi, 281. NcD, NcU, NcC.

An investigation made by the supervisor of Negro education in Virginia for the John F. Slater Fund.

BIRNIE, C. W. "The Education of the Negro in Charleston, South Carolina, before the Civil War," *Journal of Negro History,* XII (January, 1927), 13-21. NcD, NcU, NcC.

Negro slaves sometimes were educated for the purpose of looking after the master's business affairs.

BLASCOER, FRANCES. *Colored School Children in New York.* New York: Public Education Association, 1915. Pp. vii, 176. NcD.

Throws light upon the curious and subtle ways in which race prejudice acts at once to stimulate and to inhibit the activities of the colored child. He is compelled to make special adaptations to social situations of which the white child knows nothing and of which the ordinary public school does not take account.

BOND, HORACE M. "The Cash Value of a Negro Child," *School and Society,* XXXVII (May 13, 1933), 627-30. NcD, NcU, NcC.

Racial discrimination in expending school funds in the South releases wealth to white children that otherwise would be shared by Negro school children.

BOND, HORACE M. *The Education of the Negro in the American Social Order.* New York: Prentice-Hall, 1934. Pp. xx, 501. NcD, NcU, NcC.

A vivid picture of the rise and development of the Negro in terms of his education in the American social order. The book presents also a program of action and a plea for educational planning. Perhaps the most important book yet written on the subject.

BOND, HORACE M. *Negro Education in Alabama: A Study in Cotton and Steel.* Washington, D. C.: Associated Publishers, 1939. Pp. 358. NcD, NcU, NcC.

"For Negro children involved in the plantation economy, it is reasonably certain that a change in relative provisions for education now made must wait upon fundamental changes in the structure of the economic system that now gives meaning to relations between white and black. . . . Similarly the education of Negroes now living on the fringes of the new industry in Alabama depends upon the future status of that industrial development in relation to domestic and international conditions."

BRAMELD, THEODORE. *Minority Problems in the Public Schools.* New York: Harper and Brothers, 1946. Pp. ix, 264. NcD, NcU, NcC.
A study of the handling of racial, social-economic, and religious problems in seven representative school systems.

BRAWLEY, BENJAMIN G. *A History of Morehouse College.* Atlanta, Ga.: Morehouse College, 1917. Pp. 218. NcD.
An official history.

BROWN, CHARLOTTE HAWKINS. *The Correct Thing to Do, to Say, to Wear.* Boston: Christopher Publishing House, 1941. Pp. 142. NcD, NcU.
The president of the Palmer Memorial Institute for Negroes is the author of this little book on etiquette.

CALIVER, AMBROSE. *A Personnel Study of Negro College Students: A Study of the Relations Between Certain Background Factors of Negro College Students and Their Subsequent Careers in College.* New York: Teachers College, Columbia University, 1931. Pp. viii, 146. NcD, NcU.
An analysis of the social, economic, and intellectual backgrounds of Negro college students in relation to their subsequent academic progress and to certain other activities and interests in their college careers.

CALIVER, AMBROSE. *A Background Study of Negro College Students.* Washington: U. S. Government Printing Office, 1933. Pp. vii, 132. NcD, NcU.
The social backgrounds of college students in thirty-three Negro colleges.

CALIVER, AMBROSE. *Availability of Education to Negroes in Rural Communities.* Office of Education, U. S. Department of the Interior, Bulletin No. 12, 1935. Pp. iv, 86. NcU.
The most difficult problems connected with the education of Negroes are found in rural areas.

CALIVER, AMBROSE. *Vocational Education and Guidance of Negroes.* Office of Education, U. S. Department of the Interior, Bulletin No. 38, 1937. Pp. x, 137. NcD, NcU.
A study of the opportunities and facilities for the vocational education and guidance of Negroes.

CALIVER, AMBROSE. *Education of Negro Teachers.* Office of Education, U. S. Department of the Interior, Bulletin No. 10, 1939. Pp. 123. NcU.
Can inferior teachers produce superior students?

CALIVER, AMBROSE, and GREENE, ETHEL G. *Education of Negroes: A Five Year Bibliography, 1931-1935.* Office of Education, U. S. Department of the Interior, Bulletin No. 8, 1937. Pp. vi, 63. NcD, NcU.
A descriptive bibliography of books, periodical literature, and documents appearing during the period.

CAMPBELL, THOMAS M. *The Movable School Goes to the Negro Farmer.* Tuskegee, Alabama: Tuskegee Institute Press, 1936. Pp. xiv, 170. NcD, NcU.
An account of the well-rounded education Tuskegee Institute is giving to the rural Negro, told from personal experience.

COOKE, DENNIS HARGROVE. *The White Superintendent and the Negro Schools in North Carolina.* Nashville, Tennessee: George Peabody College for Teachers, 1930. Pp. xi, 176. NcD, NcU.
As judged by their own standards the white superintendents do not give sufficient time to their Negro schools.

COOLEY, ROSSA B. *Homes of the Freed.* New York: New Republic, Inc., 1926. Pp. xiv, 199. NcD.
In 1862 the first school for freedmen was established on Southern soil. In this work Miss Cooley, the head of Penn School, tells how the school has to connect education with the industrial and cultural life of the community.

DABNEY, CHARLES WILLIAM. *Universal Education in the South.* 2 vols. Chapel Hill: The University of North Carolina Press, 1936. NcD, NcU, NcC.
The story of education in the South, state by state and institution by institution.

DAVIDSON, HENRY DAMON. *"Inching Along," or, the Life and Work of an Alabama Farm Boy.* Nashville: National Publishing Co., 1944. Pp. xvii, 177. NcD, NcU.
The autobiography of the founder and principal of the Bibb County Training School in Alabama.

DYSON, WALTER. *Howard University: The Capstone of Negro Education; A History, 1867-1940.* Washington: The Graduate School, Howard University, 1942. Pp. xiv, 553. NcD, NcU, NcC.
The history and achievements of a leading national university for Negroes.

FOREMAN, CLARK. *Environmental Factors in Negro Elementary Education.* New York: W. W. Norton & Company, Inc., 1932. Pp. 88. NcD, NcU.
The evidence indicates that as the environment of Negro pupils approaches that of white children from whom the norms of achievement are derived, the achievement of Negro pupils approaches that of white children.

FROM Servitude to Service: Being the Old South Lectures on the History and Work of Southern Institutions for the Education of the Negro. Boston: American Unitarian Association, 1905. Pp. 232. NcD, NcU.
A symposium on the work of Howard University, Berea College, Tuskegee Institute, Hampton Institute, Atlanta University, and Fisk University.

FURNIVALL, J. S. *Educational Progress in Southeast Asia.* New York: Institute of Pacific Relations, 1943. Pp. xii, 186. NcD, NcU.
An important chapter in the comparative study of the education of minority peoples.

GALLAGHER, BUELL G. *American Caste and the Negro College.* New York: Columbia University Press, 1938. Pp. xv, 463. NcD, NcU, NcC.
A Negro educator thoughtfully faces the problem of the role and function of the segregated college "in the light of its social task."

HALLIBURTON, CECIL D. *A History of St. Augustine's College, 1867-1937.* Raleigh, N. C.: St. Augustine's College, 1937. Pp. 97. NcU, NcC.
The seventy-year history of the college for Negroes, Raleigh, N. C., founded by the Freedmen's Commission of the Protestant Episcopal Church.

HOLLAND, RUPERT SARGENT, ed. *Letters and Diary of Laura M. Towne. Written from the Sea Islands of South Carolina, 1862-1884.* Cambridge: The Riverside Press, 1912. Pp. xviii, 310. NcU.
A Northern missionary's life among the Negroes of St. Helena Island during the Civil War and Reconstruction.

HOLMES, DWIGHT O. W. *The Evolution of the Negro College.* Contributions to Education No. 609. New York: Teachers College, Columbia University, 1934. Pp. xi, 221. NcD, NcU, NcC.
A study of the circumstances surrounding the establishment and development of the Negro college in the United States.

JOHNSON, CHARLES S. "The Education of the Negro Child," *American Sociological Review*, I (April, 1936), 264-72. NcD, NcU.
The function of Negro education could be that of putting order and meaning
and design into the selection of new culture traits.

JOHNSON, CHARLES S. "On the Need of Realism in Negro Education,"
Journal of Negro Education, V (January, 1936), 375-82. NcD, NcU, NcC.
True education begins in experience and becomes effective in the measure that
this experience can be related to the larger world of knowledge. The education of
Negroes fails at too many points to deal concretely with the lives of Negroes.
Poor as schools for Negroes are, the educational procedure in them is poorer.

JOHNSON, CHARLES S. *The Negro College Graduate*. Chapel Hill: The University of North Carolina Press, 1938. Pp. xvii, 399. NcD, NcU, NcC.
An extensive and factual study of Negro college graduates in the United States
from 1826 to 1936. Particular attention is given to the number, location, income,
occupations, and social and economic backgrounds of living graduates.

JOHNSON, CHARLES S. "The Negro Public Schools." Vol. 4, Section 8 in
Louisiana Educational Survey. Baton Rouge, Louisiana: Louisiana Educational Survey, 1942. NcD, NcU.
A thorough-going survey of Negro common school education in a Southern
state.

JOHNSON, CHARLES S., ed. *Education and the Cultural Process*. Papers Presented at a Symposium Commemorating the Seventy-Fifth Anniversary of the
Founding of Fisk University, April 29—May 4, 1941. Pp. iii, 136. NcD, NcU,
NcC. Reprinted from *The American Journal of Sociology*, Vol. XLVIII,
No. 6 (May, 1943). NcD, NcU, NcC.
In this symposium "the papers dealing with the special cultures clearly describe
the process of 'education without schools.' The papers dealing with educational
procedure under our highly rationalized system describe what might almost be
called 'schools without education.'"

JOHNSON, GUY B. "Education, Segregation, and Race Relations," *Quarterly
Review of Higher Education Among Negroes*, III (April, 1935), 89-94. NcD.
An address delivered at the sixty-eighth anniversary of the founding of John-
son C. Smith University.

JONES, LANCE G. E. *The Jeanes Teacher in the United States, 1908-1933*.
Chapel Hill: The University of North Carolina Press, 1937. Pp. xvi, 146.
NcD, NcU, NcC.
An account of twenty-five years' experience in the supervision of Negro rural
schools.

JONES, LAURENCE CLIFTON. *The Spirit of Piney Woods*. With an intro-
duction by George Foster Peabody. New York: Fleming H. Revell Co., 1931.
Pp. 93. NcD, NcU.
A few addresses delivered on Sunday evenings, to the students of Piney Woods
Country Life School (Mississippi) by its founder.

JONES, THOMAS JESSE. *Negro Education: A Study of the Private and
Higher Schools for Colored People in the United States*. 2 vols. Prepared in
co-operation with the Phelps-Stokes Fund. U. S. Bureau of Education, Bul-
letins 38 and 39, 1917. NcD, NcU, NcC.
In spite of the forbidding appearance of these two ponderous volumes, they
contain materials of extreme interest, importance, and significance even if many
of the facts are now somewhat out of date.

KILPATRICK, WILLIAM H. *Our Educational Task, as Illustrated in the Changing South.* Chapel Hill: The University of North Carolina Press, 1930. Pp. ix, 123. NcD, NcU.

Kilpatrick presents a philosophy of education for changing society with special reference to the South.

KNIGHT, EDGAR W. *Public Education in the South.* Boston: Ginn and Company, 1922. Pp. xii, 482. NcD, NcU, NcC.

A survey of the growth of public educational organization and practices in the South.

LONG, HOLLIS MOODY. *Public Secondary Education for Negroes in North Carolina.* New York: Teachers College, Columbia University, 1932. Pp. xi, 115. NcD, NcU, NcC.

A study of practices and trends in secondary school education, and the characteristics, achievements, interests, and aims of students.

McCROREY, HENRY L. "A Brief History of Johnson C. Smith University," *Johnson C. Smith University Bulletin*, Vol. I, No. 4 (May 30, 1935). NcU.

A short history of the institution located in Charlotte, N. C.

McCUISTION, FRED. *Higher Education of Negroes.* Nashville, Tennessee: The author, 1933. Pp. 40. NcD, NcU.

A summary of conditions in the Negro colleges of the South.

McCUISTION, FRED. *Graduate Instruction for Negroes in the United States.* Nashville, Tennessee: George Peabody College for Teachers, 1939. Pp. xviii, 172. NcD, NcU, NcC.

A thorough survey of graduate education for Negroes by one fully competent to make it. The present urgent interest in this subject is an acknowledgment of "the arrival of this group at an important new stage in educational growth."

McGINNIS, FREDERICK A. *A History and an Interpretation of Wilberforce University.* Wilberforce, Ohio: Wilberforce University, 1941. Pp. xii, 215. NcD, NcU, NcC.

Before 1861 the chief patrons of this old college for Negroes in Ohio were white slaveholders in the South.

MALHERBE, E. G., ed. *Educational Adaptations in a Changing Society.* Capetown, South Africa: Juta and Co., 1937. Pp. xv, 545. NcD, NcU.

". . . educational problems in South Africa are largely determined, as they are in the United States, by the complexity of the racial and cultural diversities of South African peoples." This report of the South African Educational Conference of 1934 provided the model for C. S. Johnson, ed., *Education and the Cultural Process.*

MYRDAL, GUNNAR. *An American Dilemma.* 2 vols. (Vol. II, Chap. 41, "The Negro School"). New York: Harper and Brothers, 1944. NcD, NcU, NcC.

". . . the white superintendent and the white school board ordinarily care little about what goes on in the Negro school. There are still counties where the superintendent has never visited the majority of his Negro schools."

NEWBOLD, N. C. "Common Schools for Negroes in the South," *Annals of the American Academy of Political and Social Science*, CXL (November, 1928), 209-23. NcD, NcU, NcC.

The South has embarked on a definite policy of rebuilding the entire Negro public school system. In addition to expenditures from taxation more than $30,000,000 were received from gifts for Negro education between 1918 and 1928.

NOBLE, STUART GRAYSON. *Forty Years of the Public Schools in Mississippi, with Special Reference to the Education of the Negro.* New York: Teachers College, Columbia University, 1918. Pp. 148. NcD, NcU.

Regarded by some as one of the most adequate of the studies of education under Reconstruction.

PARK, ROBERT E. "A Memorandum on Rote Learning," *American Journal of Sociology*, XLIII (July, 1937), 23-36. NcD, NcU, NcC.
Rote learning is a cultural as well as a pedagogical problem.

PEABODY, FRANCIS G. *Education for Life*. Garden City, N. Y.: Doubleday, Page and Co., 1919. Pp. xxiv, 393. NcD, NcU.
The story of Hampton Institute in Virginia told in connection with the Fiftieth Anniversary of its founding.

RANSOM, LEON A. "Legal Status of Negro Education under Separate School Systems," *Journal of Negro Education*, VIII (July, 1939), 395-405. NcD, NcU, NcC.
Under the law Negroes are entitled to "separate but equal" educational facilities but the question of what is equality is still unanswered.

REID, IRA DE A. *Adult Education Among Negroes*. Bronze Booklet No. 1. Washington: Associates in Negro Folk Education, 1936. Pp. 73. NcD, NcU, NcC.
The adult education movement among Negroes.

REPORT of the Governor's Commission for the Study of Problems in the Education of Negroes in North Carolina. Raleigh: State Supt. of Public Instruction, 1935. Pp. 96. NcD, NcU.
A statement of a progressive program for Negro education in the state.

RISEN, MAURICE LONDON. *Legal Aspects of Separation of Races in the Public Schools*. Thesis, Temple University, Philadelphia, 1935. Pp. 142. NcD, NcU.
A study of the issues pertinent to the separation of the races in public schools.

SAVAGE, W. SHERMAN. *The History of Lincoln University*. Jefferson City, Missouri: Lincoln University, 1939. Pp. xii, 302. NcD.
A history of one of the Negro colleges which developed out of the Civil War.

SCHRIEKE, B. J. O. "American Negro and Colonial Native: Education and Equality," *Pacific Affairs*, X (September, 1937), 289-304. NcD, NcU.
"Comparison between the opportunities for the Southern Negro, as far as education is concerned, and those existing for 'natives' in colonial tutelage, shows that it is not the legal status but the social and economic position which determines the nature and quality of educational facilities."

SHEPHERD, ROBERT H. W. *Lovedale, South Africa: Story of a Century, 1841-1941*. South Africa: The Lovedale Press, 1941. Pp. xiv, 531. NcD.
History of the first missionary school for the advance education of the natives in South Africa.

SURVEY of Negro Colleges and Universities. United States Bureau of Education, Bulletin No. 7 (1928). Washington: U. S. Government Printing Office, 1929. Pp. vi, 964. NcD, NcU, NcC.

SWINT, HENRY LEE. *The Northern Teacher in the South, 1862-1870*. Nashville: Vanderbilt University Press, 1941. Pp. ix, 221. NcD, NcU.
A study of the relations between the Negro, the Southern white, and the Yankee schoolma'am.

THRASHER, MAX BENNETT. *Tuskegee, Its Story and Its Work*. Boston: Small, Maynard and Company, 1900. Pp. xvi, 251. NcD, NcU.
The story of the lengthened shadow of one man—Booker T. Washington.

VICKERY, W. E., and COLE, S. G. *Intercultural Education in American Schools*. New York: Harper and Brothers, 1943. Pp. xviii, 214. NcD, NcU.
A discussion of the responsibility of the schools in the improvement of relations between the races.

WALKER, ANNE KENDRICK. *Tuskegee and the Black Belt*. Richmond, Va.: The Dietz Press, Inc., 1944. Pp. xx, 180. NcD, NcU, NcC.
Most Southern whites will find this book liberal in outlook. Negroes will find it somewhat more than a little condescending in attitude.

WARNER, W. LLOYD. "Formal Education and the Social Structure," *Journal of Educational Sociology*, IX (May, 1936), 524-31. NcD, NcU.
An attempt to understand how each of two communities, one Southern, and one Northern, adjust their growing children to the social strata of caste and class.

WELSH, G. H. *The Black Man's Schools*. Pretoria, South Africa: The Carnegie Visitors' Grants Committee, 1936. Pp. 55. NcD, NcU, NcC.
A South African's impressions of the education of the American Negro with reference to desirable improvements in the education of the South African Bantu.

WHITING, JOSEPH L. *Shop and Class at Tuskegee*. Boston: Chapman and Grimes, 1941. Pp. 114. NcD, NcU.
A study in vocational education during two decades at Tuskegee Institute.

WILKERSON, DOXEY. *Special Problems of Negro Education*. Advisory Committee on Education. Staff Study No. 12. Washington: U. S. Government Printing Office, 1939. Pp. xvi, 171. NcD, NcU, NcC.
During the past decade there have been striking advances in American public school education, but the advances for Negro children have not kept pace with those for white children.

WINSTON, SANFORD. *Illiteracy in the United States*. Chapel Hill: The University of North Carolina Press, 1930. Pp. xii, 168. NcD, NcU.
A comprehensive analysis of illiteracy statistics in the United States and trends since 1870. Illiteracy is considered in relation to birth-rate, infant mortality, urbanization, etc.

WOODSON, CARTER G. *The Education of the Negro Prior to 1861: The History of the Education of the Colored People of the United States from the Beginning of Slavery to the Civil War*. New York: G. P. Putnam's Sons, 1915. Pp. v, 454. NcD, NcU, NcC.
The story of the groping efforts of a primitive and enslaved race to find its way in an alien world and to substitute distant, racial, and ideal ends for immediate instinctive desires and individual interests.

WRIGHT, MARION M. THOMPSON. *The Education of Negroes in New Jersey*. New York: Teachers College, Columbia University, 1941. Pp. ix, 227. NcD, NcU.
In this important contribution to Negro educational history the author traces the education of Negroes in New Jersey against the background of social changes that bring institutional efforts into sharp relief.

4. THE NEGRO IN BUSINESS AND IN THE PROFESSIONS; MISCELLANEOUS ORGANIZATIONS

BLAYTON, JESSE B. "The Negro in Banking," *Bankers' Magazine*, CXXXIII (December, 1936), 511-14. NcD.
"Negro banks are not merely important business establishments. They are social and civic agencies as well."

BROWNING, J. B. "The Beginnings of Insurance Enterprise Among Negroes," *Journal of Negro History*, XXII (October, 1937), 417-32. NcD, NcU, NcC.
A survey of Negro insurance enterprises between 1778 and 1835.

COBB, W. MONTAGUE. *The First Negro Medical Society.* Washington, D. C.:
    Associated Publishers, 1939. Pp. x, 159. NcD, NcU.
The history of the Medico-Chirurgical Society of the District of Columbia,
1884-1939. "This work opens up another theme of interest to the student of race
and culture—the role, the organization, and the defensive maneuvering of the
minority professional."

CORWIN, E. H. L., and STURGES, G. E. *Opportunities for the Medical Educa-
    tion of Negroes.* New York: C. Scribner's Sons, 1936. Pp. xv, 293. NcD,
    NcU.
A study of the Negro medical, hospital, and health situation in the United
States as a whole with special reference to the Harlem Hospital in New York
City.

DETWEILER, FREDERICK G. *The Negro Press in the United States.* Chicago:
    The University of Chicago Press, 1922. Pp. x, 274. NcD, NcU, NcC.
The influence and themes of the Negro press from the days of slavery to the
present time.

DETWEILER, FREDERICK G. "The Negro Press Today," *American Journal
    of Sociology,* XLIV (November, 1938), 391-400. NcD, NcU.
"The Negro paper began as an extended editorial, but it has been gradually
justifying itself as a newspaper. More and more it is becoming necessary to its
people as a purveyor of news."

"FORTUNE Press Analysis: Negroes," *Fortune,* XXXI (May, 1945), 233ff. NcD,
    NcU, NcC.
"The Negro press deals single-mindedly with the problems of being a Negro
in the U. S."

FRAZIER, E. FRANKLIN. "Co-operatives; the Next Step in the Negro's Busi-
    ness Development," *Southern Workman,* LIII (November, 1924), 505-9. NcD,
    NcU, NcC.
Co-operatives are peculiarly advantageous to the Negro. Through them he
may become a producer while retaining his character as a consumer.

GLEASON, ELIZA ATKINS. *The Southern Negro and the Public Library.*
    Chicago: The University of Chicago Press, 1941. Pp. xvi, 218. NcD, NcU,
    NcC.
A scholarly investigation by the librarian of Talladega College.

HAMILTON, J. G. DE ROULHAC. "The Sons and Daughters of I Will Arise,"
    Scribner's Magazine, LXXX (September, 1926), 325-31. NcD, NcU.
A racy and frothy interpretation of the role and function of Negro lodges,
sometimes known as "coffin clubs." The Negro lodge was an important factor
in the rise of Negro insurance.

HUNTER, JANE EDNA. *A Nickel and a Prayer.* Nashville: The Parthenon
    Press, 1940. Pp. 198. NcD, NcU.
An autobiography and the story of the Phillis Wheatley Association, an urban
institution for the care of Negro girls.

JACK, ROBERT L. *History of the National Association for the Advancement
    of Colored People.* Boston: Meador Publishing Co., 1943. Pp. xiv, 110. NcD,
    NcU, NcC.
The work, history, and ideology of the largest Negro organization in America.

JACKSON, WALLACE VAN. "Some Pioneer Negro Library Workers," *Library
    Journal,* LXIV (March 15, 1939), 215-17. NcD, NcU, NcC.
Brief life-sketches of Edward C. Williams, George W. Forbes, Thomas F. Blue,
S. W. Starks, J. A. Jackson, and Daniel A. P. Murray.

JACKSON, WALLACE VAN. "Negro Library Workers," *Library Quarterly*, X (January, 1940), 95-108. NcD, NcU, NcC.
The need for Negro library workers is great. About 83 per cent of the Negro population of the South is without access to any public library service.

LIBRARIES, Librarians, and the Negro. Atlanta: Atlanta University School of Library Service, 1944. NcD, NcU, NcC.
A bulletin of general information.

MAYO, SELZ C. *Negro Hospitals and Medical Care Facilities in North Carolina*. Raleigh: North Carolina Agricultural Experiment Station, State College, April, 1945. NcD.
A survey bulletin.

MILLER, KELLY. "The Historic Background of the Negro Physician," *Journal of Negro History*, I (April, 1916), 99-109. NcD, NcU, NcC.
"An accurate study of the healing art as practiced by Negroes in Africa as well as its continuance after transplantation in America would form an investigation of great historical interest."

MYRDAL, GUNNAR. *An American Dilemma*. 2 vols. (Vol. II, Chap. 42, "The Negro Press"). New York: Harper and Brothers, 1944. NcD, NcU, NcC.
"Most white people in America are entirely unaware of the bitter and relentless criticism of themselves. . . . Week in and week out these [criticisms] are presented to the Negro people in their own press. It is a fighting press."

NEGRO HOSPITALS: A Compilation of Available Statistics. Chicago: Julius Rosenwald Fund, 1931. Pp. 57. NcD.
A bulletin on Negro hospitals in the United States with emphasis upon the Carolinas and Tennessee.

THE NEGRO IN BUSINESS, 1935. Washington: U. S. Department of Commerce, July, 1935. Pp. 9. NcU.
A bibliography prepared by the Negro Affairs Division of the Department of Commerce.

OVINGTON, MARY WHITE. *The Walls Came Tumbling Down*. New York: Harcourt, Brace and Co., 1947. Pp. x, 307. NcD.
An interesting personal account of the author's role in the development and the work of the National Association for the Advancement of Colored People.

PALMER, EDWARD NILES. "Negro Secret Societies," *Social Forces*, XXIII (December, 1944), 207-12. NcD, NcU, NcC.
Denied participation in white American institutions, Negroes strive to duplicate them. Negro secret societies show that Negroes regard themselves as an integral part of American society.

PENN, I. GARLAND. *The Afro-American Press and Its Editors*. Springfield, Mass.: Willey and Co., 1891. Pp. 565. NcD, NcU, NcC.
The first important book on the Negro press. Attention is called to the services performed by the Negro press for the Negro community.

PIERCE, JOSEPH A. *Negro Business and Business Education*. New York: Harper and Brothers, 1947. Pp. 352. NcD.
A study sponsored by Atlanta University and the National Urban League.

RIDDLE, ESTELLE MASSEY. "Progress of Negro Nursing," *American Journal of Nursing*, XXXVIII (February, 1938), 162-69. NcD, NcU.
From the graduation of the first Negro professional nurse in 1879, the number has increased to 5,728 in 1930. But for a Negro population of 12,000,000 this is entirely inadequate.

ROMAN, CHARLES VICTOR. *Meharry Medical College: A History.* Nashville, Tennessee: Sunday School Publishing Board of the Nashville Baptist Convention, 1934. Pp. xi, 224. NcD, NcU.
A much better history of this important medical school for Negroes is needed.

STUART, MERAH STEVEN. *An Economic Detour.* New York: Wendell Malliet and Co., 1940. Pp. xxv, 339. NcD, NcU.
An inquiry into the origin and growth of Negro life insurance companies.

THOMS, (MRS.) ADAH B. *Pathfinders: A History of the Progress of Colored Graduate Nurses.* New York: Kay Printing House, 1929. Pp. xvi, 240. NcD.
Begins with an account of "Aunt Harriet," the famous nurse of Civil War days.

TRENT, W. J., JR. *Development of Negro Life Insurance Enterprises.* Salisbury, N. C.: Salisbury College, 1932. Pp. 62. NcU, NcC.
A history and an analysis of the most important segment of Negro business.

UNITED STATES, Department of Commerce. *Negro Chambers of Commerce: 1936.* Washington: Bureau of Foreign and Domestic Commerce, 1936. Pp. 21. NcD.
The structure and function of Negro chambers of commerce in the United States together with their names and locations.

VOORHIS, HAROLD VAN BUREN. *Negro Masonry in the United States.* New York: Henry Emmerson, 1940. Pp. xii, 132. NcD, NcU.
A report on the Negro in recognized and in "unrecognized" free masonry.

WAITE, E. EMERSON, JR. *Social Factors in Negro Business Enterprise.* M.A. thesis, Duke University, 1940. Pp. viii, 161. NcD.
The author is concerned especially with the Negro insurance business.

WILLIAMS, FRANCES HARRIET. *The Business Girl Looks at the Negro World.* New York: The Woman's Press, 1937. Pp. 55. NcD.
A study outline for Y. W. C. A. groups.

WOODSON, CARTER G. *The Negro Professional Man and the Community.* Washington: Association for the Study of Negro Life and History, 1934. Pp. xviii, 365. NcD, NcU, NcC.
With special emphasis upon the Negro physician and lawyer.

WORK, MONROE N. "The Negro in Business and the Professions," *Annals of the American Academy of Political and Social Science,* CXL (November, 1928), 138-44. NcD, NcU, NcC.
The ministry was the first American profession into which Negroes entered but now they are represented in all. Insurance was one of the earliest, and remains the most important form, of Negro business. In 1928 there were in existence more than 70,000 Negro business enterprises of various sorts.

XXVII. The Negro in Literature and in the Arts

1. THE NEGRO AS SUBJECT AND AS AUTHOR

BARTON, REBECCA CHALMERS. *Witnesses for Freedom: Negro Americans in Autobiography.* New York: Harper and Brothers, 1948. Pp. 294. NcD.
An interpretive appreciation of twenty-three Negroes who have contributed to American letters. The Foreword is by Alain Locke.

BRAWLEY, BENJAMIN G. *Early Negro American Writers. Selections with Biographical and Critical Introductions.* Chapel Hill: The University of North Carolina Press, 1935. Pp. ix, 305. NcD, NcU, NcC.
"Of value to English readers, not for the literary merit of the excerpts chosen, but for the evidence they provide of the ease and avidity with which the slave assimilated the European culture by which he was surrounded."

BROWN, STERLING A. "Negro Character As Seen by White Authors," *Journal of Negro Education*, II (January, 1933), 179-203. NcD, NcU, NcC.
The Negro has met with as great injustice in American literature as he has in American life. Seven Negro stereotypes in white literature are distinguished: (1) The Contented Slave, (2) The Wretched Freeman, (3) The Comic Negro, (4) The Brute Negro, (5) The Tragic Mulatto, (6) The Local Color Negro, and (7) The Exotic Primitive.

BROWN, STERLING A. *The Negro in American Fiction.* Bronze Booklet No. 6. Washington: The Associates in Negro Folk Education, 1937. Pp. 209. NcD, NcU, NcC.
A survey of the Negro in American fiction, both as character and as author.

BROWN, STERLING A. *Negro Poetry and Drama.* Bronze Booklet No. 7. Washington: The Associates in Negro Folk Education, 1937. Pp. 142. NcD, NcU, NcC.
A "survey of the Negro theme in American poetry and drama and critical commentary on the Negro's share in that creative expression."

BROWN, STERLING A., DAVIS, ARTHUR P., and LEE, ULYSSES, eds. *The Negro Caravan.* New York: The Dryden Press, 1941. Pp. xviii, 1082. NcD, NcU, NcC.
An anthology of American Negro writings covering the whole period of Negro experience in America.

CALVERTON, VICTOR F., ed. *Anthology of American Negro Literature.* New York: The Modern Library, 1929. Pp. xii, 535. NcD, NcU, NcC.
More diversified than most anthologies this one includes literature of the folk, the writings of professionals, essays in social science, and autobiographies.

CROMWELL, OTELIA, TURNER, L. D., and DYKES, EVA B. *Readings from Negro Authors.* New York: Harcourt, Brace and Co., 1931. Pp. xii, 388. NcD, NcU, NcC.
Contains poetry, stories, one-act plays, essays, and public addresses.

CUNARD, NANCY. *Negro Anthology.* London: Wishart & Company, 1934. Pp. viii, 854. NcD, NcU.
An anthology of art and literature by and about Negroes in America, the West Indies, Latin America, Africa, and Europe, compiled by the editor, in the con-

viction that "the Communist world-order is the solution of the race problem for the Negro."

DYKES, EVA BEATRICE. *The Negro in English Romantic Thought*. Washington, D. C.: The Associated Publishers, Inc., 1942. Pp. 197. NcD, NcU, NcC.

The purpose of this book is "to ascertain from the great bulk of poetry and prose of the eighteenth and early nineteenth centuries any sympathetic attitude toward the Negro and to find out reasons for this attitude."

FORD, NICK AARON. *The Contemporary Negro Novel*. Boston: Meador Publishing Co., 1936. Pp. 108. NcD, NcU, NcC.

A study of the race problem as it appears in contemporary novels written by Negroes.

GAINES, FRANCIS P. "The Racial Bar Sinister in American Romance," *South Atlantic Quarterly*, XXV (October, 1926), 396-402. NcD, NcU.

"Lacking in the large a community of multiple social gradations as background, American fictionists have found our sharply defined racial restrictions, particularly of white and black, an opportunity for exposition of the general tragedy of caste and for the specific pathos of passion warring with opposeless polity."

GLOSTER, HUGH MORRIS. *Negro Voices in American Fiction*. Chapel Hill: The University of North Carolina Press, 1948. Pp. 295. NcD, NcU.

A sort of hand-book of Negro literature from the Civil War to the present.

GREEN, ELIZABETH L. *The Negro in Contemporary American Literature: An Outline for Individual and Group Study*. Chapel Hill: The University of North Carolina Press, 1928. Pp. 98. NcD, NcU.

Now somewhat out of date but still a useful guide.

JOHNSON, CHARLES S., ed. *Ebony and Topaz: A Collectanea*. New York: Opportunity, National Urban League, 1927. Pp. 164. NcU.

A collection of poems, plays, essays, and stories "accepting the materials of Negro life for their own worth . . ."

KERLIN, ROBERT T. *The Voice of the Negro, 1919*. New York: E. P. Dutton & Co., 1920. Pp. xii, 188. NcD, NcU, NcC.

A compilation from the colored press of America for the four months immediately following the Washington riot. This is the first book, written by a white man, in which the significance of Negro prose and verse is recognized.

LOCKE, ALAIN. *The New Negro: An Interpretation*. New York: A. and C. Boni, 1925. Pp. xviii, 446. NcD, NcU, NcC.

A symposium, containing literary contributions of many of the important younger Negro writers. It is neither an apology nor an appeal but a literary expression of Negro life.

LOGGINS, VERNON. *The Negro Author: His Development in America*. Columbia University Studies in English and Comparative Literature. New York: Columbia University Press, 1931. Pp. ix, 480. NcD, NcU, NcC.

A critical study of Negro authorship from 1760 to 1900.

MOON, BUCKLIN, ed. *Primer for White Folks*. New York: Doubleday, Page and Co., 1945. Pp. xiv, 491. NcD, NcU, NcC.

An anthology of prose writings by and about Negroes.

NELSON, JOHN HERBERT. *The Negro Character in American Literature*. Bulletin of the University of Kansas, Vol. XXVII, No. 15; Humanistic Studies, Vol. IV, No. 1. Lawrence, Kansas: The Department of Journalism Press, 1926. Pp. 146. NcD, NcU.

Although Negro characters have appeared in the literature of other countries "no nation except our own has made a masterful presentation" of them.

REDDING, J. SAUNDERS. *To Make a Poet Black.* Chapel Hill: The University of North Carolina Press, 1939. Pp. x, 142. NcD, NcU, NcC.

A review and discussion of Negro literature up to 1939.

WATKINS, SYLVESTRE C., ed. *An Anthology of American Negro Literature.* New York: Modern Library, 1944. Pp. xvii, 481. NcD, NcU, NcC.

This book is intended to bring together, in the words of the editor, "those selections which represent the vigorous thinking and writing of today's Negro."

WOODSON, CARTER G. *Negro Orators and Their Orations.* Washington: Associated Publishers, 1925. Pp. xi, 711. NcD, NcU, NcC.

A comprehensive collection of the important orations delivered by Negroes of the United States, and a short sketch of each orator.

WRIGHT, RICHARD. *How "Bigger" Was Born.* New York: Harper and Brothers, 1940. Pp. 39. NcD, NcC.

The author attempts to account for the principal character in his famous novel *Native Son.*

2. FICTION BY OR ABOUT NEGROES

APPEL, BENJAMIN. *The Dark Stain.* New York: Dial Press, 1943. Pp. 395. NcD, NcU, NcC.

A novel of race hatred and conflict in Harlem.

ARMSTRONG, ORLAND KAY. *Old Massa's People.* Indianapolis: The Bobbs-Merrill Company, 1931. Pp. 357. NcD, NcU, NcC.

A story which makes a contribution to the social history of the South.

ATTAWAY, WILLIAM. *Blood on the Forge.* Garden City, N. Y.: Doubleday, Doran and Co., 1941. Pp. 279. NcD, NcU.

This novel by a Negro author dealing with white Americans, immigrant Slavs, and Negroes in the steel industry is not for those who shun the unlovely aspects of human nature.

AZEVEDO, ALUIZIO DE. *O Mulato.* Paris: Garnier, 1927. Pp. viii, 360. NcD.

In this novel of Brazil a Negro youth unsuccessfully attempts to make his way in a society full of racial prejudices.

BAKER, DOROTHY. *Young Man With a Horn.* Boston: Houghton Mifflin Co., 1938. Pp. 243. NcD, NcU.

A book of semi-fiction dealing with the psychic experiences of those who play and feel jazz music.

BAPTIST, R. HERNEKIN (pseud.). *Four Handsome Negresses: A Record of a Voyage.* New York: Jonathan Cape and Harrison Smith, 1931. Pp. 256. NcU.

A tale of four Negro women removed from village life and used to spread the Christian faith in Africa in the fifteenth century.

BELL, ED. *Tommy Lee Feathers.* New York: Farrar and Rinehart, 1938. Pp. 308. NcD, NcU.

A novel in dialect of that remarkable fullback Tommy Lee Feathers, "the Red Grain of the colored race."

BONTEMPS, ARNA. *Black Thunder.* New York: The Macmillan Co., 1936. Pp. 298. NcD, NcU, NcC.

A historical novel dealing with the slave insurrection of 1800 in Virginia led by a Negro named Gabriel.

BRAND, MILLEN. *Albert Sears.* New York: Simon and Schuster, 1947. Pp. x, 272. NcD.

Albert Sears, the principal character of this novel, lived in a mixed-neighbor-hood, between an expanding Negro ghetto and a disintegrating white residence area in Jersey City.

BROWN, WILLIAM WELLS. *Clotel; or, The President's Daughter: A Narra-tive of Slave Life in the United States.* London: Partridge and Oakey, 1853. Pp. 245. NcD.
Significant only as the first novel written by an American Negro. "Scattered throughout the book are intimate glimpses that only one who had been a slave could get."

BROWN, WILLIAM WELLS. *My Southern Home.* Boston: A. G. Brown & Co., 1882. Pp. vii, 253. NcD, NcU.
The first work by a Negro author dealing with the folklore of his people.

BUCKMASTER, HENRIETTA (pseud.). *Deep River.* New York: Harcourt, Brace & Co., 1944. Pp. 481. NcD, NcU, NcC.
"A historical novel in which events have moral values and are in themselves founded on ideas." The story is about the anti-slavery fight of the daughter of a Georgia slave-owner.

CABLE, GEORGE W. *Old Creole Life.* New York: Charles Scribner's Sons, 1937. Pp. xv, 303. NcD, NcU, NcC.
Early nineteenth-century Louisiana in vivid local color.

CABLE, GEORGE W. *The Grandissimes: A Story of Creole Life.* New York: Charles Scribner's Sons, 1916. Pp. ix, 448. NcD, NcU, NcC.
A long novel of old Louisiana with some unusual Negro types.

CARTER, HODDING. *The Winds of Fear.* New York: Farrar and Rinehart, 1944. Pp. 278. NcD, NcC.
". . . no great shakes as a novel, it is nevertheless one of the clearest pictures of the mounting racial tension in the South thus far to appear."

CASPARY, VERA. *The White Girl.* New York: J. H. Sears and Co., 1929. Pp. 305. NcU.
A problem in race crossing and mistaken identity.

CATHER, WILLA S. *Sapphira and the Slave Girl.* New York: A. A. Knopf, 1940. Pp. 295. NcD, NcU, NcC.
A story of Virginia just before the Civil War. It deals with the jealousy of Sapphira for the mulatto girl whom she suspects of being her husband's mistress.

CHESNUTT, CHARLES W. *The Wife of His Youth, and Other Stories of the Color Line.* Boston: Houghton Mifflin and Co., 1899. Pp. 323. NcD, NcU.
A collection of stories dealing mainly with the race problem.

CHESNUTT, CHARLES W. *The House Behind the Cedars.* Boston: Hough-ton Mifflin and Co., 1900. Pp. 294. NcD, NcU, NcC.
A novel of the color line.

CHESNUTT, CHARLES W. *The Marrow of Tradition.* Boston: Houghton Mifflin and Co., 1901. Pp. 329. NcD, NcU, NcC.
This novel, regarded by many as Chesnutt's best, is based upon the Wilming-ton, N. C., race riot.

CHESNUTT, CHARLES W. *The Colonel's Dream.* New York: Doubleday, Page and Co., 1905. Pp. 249. NcU.
The small town which is the scene of this novel is characteristic of the idle and unprosperous post-Civil War Southern towns in which prejudice between the races grew and flourished.

CHILDERS, JAMES S. *A Novel about a White Man and a Black Man in the Deep South*. New York: Farrar and Rinehart, Inc., 1936. Pp. 276. NcD, NcU, NcC.
A novel intended to show that the race problem will be solved by men of good will.

CHOPIN, KATE. *Bayou Folk*. Boston: Houghton Mifflin and Co., 1894. Pp. 313. NcD, NcU.
A collection of stories laid in and around Natchitoches in Louisiana.

CLEMENS, SAMUEL L. (MARK TWAIN, pseud.). *The Adventures of Huckleberry Finn*. Vol. XIII in *The Writings of Mark Twain*. Hartford, Connecticut: American Publishing Co., 1899. Pp. xiii, 395. NcD, NcU.
The story of the friendship between a specimen of river "white trash" and a runaway Negro slave. A novel full of insight into race relations.

COLEMAN, RICHARD. *Don't You Weep, Don't You Moan*. New York: The Macmillan Co., 1935. Pp. 288. NcD, NcU, NcC.
Charleston (S. C.) Negroes' domestic relations.

CONRAD, JOSEPH. *The Nigger of The Narcissus*. Garden City, N. Y.: Doubleday, Doran and Co., 1936. Pp. xvi, 173. NcD, NcU, NcC.
Negro seamen powerfully portrayed.

COOK, FANNIE. *Mrs. Palmer's Honey*. New York: Doubleday and Co., 1946. Pp. 280. NcD, NcU, NcC.
This novel by a white woman is the winner of the first George Washington Carver Award. It is the story of Honey Hoop, Mrs. Palmer's servant.

COURLANDER, HAROLD. *The Caballero*. New York: Farrar and Rinehart, 1940. Pp. 443. NcD, NcC.
Fiction based upon the author's observations in Haiti concerning the clash of the mulatto and the black, the patois, and the peasant culture of the Caribbean area.

CULLEN, COUNTEE. *One Way to Heaven*. New York: Harper and Brothers, 1932. Pp. 280. NcD, NcU, NcC.
A novel dealing with the religion and superstitions of Negroes in Harlem, especially those of the servant class.

DARGAN, (MRS.) OLIVE. *Call Home the Heart*. New York: Longmans, Green and Co., 1932. Pp. 432. NcD, NcU.
A white mountain woman who saves a Negro labor organizer from a lynch mob is revolted by close contact with Negroes. "Mountain people are always white."

DICKERMAN, HALLIE FERRON. *Stephen Kent*. New York: Hartney Press, 1935. Pp. vii, 333. NcD.
A frank treatment of miscegenation.

DIXON, THOMAS. *The Flaming Sword*. Atlanta: Monarch Publishing Co., 1939. Pp. 562. NcD, NcU.
"A vehement melodrama depicting the destruction of American democracy by the red menace . . . to be accomplished . . . primarily through communistic corruption of the black race."

DRYSDALE, ISABEL. *Scenes in Georgia*. Philadelphia: American Sunday School Union, 1827. Pp. 83. NcD.
The Aunt Chloe of this old novel is probably the first successful Negro mammy in American fiction.

DUBOIS, W. E. B. *Dark Princess*. New York: Harcourt, Brace and Co., 1928. Pp. 311. NcD.

This novel represents what Rebecca Chalmers Barton describes as "the climax of what might be called the urban-cosmopolitan tendency" in Negro fiction.

DUBOIS, WILLIAM PÈNE. *The Three Policemen*. New York: The Viking Press, 1938. Pp. 92. NcD.

Bottsford is the hero of this story. His bravery and intelligence entitle him to become first emperor of Fabre Island.

DUNBAR, PAUL LAWRENCE. *Folks From Dixie*. New York: Dodd, Mead and Co., 1898. Pp. 263. NcD, NcU.

This collection of short stories pictures a self-contained little plantation community almost completely absorbed in its own experiences.

DUNBAR, PAUL LAWRENCE. *The Uncalled*. New York: Dodd, Mead and Co., 1898. Pp. 255. NcD, NcU.

The first non-racial novel to be written by an American Negro. The hero is Dunbar himself.

DUNBAR, PAUL LAWRENCE. *The Sport of the Gods*. New York: Dodd, Mead and Co., 1902. Pp. 255. NcD, NcU.

The tragedy of the Negro provincial in the big city.

DUNBAR, PAUL LAWRENCE. *The Best Short Stories of Paul Lawrence Dunbar*. Selected and edited with an introduction by Benjamin Brawley. New York: Dodd, Mead and Co., 1938. Pp. xvii, 258. NcD, NcU, NcC.

Best remembered as a poet, Dunbar also produced some excellent short stories.

EHRLICH, LEONARD. *God's Angry Man*. New York: Simon and Schuster, 1932. Pp. xv, 363. NcD, NcU, NcC.

A novel about John Brown and the abolition movement.

FAST, HOWARD. *Freedom Road*. New York: Duell, Sloan and Pearce, 1944. Pp. 261. NcD, NcU, NcC.

A historical novel of the Reconstruction period in South Carolina.

FAULKNER, WILLIAM. *Go Down Moses*. New York: Random House, 1942. Pp. 383. NcD, NcU, NcC.

Seven stories dealing with the relationships between Negroes and whites in Mississippi.

FAUSET, JESSIE R. *Plum Bun: A Novel without a Moral*. New York: Frederick A. Stokes Co., 1929. Pp. 379. NcD, NcU, NcC.

A novel dealing with "passing" over the color line. The struggle is between family affection, on the one hand, and a larger role in the white world, on the other.

FAUSET, JESSIE R. *The Chinaberry Tree: A Novel of American Life*. New York: Frederick A. Stokes Co., 1931. Pp. 341. NcD, NcU, NcC.

The private lives of educated Negroes and the story of two illegitimate children. Middle class Negro life in the North.

FAUSET, JESSIE R. *Comedy, American Style*. New York: Frederick A. Stokes Co., 1933. Pp. 327. NcD, NcU, NcC.

A distinct contribution to problematic fiction about the Negro. This novel deals with the problems of a near-white, well-to-do Negro family in Philadelphia.

FISHER, DOROTHY CANFIELD. *The Bent Twig*. New York: Grosset and Dunlap, 1915. Pp. vi, 480. NcD, NcU, NcC.

A novel dealing with race prejudice in a midwestern town.

FISHER, RUDOLPH. *The Walls of Jericho*. New York: A. A. Knopf, 1928. Pp. 307. NcD, NcU.

The action of this novel is laid in the dance-halls, cabarets, and poolrooms of Harlem.

FISHER, RUDOLPH. *The Conjure Man Dies: A Mystery Tale of Dark Harlem.* New York: Covici, Friede, 1932. Pp. 316. NcD, NcU.
The first complete detective story to be written by a Negro author.

FLANNAGAN, ROY. *Amber Satyr.* Garden City, N. Y.: Doubleday, Doran and Co., 1932. Pp. 304. NcD.
The tragic story of a Negro-Indian mixture in Virginia.

FULLER, EDMUND. *A Star Pointed North.* New York: Harper and Brothers, 1946. Pp. vii, 361. NcD, NcU, NcC.
A historical novel based upon the life of Frederick Douglass.

GORDON, TAYLOR. *Born to Be.* New York: Covici, Friede, 1929. Pp. xvi, 236. NcD, NcU, NcC.
In his Foreword Carl Van Vechten calls this book "a 'human document' of the first order, to be studied by sociologists for years to come."

GRAHAM, KATHERYN CAMPBELL. *Under the Cottonwood: A Saga of Negro Life in which the History, Traditions and Folklore of the Negro of the Last Century are Vividly Portrayed.* New York: Wendell Malliet and Co., 1941. Pp. 262. NcD, NcU, NcC.
A disguised autobiography of the author whose family, after the Civil War, went west with their former owners. An important naïve document for the study of Negro life.

GRANBERRY, EDWIN. *Strangers and Lovers.* New York: Macaulay Co., 1928. Pp. 320. NcD.
The mutual hostility of Negroes and poor whites in the pine barrens and swamps of Florida.

HALSEY, MARGARET. *Some of My Best Friends Are Soldiers.* New York: Simon and Schuster, 1944. Pp. 207. NcD.
"A kind of novel," the author calls it, concerning discrimination against Jews and Negroes.

HARRIS, JOEL CHANDLER. *Mingo, and Other Sketches in Black and White.* Boston: J. R. Osgood and Company, 1884. Pp. 273. NcD, NcU.
A story showing caste dominance and the hunger of the planter for more land.

HEDDEN, WORTH TUTTLE. *The Other Room.* New York: Crown Publishers, 1947. Pp. 274. NcD.
For this novel a former North Carolina author received a *Saturday Review of Literature* award. It deals with the race problem in New Orleans.

HENDERSON, GEORGE WYLIE. *Ollie Miss.* New York: Frederick A. Stokes Co., 1935. Pp. 276. NcD, NcU, NcC.
The story of a Negro peasant woman, with an unsentimental picture of the life of the Negro landowners and sharecroppers in Alabama.

HETH, EDWARD H. *Light Over Ruby Street.* New York: Smith and Durrell, Inc., 1940. Pp. vi, 294. NcD.
The story has to do with whites who visit Ruby Street in the Negro section of a city for no good purpose.

HEYWARD, DUBOSE. *Porgy.* New York: George H. Doran Co., 1925. Pp. 196. NcD, NcU, NcC.
A story of Negro life in Charleston, South Carolina. Heyward pleads for "great hearts to understand."

HEYWARD, DUBOSE. *Mamba's Daughters: A Novel of Charleston.* Garden City, N. Y.: Doubleday, Doran and Co., 1929. Pp. 311. NcD, NcU, NcC.
A novel showing the art of acquiring "white folks."

HILDRETH, RICHARD. *The Slave; or, Memoirs of Archy Moore.* 3rd ed.
2 vols. in 1. New York: American Anti-Slavery Society, 1840. NcD, NcU.
This book, the first use of the novel for anti-slavery opinions, was originally
published in 1836, later renamed and published as *The White Slave* (1852). It
was the most effective piece of abolition fiction of the early period.

HILL, JOHN H. *Princess Malah.* Washington, D. C.: Associated Publishers,
Inc., 1933. Pp. 330. NcD, NcU, NcC.
A historical novel by a Negro author written in the plantation tradition.

HIMES, CHESTER B. *If He Hollers Let Him Go.* New York: Doubleday,
Doran and Co., 1945. Pp. 249. NcD, NcC.
Richard Wright says of this novel, "Himes lights up race relations among ship-
yard workers in a neon glare."

HUGHES, LANGSTON. *Not Without Laughter.* New York: A. A. Knopf, 1933.
Pp. 324. NcD, NcU, NcC.
A novel dealing with the conflicts in a migrant Negro family in a Kansas town
growing out of the struggles of the members of the family to achieve a place
for themselves in the small Negro community.

HUGHES, LANGSTON. *The Ways of White Folks.* New York: A. A. Knopf,
1934. Pp. 248. NcD, NcU, NcC.
Short stories dealing with the relations between Negroes and whites from a
point of view inaccessible to white writers.

HURSTON, ZORA NEALE. *Jonah's Gourd Vine.* Philadelphia: J. B. Lippincott, 1934. Pp. 316. NcD, NcU, NcC.
The story of a Negro preacher whose weakness for women causes his down-
fall. Pictures the all-Negro towns of Florida.

JOHNSON, JAMES WELDON. *The Autobiography of an Ex-Coloured Man.*
New York: A. A. Knopf, 1927. Pp. xii, 211. NcD, NcU, NcC.
This fictionalized autobiography was first published anonymously in 1912. In
it we are shown the sophisticated Negro moving from one city to another and
from one continent to another.

JOHNSON, JOSEPHINE. *Jordanstown.* New York: Simon and Schuster, 1937.
Pp. 259. NcD, NcU.
A novel significant for its analysis of the integration of Negro and white lives
in a small town in the South.

JOSEPH, ARTHUR (JOHN ARTHUR, pseud.). *Dark Metropolis.* Boston:
Meador Publishing Co., 1936. Pp. 154. NcD.
A novel of Harlem.

KENNEDY, ROBERT EMMET. *Black Cameos.* New York: A. and C. Boni,
1924. Pp. xxv, 210. NcD, NcU.
Dialect stories of Negro life in Gretna, a Negro suburb of New Orleans.

KENNEDY, ROBERT EMMET. *Gritney People.* New York: Dodd, Mead
and Co., 1927. Pp. 250. NcD, NcU, NcC.
Stories by and about the Negro people of a community near New Orleans.

LARSEN, NELLA. *Passing.* New York: A. A. Knopf, 1929. Pp. 215. NcD,
NcU, NcC.
The story of Clare, a colored girl who "passes" and does not thereby find
happiness.

LEE, GEORGE W. *River George.* New York: The Macaulay Company, 1937.
Pp. 275. NcD, NcU.
A Negro author tells a story of the troubles of a sharecropper's life.

LEWIS, SINCLAIR. *Kingsblood Royal.* New York: Random House, 1947. Pp. 348. NcD, NcU, NcC.
This book is advertised as the story of the man who resigned from the white race.

McKAY, CLAUDE. *Home to Harlem.* New York: Harper and Brothers, 1928. Pp. 340. NcD, NcU, NcC.
A novel which pictures Harlem as a world of pure sensation and abandon. With one exception, the characters are never bothered by ideas.

McKAY, CLAUDE. *Banjo.* New York: Harper and Brothers, 1929. Pp. 326. NcD, NcU, NcC.
The scene of this novel is sensuous and vagabond Marseilles. Negroes are too occupied with their own intense living to pay much attention to issues of race and prejudice.

McKAY, CLAUDE. *Banana Bottom.* New York: Harper and Brothers, 1933. Pp. 317. NcD, NcC.
A novel of Jamaica stressing economic and social questions.

MARAN, RENÉ. *Batouala.* New York: Seltzer, 1922. Pp. 207. NcD, NcU, NcC.
A novel which comes to grips with reality in a masterful way.

MEADE, JULIAN R. *The Back Door.* New York: Longmans, Green and Co., 1938. Pp. 310. NcD, NcU, NcC.
A problem novel of the black population in the South—of "Back-Door" people —Negroes whose lot it is to serve the whites in their kitchens and tobacco factories.

MEANS, FLORENCE C. *The Singing Wood.* Boston: Houghton Mifflin Co., 1937. Pp. vi, 241. NcD.
At a large university in California, Cordelia, a young Negro girl, meets and experiences some partial solutions of race problems. Lodusky Day, a white student, is the heroine of the story.

MEANS, FLORENCE C. *Shuttered Windows.* Boston: Houghton Mifflin Co., 1938. Pp. 205. NcD, NcC.
The story of Harriet Freeman, a sixteen-year-old colored girl who was educated in the North and who found adjustment hard when she returned to visit her grandmother on a sea island off the coast of South Carolina.

MELVILLE, HERMAN. *Benito Cereno.* London: The Nonesuch Press, 1926. Pp. 122. NcD, NcC.
An old novel dealing with the African slave trade but its scenes and characters are still alive and new.

MILLEN, GILMORE. *Sweet Man.* New York: Viking Press, 1930. Pp. 299. NcU.
The adventures of John Henry, son of a mulatto and a white man, which end in tragedy.

MILLIN, SARAH GERTRUDE. *God's Stepchildren.* New York: Boni and Liveright, 1924. Pp. 319. NcD, NcU, NcC.
In this novel of South Africa the course of four generations of race mixture is unrolled. In spite of successive bleaching the conclusion is that black blood and white cannot mix.

MOODY, MINNIE HITE. *Death is a Little Man.* New York: J. Messner, 1936. Pp. 274. NcU.
An informed and sympathetic novel of Negro life in the Atlanta Bottoms.

MOON, BUCKLIN. *The Darker Brother.* New York: Doubleday, Doran and
Co., 1943. Pp. 246. NcD, NcU, NcC.
Jonathan Daniels says, "Nowhere has the story of the American Negro been
so effectively told as in this hard-boiled and heart-touching novel." The story
of a young Negro from the South in the slums of Harlem.

MOTLEY, WILLARD. *Knock on Any Door.* New York: D. Appleton-Century
Co., 1947. Pp. 504. NcD.
A Negro author writes a non-racial novel of one Nick Romano who lived by
the code: "Live fast, die young, have a good looking corpse."

MURRAY, CHALMERS S. *Here Comes Joe Mungin.* New York: G. P. Putnam's Sons, 1924. Pp. 316. NcD, NcU.
A novel about the Gullah Negroes of South Carolina by a white author who
is neither sorry for nor critical of them. Described by a reviewer as "the fight-
ingest, wenchingest, sweatingest novel of the season."

NISBET, ALICE. *Send Me an Angel.* Chapel Hill: The University of North
Carolina Press, 1946. Pp. 122. NcD, NcU, NcC.
The story of Delilah, a Negro woman who lives on Mr. Ed's place.

O'DONNELL, EDWIN P. *Green Margins.* Boston: Houghton Mifflin Co., 1936.
Pp. 499. NcD.
The setting of these stories is the delta south of New Orleans where Slavonians,
Filipinos, French, Italians, Cajuns, and Negroes fish, trap, and struggle for a
living.

ODUM, HOWARD W. *Rainbow Round my Shoulder: The Blue Trail of Black
Ulysses.* Indianapolis: The Bobbs-Merrill Co., 1928. Pp. 322. NcD, NcU.
The story of Left Wing Gordon, a rambling, roving, singing man. "I done walk
till feets gone to rollin'. Jes lak a wheel, Lawd, jes lak a wheel."

PAGE, MYRA. *Gathering Storm.* New York: International Publishing Co.,
1932. Pp. 374. NcU.
A revolutionary novel. Textile "lintheads" and Negroes uniting constitute the
"gathering storm."

PAGE, THOMAS NELSON. *In Ole Virginia.* New York: Charles Scribner's
Sons, 1928. Pp. 230. NcD, NcU, NcC.
A well-known collection of stories in Negro dialect in which slavery is idealized.

PARKER, DOROTHY. "An Arrangement in Black and White," in *Here Lies.*
New York: The Viking Press, 1939. NcD.
Race prejudice in pink.

PATON, ALAN. *Cry, the Beloved Country: A Story of Comfort in Desolation.*
New York: Charles Scribner's Sons, 1948. Pp. ix, 278. NcD, NcU.
A distinguished novel depicting the disintegration of native society in South
Africa.

PATTERSON, PERNET. *The Road to Canaan.* New York: Minton, Balch
and Co., 1931. Pp. vii, 240. NcD.
A collection of eight stories dealing with Negro life in and near Richmond,
Virginia.

PAYNTER, JOHN H. *Fugitives of the Pearl.* Washington: Associated Publishers, 1930. Pp. xi, 209. NcD, NcU.
A historical romance by a Negro author.

PEACOCKE, JAMES S. *The Creole Orphans; or, Lights and Shadows of
Southern Life: A Tale of Louisiana.* New York: Derby and Jackson, 1856.
Pp. 365. NcD.

A novel dealing candidly with the mixing of blood in the society of the Louisiana plantations.

PEEPLES, EDWIN A. *Swing Low.* Boston: Houghton Mifflin Co., 1945. Pp. 293. NcD, NcU, NcC.

In this social novel Willy Mack, Negro, loved the smell of plantation mules. But he married Amy and went to live in Atlanta.

PETERKIN, JULIA. *Green Thursday.* New York: A. A. Knopf, 1924. Pp. 188. NcD, NcU.

A group of connected short stories dealing with the Negroes of Blue Brook Plantation.

PETERKIN, JULIA. *Black April.* Indianapolis: The Bobbs-Merrill Co., 1927. Pp. 316. NcD, NcU.

A novel picturing the folk life of the Negroes of Blue Brook Plantation and its Negro foreman, Black April.

PETERKIN, JULIA. *Scarlet Sister Mary.* Indianapolis: The Bobbs-Merrill Co., 1928. Pp. 345. NcD, NcU.

A Pulitzer Prize novel stressing the exotic and the primitive in the life of plantation Negroes. The story concerns the joyous life of a Negro "charity girl."

PETRY, ANN. *The Street.* Boston: Houghton Mifflin Co., 1946. Pp. 435. NcD, NcU, NcC.

Another novel of Harlem in which sorry conditions are revealed in unpretentious and adroit prose.

POPE, EDITH. *Colcorton.* New York: Charles Scribner's Sons, 1944. Pp. 330. NcD.

The scene of this novel is present-day Florida and the theme is miscegenation.

RAYFORD, JULIAN L. *Cotton Mouth.* New York: Charles Scribner's Sons, 1941. Pp. 400. NcD, NcU, NcC.

A novel dealing with Negro-white relationships in the Deep South.

ROBINSON, ROWLAND E. *Out of Bondage and other Stories.* Rutland, Vermont: Charles E. Tuttle Co., 1936. Pp. 255. NcD, NcC.

Stories dealing with the Negro and his flight from bondage.

RYLEE, ROBERT. *Deep Dark River.* New York: Farrar and Rinehart, Inc., 1935. Pp. 308. NcD, NcU, NcC.

A vivid description of the tragedy of Mississippi injustices and persecutions told by a white Southerner.

SANFORD, JOHN B. *The People From Heaven.* New York: Harcourt, Brace and Co., 1943. Pp. 232. NcD, NcU.

An unconventional novel against racial intolerance rendered ineffective by a self-conscious vehemence.

SAXON, LYLE. *Children of Strangers.* Boston: Houghton Mifflin Company, 1937. Pp. 294. NcD, NcU, NcC.

The "children of strangers" of this novel are the mulattoes on the Louisiana plantation where the story unfolds. The mulatto community, isolated from whites and blacks alike, is a race apart living to itself on its own land.

SCHUYLER, GEORGE S. *Black No More.* New York: The Macaulay Co., 1931. Pp. 250. NcD, NcU.

A satire on race prejudice and the color line.

SMITH, ARTHUR D. HOWDEN. *The Dead Go Overside.* New York: Greystone Press, 1938. Pp. 388. NcD, NcC.

A novel of mystery, romance, and adventure, filled with the color of slave centers in Africa and a background of a roving sea.

SMITH, LILLIAN. *Strange Fruit.* New York: Reynal and Hitchcock, 1944. Pp. 371. NcD, NcU, NcC.
A first novel by a Southern white woman dealing with love across the color line.

SPIVAK, JOHN L. *Georgia Nigger.* New York: Brewer, Warren and Putnam, 1932. Pp. 241. NcD.
Story of a Negro's attempt to escape from peonage.

STANLEY, MARIE. *Gulf Stream.* New York: Coward McCann, Inc., 1930. Pp. 304. NcD, NcU.
A novel about race mixture and the color line in an Alabama community.

STEIN, GERTRUDE. *Three Lives.* New York: The Modern Library, 1933. Pp. xi, 279. NcD, NcU, NcC.
The love affairs of Melanctha, a part-white girl.

STEPHENS, NAN BAGLEY. *Glory.* New York: John Day Co., 1932. Pp. 311. NcU.
An intimate story of Negro life in a small Georgia town.

STOWE, HARRIET BEECHER. *Uncle Tom's Cabin.* New York: Edward McCann Co., 1929. Pp. 446. NcD, NcU, NcC.
President Lincoln said to the author of *Uncle Tom's Cabin,* "So you are the little woman who brought on the great war."

STRAUSS, THEODORE. *Night at Hogwallow.* Boston: Little, Brown and Co., 1937. Pp. 174. NcD, NcC.
Hair-raising melodrama. But this novel gives a good picture of the lynching mob at work.

STRIBLING, THOMAS S. *Birthright.* New York: The Century Co., 1922. Pp. 309. NcD, NcU, NcC.
A protest against the assumption that all Negroes are carefree and happy.

SYLVESTER, HARRY. *Dearly Beloved.* New York: Duell, Sloan and Pearce, 1942. Pp. 262. NcU.
The locale of this novel is a Catholic community in Maryland. The effort of a young white man to establish a cooperative intended to include Negroes precipitated considerable racial feeling.

THURMAN, WALLACE. *The Blacker the Berry.* New York: The Macaulay Co., 1929. Pp. 262. NcD, NcU.
The heroine of this novel is coal black, and there seems to be no place in the world for a black girl.

THURMAN, WALLACE. *Infants of the Spring.* New York: The Macaulay Co., 1932. Pp. 284. NcD, NcU.
A sparkling satire on race relations in a large urban center.

THURMAN, WALLACE, and FURMAN, A. L. *The Interne.* New York: The Macaulay Co., 1932. Pp. 252. NcD, NcC.
A non-racial novel by Negro authors.

TINKER, EDWARD L. *Toucoutou.* New York: Dodd, Mead and Company, 1928. Pp. 312. NcU.
A story of race prejudice in New Orleans in the 1850's accompanied by a large amount of picturesque detail.

TOOMER, JEAN. *Cane.* New York: Boni and Liveright, 1923. Pp. xi, 239. NcD, NcU.
Cane is a collection of stories which, half prose, half poetry, touch the edges of areas in Negro life that have seldom found their way into literature.

TOURGÉE, ALBION WINEGAR. *A Fool's Errand. By One of the Fools.* New York: Fords, Howard and Hulbert, 1880. Pp. 361. NcD, NcU.
This novel has been called "the Uncle Tom's Cabin of Reconstruction."

TOURGÉE, ALBION WINEGAR. *Hot Plowshares.* New York: Fords, Howard and Hulbert, 1883. Pp. 610. NcD, NcU.
A story of the "suffering produced by race mixture, a kind of pall which the plantation throws over its blacks even after they have escaped to free countries."

TRACY, DON. *How Sleeps the Beast.* London: Constable, 1937. Pp. 279. NcD.
A novel which excellently depicts the moods and the social mechanism of lynching.

TURPIN, WATERS EDWARD. *These Low Grounds.* New York: Harper and Brothers, 1937. Pp. 344. NcD, NcU.
The story of four generations of Negroes on the Eastern shore.

VAN VECHTEN, CARL. *Nigger Heaven.* New York: A. A. Knopf, 1926. Pp. 286. NcD, NcU, NcC.
The first novel to utilize the material presented by the crowded Negro communities of Northern cities. The exotic and the primitive are emphasized.

WALROND, ERIC. *Tropic Death.* New York: Boni and Liveright, 1926. Pp. 283. NcD, NcU.
Exotic stories of marine and peasant life in the Caribbean region.

WELD, JOHN. *Sabbath Has No End.* New York: Charles Scribner's Sons, 1942. Pp. 329. NcD, NcU.
The theme of this conventional novel is James Weldon Johnson's statement, "In the core of the heart of the American race problem the sex factor is rooted."

WHEATON, ELIZABETH LEE. *Mr. George's Joint.* New York: E. P. Dutton and Co., 1941. Pp. 375. NcD, NcU, NcC.
A Southern white woman tells the story of what goes on in a Negro "jinte."

WHITE, WALTER. *The Fire in the Flint.* New York: A. A. Knopf, 1924. Pp. 300. NcD, NcU.
The scene of this powerful lynching novel is a small Southern town.

WHITE, WALTER. *Flight.* New York: A. A. Knopf, 1926. Pp. 300. NcD, NcU, NcC.
In this cosmopolitan novel an octoroon girl passes over into white society but later returns to her own people.

WHITTAKER, JAMES (GEOFFREY BARNES, pseud.). *Dark-Lustre.* New York: Alfred H. King, Inc., 1932. Pp. 288. NcD.
A study in black and white telling the story of the tangled lives of three people.

WRIGHT, RICHARD. *Uncle Tom's Children.* New York: Harper and Brothers, 1938. Pp. 384. NcD, NcU, NcC.
Four novellas. "The core of Wright's stories is the conflict between the Negro's instinct for self-preservation and an impersonal, unpredictable lynch machine."

WRIGHT, RICHARD. *Native Son.* New York: Harper and Brothers, 1940. Pp. 359. NcD, NcU, NcC.
The tragic story of Bigger Thomas, whipped before he was born. No novel portraying more forcefully the actual, dangerous status of the Negro in American life has been written.

ZINBERG, LEN. *Walk Hard—Talk Loud.* New York: The Bobbs-Merrill Company, 1940. Pp. 354. NcD.
A plain-spoken novel dealing with the aspirations of a young Negro in the prize fight ring.

3. POETRY BY OR ABOUT NEGROES

ANDERSON, GEORGE K., and WALTON, EDA LOU, eds. *This Generation.*
Chicago: Scott, Foresman and Company, 1939. Pp. 762-68. NcD, NcC.
Eight fine poems by Sterling Brown in this collection of British and American
literature.

BENÉT, STEPHEN VINCENT. *John Brown's Body.* Garden City, N. Y.:
Doubleday, Doran and Co., 1930. Pp. 376. NcD, NcU, NcC.
A long poem of the Civil War including Negro characters.

BONTEMPS, ARNA, ed. *Golden Slippers.* New York: Harper and Brothers,
1941. Pp. xii, 220. NcD, NcU.
An anthology of Negro poetry compiled for younger people.

BRAITHWAITE, W. S. B., ed. *Anthology of Magazine Verse, 1913........, and
Yearbook of American Poetry.* Various publishers, 1913......... NcD, NcU,
NcC.
Anthologies of American magazine verse selected and edited by a Negro who
is keenly sensitive to the best in our poetry.

BROOKS, GWENDOLYN. *A Street in Bronzeville.* New York: Harper and
Brothers, 1945. Pp. vi, 57. NcD, NcU, NcC.
Ballads, blues, and portraits in verse.

BROWN, STERLING A. *Southern Road.* New York: Harcourt, Brace and Co.,
1932. Pp. xv, 135. NcD, NcU, NcC.
A first volume of verse. "An attempt at folk portraiture of Southern characters."

CRADY, KATE M. *Free Steppin'.* Dallas, Texas: Mathis, Van Nort and Co.,
1938. Pp. 83. NcD, NcU, NcC.
Negro life in dialect verse by a Southern white woman.

CULLEN, COUNTEE. *Color.* New York: Harper and Brothers, 1925. Pp. xvii,
108. NcD, NcU, NcC.
Cullen's work "is the most polished lyricism of modern Negro poetry."

CULLEN, COUNTEE, ed. *Caroling Dusk: An Anthology of Verse by Negro
Poets.* New York: Harper and Brothers, 1927. Pp. 237. NcD, NcU, NcC.
Significant for its recognition of younger and heretofore almost unknown Negro
poets this anthology is otherwise not outstanding.

CULLEN, COUNTEE. *Copper Sun.* New York: Harper and Brothers, 1927.
Pp. 89. NcD, NcU, NcC.
Fifty-eight versatile poems.

CULLEN, COUNTEE. *The Black Christ and Other Poems.* New York: Harper
and Brothers, 1929. Pp. viii, 110. NcD, NcU, NcC.
A narrative poem telling the story of a young Negro who was lynched for
the crime of another.

CULLEN, COUNTEE. *The Medea and Some Other Poems.* New York: Harper
and Brothers, 1935. Pp. vi, 97. NcD, NcU, NcC.
The poet's version of the Medea of Euripides. This book also contains ten
sonnets.

CULLEN, COUNTEE. *The Lost Zoo (a Rhyme for the Young but not too
Young) by Christopher Cat and Countee Cullen.* New York: Harper and
Brothers, 1940. Pp. 72. NcD, NcU, NcC.
Rhymed nonsense about cats and cat character.

DAVIS, FRANK M. *Black Man's Verse.* Chicago: Black Cat Press, 1935. Pp. 83.
NcD, NcU.
Comments in free verse on the abuses of democracy.

DAVIS, FRANK M. *I Am the American Negro*. Chicago: Black Cat Press, 1937. Pp. 69. NcD, NcU.
A vigorous book of social protest written in prose poetry.

DAVIS, FRANK M. *Through Sepia Eyes*. Chicago: Black Cat Press, 1938. Pp. 10. NcD.
Four short stinging poems.

ELEAZER, ROBERT B., comp. *Singers in the Dawn*. Atlanta, Ga.: Conference on Education and Race Relations, 1934. Pp. 23. NcD, NcU.
A brief anthology of American Negro poetry.

HAWKINS, WALTER EVERETT. *Chords and Discords*. Boston: R. G. Badger, 1920. Pp. 100. NcU.
". . . the 'chords' are conventional lyrics about love and duty, but the 'discords' foreshadow new Negro poetry."

HILL, MILDRED MARTIN. *A Traipsin' Heart*. New York: Wendell Malliet and Company, 1942. Pp. 61. NcD, NcU, NcC.
These poems by a Durham, North Carolina, Negro woman represent an honest effort to express her emotions about nature and about her people. One of the best of the collection, "La Belle Mere," was written after a visit to the Sara P. Duke Gardens.

HORTON, GEORGE M. *Poetical Works*. Hillsboro, N. C.: D. Heartt, 1845. Pp. 96. NcU.
A rare copy of the rhymes of a Negro slave janitor at the University of North Carolina. The University of North Carolina library also has "Hope of Liberty" and various miscellaneous poems by Horton.

HUGHES, LANGSTON. *The Weary Blues*. New York: A. A. Knopf, 1926. Pp. 109. NcD, NcU.
Poems that show the fine qualities of force, passion, directness, and sensitive perception.

HUGHES, LANGSTON. *Fine Clothes to the Jew*. New York: A. A. Knopf, 1927. Pp. 89. NcD, NcU, NcC.
Poems interpreting the life of the man farthest down.

HUGHES, LANGSTON. *The Dream Keeper and Other Poems*. New York: A. A. Knopf, 1932. Pp. 77. NcD, NcU, NcC.
A collection of poems expressly written for young people. They include lyrics of great beauty, stanzas in serious vein, rollicking songs, and typical blues.

HUGHES, LANGSTON. *Scottsboro Limited*. New York: The Golden Stair Press, 1932. Pp. 20. NcD.
Four poems and a play in verse.

HUGHES, LANGSTON. *Shakespeare in Harlem, and Other Poems*. New York: A. A. Knopf, 1942. Pp. 124. NcD, NcU, NcC.
The author himself calls this "a book of light verse." The excellent drawings are by E. McKnight Kauffer.

HUGHES, LANGSTON. *Jim Crow's Last Stand*. New York: Negro Publishing Society of America, 1943. NcD.
A book of poems dedicated to "one nation, indivisible, with liberty and justice for all."

JOHNSON, GEORGIA DOUGLAS. *The Heart of a Woman and Other Poems*. Boston: The Cornhill Co., 1918. Pp. xii, 62. NcD.
The author of these poems has "set herself the task of documenting the feminine heart."

JOHNSON, GEORGIA DOUGLAS. *An Autumn Love Cycle.* New York: H.
Vinal, Ltd., 1928. Pp. xix, 70. NcD, NcU.
Another volume of competent poetry.

JOHNSON, JAMES WELDON. *Fifty Years and Other Poems.* Boston: The
Cornhill Co., 1917. Pp. xiv, 93. NcD, NcU.
Earlier poems of the great Negro man of letters.

JOHNSON, JAMES WELDON. *God's Trombones. Seven Negro Sermons in
Verse.* New York: The Viking Press, 1927. Pp. 56. NcD, NcU, NcC.
The Southern Negro has achieved a folk product, perhaps to be found in no
other group. This is the folk sermon. In the Preface, James Weldon Johnson
suggests how these sermons originated and spread from one community to another like other folk creations. The poet here reproduces in verse the sonorous
and apocalyptic eloquence of the old-time Negro preacher.

JOHNSON, JAMES WELDON. *The Book of American Negro Poetry.* New
York: Harcourt, Brace and Co., 1931. Pp. xii, 300. NcD, NcU, NcC.
An anthology of verse by Negroes. Preface is an essay on the creative genius
of the Negro.

JOHNSON, JAMES WELDON. *Saint Peter Relates an Incident.* New York:
The Viking Press, 1935. Pp. ix, 105. NcD, NcU, NcC.
A satire on the treatment accorded Negro Gold Star Mothers. Contains an
account of the writing of the title poem, also an account of the writing of the
Negro National Anthem "Lift Every Voice and Sing."

KERLIN, ROBERT T. *Contemporary Poetry of the Negro.* The Hampton
Bulletin, Vol. XVII, No. 1 (February, 1921). Pp. 22. NcD.
"A people that is producing poetry is not perishing, but is astir with life, with
vital impulses, with life-giving visions."

KERLIN, ROBERT T. *Negro Poets and Their Poems.* New and enl. ed. Washington: Associated Publishers, 1935. Pp. xxi, 342. NcD, NcU, NcC.
A literary history and an anthology of verse by Negro writers.

LEONARD, WILLIAM ELLERY. *The Lynching Bee and Other Poems.* New
York: B. W. Huebsch, Inc., 1920. Pp. 84. NcU.
Poems that attempt "to phrase the ominous turmoil of our times."

LOCKE, ALAIN, ed. *Four Negro Poets.* The Pamphlet Poet Series. New York:
Simon and Schuster, 1927. Pp. 31. NcD, NcU.
A little anthology of the more racially distinctive poems of Claude McKay,
Jean Toomer, Countee Cullen, and Langston Hughes.

McGIRT, JAMES EPHRAIM. *Avenging the Maine, a Drunken A.B., and Other
Poems.* Raleigh: Edwards and Broughton, 1900. Pp. 119. NcD, NcU, NcC.
In the dark ages of Negro poetry a North Carolina Negro produced this and
other volumes.

McKAY, CLAUDE. *Constab Ballads.* London: Watts and Company, 1912. Pp.
94. NcD.
These poems were written when the well-known Negro author was a not-very-
good constable in Jamaica.

McNEILL, JOHN CHARLES. *Lyrics From Cotton Land.* Charlotte, N. C.:
The Stone and Barringer Co., 1922. Reprinted by the University of North
Carolina Press. Pp. xviii, 189. NcD, NcU.
A Southern white local color poet.

MARCH, JOSEPH MONCURE. *The Set-Up.* New York: Covici, Friede, 1928.
Pp. 184. NcD.
A white poet writes a poem on the career of a Negro prize fighter.

MURPHY, BEATRICE M., ed. *Negro Voices: An Anthology of Contemporary Verse.* New York: Henry Harrison, 1938. Pp. 173. NcD, NcU, NcC.
"The present book serves two purposes. It gives the reader new poems by his old favorites and presents to the audience a number of new poets."

PORTER, DOROTHY B. *North American Negro Poets: A Bibliographical Checklist of Their Writings, 1760-1944.* Hattiesburg, Mississippi: The Book Farm, 1945. Pp. 90. NcD, NcU, NcC.
This bibliography supplements as well as brings up to date A. A. Schomburg's *A Bibliographical Checklist of Negro Poetry* (New York, 1916).

SPRATLIN, VALAUREZ BURWELL. *Juan Latino, Slave and Humanist.* New York: Spinner Press, 1938. Pp. xiii, 216. NcD, NcU, NcC.
A biographical and critical study of the sixteenth-century Negro poet.

THOMAS, CHARLES CYRUS. *A Black Lark Caroling.* Dallas: The Kaleidograph Press, 1936. Pp. xii, 73. NcD.
A collection of poems attempting to interpret the inner line of the Negro as the song interprets a lark.

TOLSON, MELVIN B. *Rendezvous with America.* New York: Dodd, Mead and Co., 1944. Pp. xii, 121. NcU, NcC.
Harry Hansen, reviewing this book of verse, says: "Both the title poem and those that follow are like music that is easy to sing. . . . The lines are full of memories of American accomplishments that are now the heritage of all who live here."

WALKER, MARGARET. *For My People.* New Haven: Yale University Press, 1942. Pp. 58. NcD, NcU, NcC.
The author, a professor of English at Livingstone College, Salisbury, North Carolina, is the first Negro poet to win an award in the Yale Series of Younger Poets. The *Time* reviewer says, ". . . she writes with civilized simplicity about the humanity of her people."

WHEATLEY, PHILLIS. *Memoir and Poems.* 3rd ed. Boston: Isaac Knapp, 1838. Pp. 155. NcU, NcC.
Life and poems of an African-born slave girl reared in a colonial New England home.

WHITE, NEWMAN I., and JACKSON, WALTER C., eds. *An Anthology of Verse by American Negroes.* Durham: Trinity College Press, 1924. Pp. xi, 250. NcD, NcU, NcC.
The introduction and the biographical and critical notes add much to the value of this anthology.

WIGGINS, LIDA KECK. *The Life and Works of Paul Lawrence Dunbar.* Napersville, Illinois: J. L. Nichols and Co., 1907. Pp. 430. NcD, NcU.
In an introduction to this book William Dean Howells says Dunbar's "brilliant and unique achievement was to have studied the American Negro objectively." Yet the great Negro poet paid little attention to the change and turmoil which characterized the world of the Negro during the period in which he wrote.

4. THE NEGRO AND NEGRO LIFE ON THE STAGE

BASSHE, EM JO. *Earth.* New York: The Macaulay Co., 1927. Pp. xiii, 122. NcD, NcU.
A play dealing with religious ecstasy among Negroes.

BOND, FREDERICK W. *The Negro and the Drama. The Direct and Indirect Contribution Which the American Negro Has Made to Drama and the Legitimate Stage, With the Underlying Conditions Responsible.* Washington, D. C.: Associated Publishers, Inc., 1940. Pp. x, 213. NcD, NcU, NcC.

An outline of Negro dramatic art from minstrelsy to the Federal Theatre movement among Negroes.

BOUCICAULT, DION. *The Octoroon, or Life in Louisiana.* Chicago: Dramatic Publishing Co., c. 1895. Pp. 43. NcD, NcC.
A tragedy of mixed blood. Important in the history of race drama in America.

CONNELLY, MARCUS C. *The Green Pastures.* New York: Farrar and Rinehart, Inc., 1930. Pp. xiii, 150. NcD, NcU, NcC.
A fable in two parts supposedly based upon the religious beliefs of illiterate Negroes in the deep South and inspired by Roark Bradford's "Ol Man Adam an' his Chillun."

COTTER, JOSEPH S., SR. *Caleb, The Degenerate. A Play in Four Acts. A Study of the Types, Customs, and Needs of the American Negro.* New York: Henry Harrison, 1940. Pp. 64. NcD.
This play, dealing with the question of the best policy in the education of Negroes, is the first published serious drama written by a Negro.

CULBERTSON, ERNEST H. *Goat Alley: A Tragedy of Negro Life.* Cincinnati, Ohio: Stewart Kidd Co., 1922. Pp. 155. (One-act version in *Twenty Contemporary One-Act Plays.* New York: Appleton, 1922.) NcD, NcU.
A play depicting the drab misery of Negro slum life.

EDMONDS, RANDOLPH. *Shades and Shadows.* Boston: Meador Publishing Co., 1930. Pp. 171. NcD.
Contains the dramatic stories: "The Devil's Price," "Hewers of Wood," "Shades and Shadows," "Everyman's Land," "The Tribal Chief," and "The Phantom Treasure." These stories, although written in the form of drama, are for reading rather than for the stage.

EDMONDS, RANDOLPH. *Six Plays for a Negro Theatre.* Boston: Walter H. Baker Co., 1934. Pp. 155. NcD, NcU, NcC.
Melodramatic plays of folk-life.

GILBERT, DOUGLAS. *American Vaudeville: Its Life and Times.* New York: Whittlesey House, 1940. Pp. x, 428. NcD, NcU.
A valuable account of a phase of American life and amusement now past but not forgotten. The part played by the Negro in vaudeville is included.

GREEN, PAUL. *Lonesome Road: Six Plays for the Negro Theatre.* New York: R. M. McBride and Co., 1926. Pp. xx, 217. NcD, NcU, NcC.
Life of Negroes in North Carolina.

GREEN, PAUL. *The Field God and In Abraham's Bosom.* New York: R. M. McBride and Co., 1927. Pp. 317. NcD, NcU, NcC.
In Abraham's Bosom was the Pulitzer Prize play of 1926. It is the story of a Negro whose aim was to educate himself and his race.

GREEN, PAUL, and WRIGHT, RICHARD. *Native Son. (The Biography of a Young American). A Play in Ten Scenes.* New York: Harper and Brothers, 1941. Pp. ix, 148. NcD, NcU, NcC.
A play adapted from the novel by Richard Wright.

HEYWARD, DUBOSE. *Brass Ankle.* New York: Farrar and Rinehart, Inc., 1931. Pp. 133. NcD, NcU.
A three-act tragedy of mixed blood and race prejudice in a small town.

HUTTON, LAURENCE. "The American Stage Negro," in *Curiosities of the American Stage.* New York: Harper and Brothers, 1891. NcD, NcU.
An early account of white blackface comedians and Negro minstrelsy.

ISAACS, EDITH J. R. *The Negro in the American Theatre.* New York: Theatre Arts, Inc., 1947. Pp. 143. NcD.
A chronological record of the Negro's progress in the American theatre.

LAWSON, HILDA J. *The Negro in American Drama.* Abstract of Thesis
  (Ph.D), University of Illinois, 1939. Pp. 13. NcD, NcU.
A bibliography of contemporary Negro drama.

LOCKE, ALAIN. "The Negro and the American Theatre," in Edith Isaacs, ed.,
  Theatre: Essays on the Arts of the Theatre. Boston: Little, Brown and Co.,
  1927. Pp. 290-303. NcD, NcU.
An appraisal of the Negro's contributions to the theatre as actor and as
playwright.

LOCKE, ALAIN, and GREGORY, MONTGOMERY. *Plays of Negro Life: A
  Source-book of Native American Drama.* New York: Harper and Brothers,
  1927. Pp. 430. NcD, NcU, NcC.
Twenty plays by Negro and white authors. It may appear to some that the
best plays on Negro life are not written by Negroes but by whites. The Negro
writer has not been as successful in drama as in verse.

MATTHEWS, BRANDER. "The Rise and Fall of Negro Minstrelsy," *Scribner's Magazine,* LVII (June, 1915), pp. 754-59. NcD, NcU.
One of the best short accounts of a cultural development "which is absolutely
natural to these States and which could not have come into existence anywhere
else in the civilized world."

MEYER, ANNIE NATHAN. *Black Souls: A Play in Six Scenes.* New Bedford,
  Mass.: Reynolds Press, 1932. Pp. 99. NcD, NcU.
A dramatic presentation of the problems of the American Negro emancipated
into a society which will not receive him.

"NEGRO Minstrelsy, Ancient and Modern," *Putnam's Monthly,* V (January,
  1855), 72-79. NcD, NcU.
Some early reflections on the growth of a new art form.

NEVINS, ROBERT. "Stephen C. Foster and Negro Minstrelsy," *Atlantic
  Monthly,* XX (November, 1867), 608-16. NcD, NcU, NcC.
After Dan Rice's first blackface act little advance was made in Negro min-
strelsy until the advent of Stephen Foster.

O'NEILL, EUGENE. *The Emperor Jones.* New York: D. Appleton-Century
  Co., 1924. Pp. 54. NcD, NcU, NcC.
A story with its setting on an island of the West Indies, presented in eight
scenes or episodes instead of through the conventional acts. This student edition
contains a study guide for the screen version of the play. "Striking on two
counts . . . a departure from the old rules of play writing, and it introduced a
memorable Negro figure on the stage."

PETERS, PAUL, and SKLAR, GEORGE. *Stevedore: A Play in Three Acts.*
  New York: Covici, Friede, 1934. Pp. 123. NcD, NcU.
A play based upon a dispute between Negro stevedores and their employers in
New Orleans and the race riot which developed from it.

POLLARD, EDWARD A. *Black Diamonds Gathered in the Darkey Homes of
  the South.* New York: Pudney and Russell, 1859. Pp. xiv, 122. NcD, NcU.
Deals with plantation shows in which Negroes figured before the Civil War.

RICHARDSON, WILLIS. *Plays and Pageants from the Life of the Negro.*
  Washington: Associated Publishers, Inc., 1930. Pp. x, 373. NcD, NcU, NcC.
A collection of plays and pageants written by Negroes without the use of
dialect, and suitable for young people of school age.

RICHARDSON, WILLIS, and MILLER, MAY, eds. *Negro History in Thirteen
  Plays.* Washington: Associated Publishers, Inc., 1935. Pp. vii, 333. NcD,
  NcU, NcC.

A collection of Negro plays adapted for children of the elementary and junior high school age.

SCHLICK, FREDERICK. *Bloodstream: A Play in Three Acts.* Boston: Walter H. Baker Co., 1934. Pp. 96. NcD.
A tragedy of Negro and white convict labor in the mines.

TORRENCE, FREDERIC RIDGELY. *Three Plays for a Negro Theatre.* New York: The Macmillan Co., 1917. Pp. 111. NcD, NcU.
The three plays dramatizing the inarticulate Negro folk are "Granny Maumee," "The Rider of Dreams," and "Simon the Cyrenian."

WARE, ALICE HOLDSHIP. *Mighty Wind a' Blowin'.* New York: New Theatre League, Repartory Department, 1936. Pp. 26. NcD.
A one-act play of the plight of sharecroppers, white and black.

WEXLEY, JOHN. *They Shall Not Die: A Play in Three Acts.* New York: A. A. Knopf, 1934. Pp. 191. NcD, NcU.
A dramatization of the Scottsboro case.

WITTKE, CARL F. *Tambo and Bones: A History of the American Minstrel Stage.* Durham: Duke University Press, 1930. Pp. ix, 269. NcD, NcU.
Useful as a reference work on minstrelsy in the United States.

5. RACE LITERATURE FOR AND ABOUT CHILDREN

AKIN, EMMA E. *Ideals and Adventures.* Oklahoma City, Oklahoma: Harlow Publishing Corp., 1938. Pp. 251. NcD, NcU, NcC.
Simple stories of successful Negro Americans for boys and girls.

ANDREWS, JANE. *The Seven Little Sisters who Live on the Round Ball that Floats in Air.* Boston: Ginn and Co., 1924. Pp. v, 119. NcD.
Emphasizes that all children regardless of race are brothers and sisters.

BAKER, AUGUST. *Books About Negro Life For Children.* Rev. ed. New York: Bureau for Intercultural Education, 1946. Pp. 16. NcD.
It is the purpose of this bibliography "to bring together books for children that give an unbiased, accurate, well-rounded picture of Negro life in all parts of the world."

BEIM, LORRAINE, and BEIM, JERROLD. *Two is a Team.* New York: Harcourt, Brace and Co., 1945. Pp. 61. NcD.
Story of two little boys, one white, the other colored.

BERRY, ERICK (pseud.). *Juma of the Hills.* New York: Harcourt, Brace and Co., 1932. Pp. xi, 260. NcD.
Story of West Africa.

BEST, HERBERT. *Garram the Hunter.* Garden City, N. Y.: Doubleday, Doran and Co., 1930. Pp. viii, 332. NcD, NcU, NcC.
Story of an African boy and his dog.

BEST, HERBERT. *Garram the Chief.* Garden City, N. Y.: Doubleday, Doran and Co., 1932. Pp. viii, 261. NcD.
Story of the hill tribes.

BONTEMPS, ARNA. *Sad-Faced Boy.* Boston: Houghton Mifflin Co., 1937. Pp. 119. NcD, NcU, NcC.
Slumber, sad-faced boy, and his two brothers hitch-hiked to New York where they organized a Harlem band. After many adventures, they returned to their Alabama home convinced that there is no place like home.

BONTEMPS, ARNA, and HUGHES, LANGSTON. *Popo and Fifina, Children of Haiti.* New York: The Macmillan Co., 1932. Pp. 100. NcD, NcU, NcC.
The daily experiences of two Haitian children reflect the life of the people in an interesting way.

BRADLEY, MARY HASTINGS. *Alice in Jungleland.* New York: D. Appleton and Co., 1940. Pp. 170. NcD.
Stories about the African travels of the author's daughter.

BRAUNE, ANNA. *Honey Chile.* Garden City, N. Y.: Doubleday, Doran and Co., 1937. Pp. 152. NcD, NcU.
An excellent story for children of six or seven years of age. The record of a happy day on an Alabama plantation.

BROWN, JEANETTE PERKINS. *The Family Goes Traveling.* New York: Friendship Press, 1936. Pp. 31. NcD.
Text and photographs about a Negro family.

CENDRARS, BLAISE. *Little Black Stories for Little White Children.* New York: Payson and Clarke, 1929. Pp. 138. NcD.
Stories the African children tell to amuse themselves while they sit around the fire and keep watch for protection against wild beasts.

CREDLE, ELLIS. *The Flop-Eared Hound.* New York: Oxford University Press, 1938. Pp. 61. NcD, NcU, NcC.
Story centers around Shadrock, also known as "Little Bootjack," and his flop-eared hound. Simply told. The photographic illustrations are masterpieces in their own right.

CUTHBERT, MARION. *We Sing America.* New York: The Friendship Press, 1936. Pp. 117. NcD, NcC.
This book treats pleasant and unpleasant facts about the Negro in a simple yet forthright manner.

ENRIGHT, ELIZABETH. *Kintu, a Congo Adventure.* New York: Farrar and Rinehart, 1935. Pp. 54. NcD, NcU, NcC.
The colorful story of a little African boy who had many exciting adventures in the jungle.

EVANS, EVA KNOX. *Araminta.* New York: Minton, Balch and Co., 1935. Pp. 84. NcD, NcC.
Araminta, a city child, visits her grandparents in the country and learns much about nature and the simple ways of living.

EVANS, EVA KNOX. *Jerome Anthony.* New York: G. P. Putnam's Sons, 1936. Pp. 86. NcD, NcC.
Araminta's country playmate, Jerome Anthony, visits the city and learns much about it.

EVANS, EVA KNOX. *Araminta's Goat.* New York: G. P. Putnam's Sons, 1938. Pp. 92. NcD, NcC.
The fun Araminta has when she visits the country again.

EVANS, EVA KNOX. *Key Corner.* New York: G. P. Putnam's Sons, 1938. Pp. 206. NcD, NcC.
The experiences of rural colored children in Georgia.

GEDO, LEOPOLD. *Who is Johnny?* Translated by Kate Seredy. New York: Viking Press, 1939. Pp. 243. NcD, NcC.
Of this story Josephine Schuyler says, "This is without doubt the most interesting and charming book ever written about a colored child."

GOVAN, CHRISTINE NOBLE. *Those Plummer Children.* Boston: Houghton Mifflin Co., 1934. Pp. 196. NcD, NcC.
Not many books for boys and girls contain so much genuine humor, and there are few stories that show so vividly and engagingly the relationship between Southern white people and the Negroes who are members of the household. The background of a small Southern town is authentic. Grades 5-7.

HADER, B. H., and HADER, ELMER. *Jamaica Johnny*. New York: The Macmillan Co., 1935. Pp. 90. NcD, NcC.
An interesting story about a little Negro boy in Jamaica. He helped his uncle on the farm, but he did not like to go to school until something happened.

JACKSON, JESSE. *Call Me Charley*. New York: Harper and Brothers, 1945. Pp. 156. NcD.
A story about Charley, the only Negro boy in Arlington Heights.

LANG, DON. *On the Dark of the Moon*. New York: Oxford University Press, 1943. Pp. 235. NcD, NcC.
A book about a small Negro boy who has a talent for trouble and a way with raccoons.

LATTIMORE, ELEANOR F. *Junior: A Colored Boy of Charleston*. New York: Harcourt, Brace and Co., 1938. Pp. 129. NcD, NcC.
A story of James Robinson, Junior, who sells vegetables and shrimps, shines shoes, and washes windows in order to help his family while his father has no work.

NEWSOME, EFFIE L. *Gladiola Garden*. Washington, D. C.: Associated Publishers, 1940. Pp. xv, 167. NcD.
Mrs. Newsome has been called the Negro race's "foremost creator of children's poetry and yet there is nothing 'racial' about her work."

NOLEN, ELEANOR W. *A Shipment for Susannah*. New York: Thomas Nelson and Sons, 1938. Pp. 82. NcD, NcC.
Story covering the pleasant association of Susannah, a Negro slave, and her little mistress, Nellie Custis, on Mt. Vernon Plantation. The story runs smoothly and engagingly as it relates how Susannah learns to perform household duties and how a special gift for Susannah was included in General Washington's annual shipment from London.

SHACKELFORD, JANE D. *My Happy Days*. Washington: Associated Publishers, 1944. Pp. 121. NcD, NcU, NcC.
A portrayal of the home, school, and community activities of an eight-year-old Negro boy.

SHARPE, STELLA GENTRY. *Tobe*. Chapel Hill: The University of North Carolina Press, 1939. Pp. 121. NcD, NcU, NcC.
Tobe was written by a North Carolina farm woman because a little Negro boy said to her, "I wish there was a book where colored folks talked like people."

TUNIS, JOHN R. *All American*. New York: Harcourt, Brace and Company, 1942. Pp. 245. NcD, NcU.
Difficulties on a high-school football team because of the presence of a Negro boy and a Jewish boy.

VAN VROOMAN, MARIA. *Shine*. New York: E. P. Dutton, 1939. Pp. 50. NcD, NcU.
Amusing adventures of a six-year-old Negro boy.

WHITE, WILLIAM C. *Mouseknees*. New York: Random House, 1939. Pp. 144. NcD, NcC.
Tells of the surprising adventures of a little West Indian who was a table boy at the hotel and his efforts to find out the truth about certain things.

WHITING, HELEN ADELE. *Negro Art, Music and Rhyme for Young Folks* (Book II). Washington, D. C.: Associated Publishers, 1938. Pp. 38. NcD, NcU, NcC.
Simple accounts of the contribution Negroes have made to civilization in the arts. Adapted for very young children.

WHITING, HELEN ADELE. *Negro Folk Tales for Pupils in the Primary Grades* (Book I). Washington, D. C.: Associated Publishers, 1938. Pp. 28. NcD, NcU, NcC.
A collection of African and American Negro folk tales for very young children.

WORTHINGTON, FRANK. *The Little Wise One.* Boston: Houghton Mifflin Co., 1932. Pp. 141. NcD.
African animal stories around the campfire. The author believes these stories have figured in folklore from Aesop to Joel Chandler Harris.

6. NEGRO MUSIC AND MUSICIANS

ALLEN, WILLIAM F., WARE, CHARLES P., and GARRISON, LUCY McKIM. *Slave Songs of the United States.* New York: Peter Smith, 1929. Pp. xliv, 115. NcD, NcU, NcC.
A collection of 136 songs arranged by geographical areas. Originally published in 1867. Of this important pioneer collection *Lippincott's Magazine* (Philadelphia) said in March, 1868: "It was hardly worth while to try to perpetuate this trash, vulgarity and profanity by putting it into print."

ARMSTRONG, LOUIS. *Swing that Music.* New York: Longmans, Green and Co., 1936. Pp. xii, 136. NcU.
An autobiography, and an interpretation of "swing" by a leader of the art.

BALLANTA, N. G. J., comp. *St. Helena Island Spirituals.* New York: G. Schrimer, 1925. Pp. xviii, 93. NcD, NcU.
Many of these 115 spirituals, says Guy B. Johnson, "were undoubtedly secular songs before the Church began its work among the Negroes."

BLESH, RUDI. *Shining Trumpets: A History of Jazz.* New York: A. A. Knopf, 1946. Pp. xvi, 365. NcD, NcU.
An illustrated history.

BURLIN, NATALIE CURTIS. *Negro Folk-Songs.* 4 vols. New York: G. Schrimer, 1918-19. NcD, NcU.
The spirituals of Volumes I and II and the work and play songs of Volumes III and IV were recorded at Hampton Institute.

COURLANDER, HAROLD. *Haiti Singing.* Chapel Hill: The University of North Carolina Press, 1939. Pp. xii, 273. NcD, NcU, NcC.
A collection of folklore, melodies, drum rhythms, and dances from Haiti. There are fine introductory chapters on Voodoo.

DETT, ROBERT NATHANIEL. *Religious Folk-Songs of the Negro.* Hampton, Virginia: Hampton University Press, 1927. Pp. xxvii, 236, ii, xiii. NcD, NcU, NcC.
A new edition, rearranged with an introductory essay on Negro music by the director of the Hampton Institute Chorus, of "the Cabin and Plantation Song," first published by Hampton Institute in 1874.

EWEN, DAVID. *Men of Popular Music.* Chicago: Ziff-Davis Publishing Company, 1944. Pp. 213. NcD, NcC.
Sketches of some white and Negro popular musicians of the past forty years.

GELLERT, LAWRENCE, and SIEGMEISTER, ELIE. *Negro Songs of Protest.* New York: American Music League, 1936. Pp. 47. NcD, NcU.
"Sistren an' brethren, stop foolin' wid pray
When black face is lifted, Lord turnin' way."

GOFFIN, ROBERT. *Jazz: From the Congo to the Metropolitan.* New York: Doubleday, Doran and Co., Inc., 1944. Pp. xii, 254. NcD, NcU, NcC.
A history and criticism of hot jazz.

GRISSOM, MARY A. *The Negro Sings a New Heaven.* Chapel Hill: The University of North Carolina Press, 1930. Pp. 101. NcD, NcU.
A collection of original melodies selected from religious services of worship today in and around Louisville, Kentucky, and certain rural sections in Adair County.

HANDY, W. C. *Blues: An Anthology.* New York: A. and C. Boni, 1926. Pp. 180. NcD, NcU.
Abe Niles adds a short history and an analysis to this collection of "blues" songs.

HARE, MAUD CUNEY. *Negro Musicians and Their Music.* New ed. Washington: Associated Publishers, 1936. Pp. xii, 439. NcD, NcU, NcC.
Negro music is traced from early African influences to the interpretative music in America today.

HOBSON, WILDER. *American Jazz Music.* New York: W. W. Norton and Company, Inc., 1939. Pp. 230. NcD, NcC.
Discusses the "musical underground" in connection with the origin of the various 1933 styles.

JACKSON, GEORGE PULLEN. *White Spirituals in the Southern Uplands.* Chapel Hill: The University of North Carolina Press, 1933. Pp. xv, 444. NcD, NcU.
Termed spirituals by their mountain white singers these songs are, in fact, much like those sung by the Negroes. This book is an important contribution to the literature on folk culture.

JACKSON, GEORGE PULLEN. *White and Negro Spirituals: Their Life Span and Kinship.* New York: J. J. Augustin, 1944. Pp. xiii, 349. NcD, NcU, NcC.
A history of 200 years of song-making and singing among the country folk of the South.

JESSYE, EVA A. *My Spirituals.* New York: Robbins-Engel, Inc., 1927. Pp. 81. NcD, NcU.
A collection of seventeen songs.

JOHNSON, GUY B. "Double Meaning in the Popular Negro Blues," *Journal of Abnormal and Social Psychology,* XXII (April-June, 1927), 12-20. NcD, NcU.
"Folk song students know that many standard folk songs have come up out of the slime. But it is doubtful if any group has ever carried its ordinary vulgarities over into respectable sane life so completely and successfully as the American Negro."

JOHNSON, JAMES WELDON, ed. *The Book of American Negro Spirituals.* Musical arrangements by J. Rosamond Johnson, additional numbers by Lawrence Brown. New York: The Viking Press, 1925. Pp. 187. NcD, NcU, NcC.
Arrangements of sixty-one of the best of the old spirituals intended to preserve the natural rhythmic qualities of Negro song. The editor, in the Preface, summarizes the history, development, and importance of the spirituals.

JOHNSON, JAMES WELDON, ed. *The Second Book of Negro Spirituals.* New York: The Viking Press, 1926. Pp. 189. NcD, NcU, NcC.
A companion volume to *The Book of American Negro Spirituals.*

JOHNSON, JOHN ROSAMOND, ed. *Rolling Along in Song.* New York: The Viking Press, 1937. Pp. 224. NcD, NcU, NcC.
A chronological survey of American Negro music, with eighty-seven arrangements of Negro songs, including ring shouts, spirituals, work songs, plantation ballads, chain-gang, jail-house, and minstrel songs, street cries, and blues.

KENNEDY, ROBERT EMMET. *Mellows. A Chronicle of Unknown Singers.* New York: A. and C. Boni, 1925. Pp. 183. NcD, NcU.

"Mellows" is the word which the Negroes of Louisiana apply to what are elsewhere called spirituals.

KENNEDY, ROBERT EMMET. *More Mellows.* New York: Dodd, Mead and Co., 1931. Pp. 178. NcD.

Thirty-seven songs grouped as: (1) unharmonized spirituals; (2) ballets without the music; (3) harmonized spirituals; (4) harmonized folk-songs.

KREHBIEL, HENRY EDWARD. *Afro-American Folksongs.* New York: G. Schrimer, 1914. Pp. xii, 176. NcD, NcU, NcC.

A study of Negro songs from the point of view of the expert musician.

LOCKE, ALAIN. *The Negro and His Music.* Washington: Associates in Negro Folk Education, 1936. Pp. 142. NcD, NcU, NcC.

An insightful history and survey of the folk sources in Negro music with the conclusion that "there is now no deep divide between our folk music and the main stream of world music."

LOMAX, JOHN A., and LOMAX, ALAN. *American Ballads and Folk Songs.* New York: The Macmillan Co., 1934. Pp. xxxix, 625. NcD, NcU, NcC.

Any song that springs up in America among any element of the population is good enough for the Lomaxes. White and black Southerners contribute generously to this collection.

LOMAX, JOHN A., and LOMAX, ALAN. *Negro Folk Songs as Sung by Lead Belly.* New York: The Macmillan Co., 1936. Pp. xiv, 242. NcD, NcU, NcC.

The story of "Lead Belly," king of guitar players, and many of his songs.

MARSH, J. B. T. *The Story of the Jubilee Singers with Their Songs.* Rev. ed. Boston: Houghton, Osgood and Co., 1880. Pp. viii, 265. NcD, NcU.

The story of Fisk University is almost inseparable from the story of her Jubilee singers.

METFESSEL, MILTON FRANKLIN. *Phonophotography in Folk Music: American Negro Songs in New Notation.* Chapel Hill: The University of North Carolina Press, 1928. Pp. x, 181. NcD, NcU.

American Negro songs studied by means of sound photography.

MEZZROW, MEZZ, and WOLFE, BERNARD. *Really the Blues.* New York: Random House, 1946. Pp. 388. NcD, NcC.

Mezzrow, a white jazz musician, lived as a Negro. Bernard Wolfe helped him tell his story.

MILLIGAN, HAROLD VINCENT. *Stephen Collins Foster. A Biography of America's Folk-Song Composer.* New York: G. Schrimer, 1920. Pp. viii, 116. NcD, NcU.

A biography of the Joel Chandler Harris of American music.

NILES, J. J. *Singing Soldiers.* New York: Charles Scribner's Sons, 1927. Pp. xii, 171. NcD, NcU.

Songs of the Negro troops with the American Expeditionary Force during the First World War. Except among the Negroes, original songs created by American soldiers are said to have been rare. Sample: The emotions produced by the burial of an officer is recorded in "I've got a grave-diggin' feelin' in my heart."

ODUM, HOWARD W., and JOHNSON, GUY B. *The Negro and His Songs: A Study of the Typical Negro Songs of the South.* Chapel Hill: The University of North Carolina Press, 1925. Pp. vii, 306. NcD, NcU, NcC.

Spirituals, social, and work songs discussed from a sociological and historical point of view. The words of two hundred songs are given.

ODUM, HOWARD W. and JOHNSON, GUY B. *Negro Workaday Songs.*
Chapel Hill: The University of North Carolina Press, 1926. Pp. xii, 278. NcU.
Secular and mundane songs sung by Negroes here, there, and everywhere.

PANASSIÉ, HUGUES. *Hot Jazz: The Guide to Swing Music.* New York: N.
Witmark and Sons, 1936. Pp. xvi, 363. NcD.
Translated from the French *Le Jazz Hot.*

PANASSIÉ, HUGUES. *The Real Jazz.* New York: Smith and Durrell, 1943.
Pp. xiv, 326. NcD, NcU.
The author considers jazz music essentially a Negro creation and very difficult
for whites to comprehend or correctly interpret.

PARRISH, LYDIA. *Slave Songs of the Georgia Sea Islands.* New York:
Creative Age Press, Inc., 1942. Pp. xxxi, 256. NcD, NcU.
Following an introduction written by the eminent music critic, Olin Downes,
Miss Parrish has a chapter on the character of Negro slave songs. This is fol-
lowed by a delightful array of songs and singers.

RAMSEY, FREDERICK, JR., and SMITH, CHARLES EDWARD, eds. *Jazz-
men.* New York: Harcourt, Brace and Co., 1939. Pp. xv, 360. NcD.
Little-known and well-known masters, old and new.

SANDBURG, CARL, comp. *The American Songbag.* New York: Harcourt,
Brace and Company, 1927. Pp. xxiii, 495. NcD, NcU, NcC.
Mr. Sandburg says this is more than a collection of tunes and words; it is a
contribution to American history. Songs and ballads of the Negro are included.

SARGEANT, WINTHROP. *Jazz: Hot and Hybrid.* New ed. New York: E. P.
Dutton and Co., 1946. Pp. 287. NcD.
Of this book Alain Locke says, "It is the best and most scholarly analysis of
jazz and Negro secular folk music to date."

SCARBOROUGH, DOROTHY. *On the Trail of Negro Folk-Songs.* Cambridge:
Harvard University Press, 1925. Pp. 289. NcD, NcU, NcC.
An important feature of this work, which is devoted entirely to secular songs,
is the author's discussion of the Negro's part in the transmission of traditional
English and Scottish songs and ballads.

STEIG, HENRY. *Send Me Down.* New York: A. A. Knopf, 1941. Pp. 461.
NcD.
An authentic and penetrating analysis of Negro jazz and jazz-makers in the
form of fiction.

TALLEY, THOMAS W. *Negro Folk Rhymes, Wise and Otherwise.* New York:
The Macmillan Co., 1922. Pp. 347. NcD, NcU.
This volume is confined exclusively to secular songs. The author offers in-
formation in regard to the circumstances under which the rhymes originated.

TRENT-JOHNS, ALTONA. *Play Songs of the Deep South.* Washington:
Associated Publishers, 1945. Pp. 33. NcD, NcU.
Words and music of some singing games as played and sung by Negro children
in the South.

TROTTER, JAMES MONROE. *Music and Some Highly Musical People.* Boston: Lee and Shepard, 1880. Pp. 505. NcD, NcU, NcC.
American Negro musical celebrities of the past.

TURNER, LUCILE PRICE. "Negro Spirituals in the Making," *Musical Quarterly,* XVII (October, 1931), 480-85. NcD, NcU.
Most Negro spirituals have been composed in church by the entire congregation. They are based upon themes evolved by individuals when engaged in
manual labor.

WHEELER, MARY, comp. *Steamboatin' Days.* Baton Rouge: Louisiana State University Press, 1944. Pp. 121. NcD, NcU.
Words and music of the songs of the packet boat era on the Mississippi and its tributaries. They were gathered from Negroes who had worked "on the rivuh."

WHITE, NEWMAN I. *American Negro Folk-Songs.* Cambridge: Harvard University Press, 1928. Pp. 700. NcD, NcU, NcC.
A comprehensive reference work including the words of over eight hundred songs, many of which are annotated and traced to their origins. With a bibliography of books which deal directly with the folk song.

WORK, JOHN W. *Folk-Songs of the American Negro.* Nashville, Tennessee: Fisk University Press, 1915. Pp. 131. NcD, NcU.
A book of spirituals recorded at Fisk University.

WORK, JOHN W. *American Negro Songs.* New York: Howell, Soskin & Company, 1940. Pp. vii, 259. NcD, NcU, NcC.
A collection of 230 songs, preceded by a discussion of their origins.

7. ART BY OR ABOUT NEGROES

COVARRUBIAS, MIGUEL. *Negro Drawings.* New York: A. A. Knopf, 1927. Pp. 78. NcD.
A version of Harlem types and atmosphere.

CRITE, ALLAN R. *Were You There When They Crucified My Lord?* Cambridge, Mass.: Harvard University Press, 1944. Pp. 93. NcD, NcU, NcC.
The Negro spiritual translated into thirty-nine brush drawings.

EXHIBIT of Fine Arts. Productions of American Negro Artists. New York: Harmon Foundation, 1928. Pp. 11. NcU.
Showing the Negro taking his place in American art.

GUILLAUME, PAUL, and MUNRO, THOMAS. *Primitive Negro Sculpture.* New York: Harcourt, Brace and Co., 1926. Pp. 134. NcD, NcU.
An appreciation of primitive Negro sculpture and an effort to understand its influence on contemporary art movements.

HIRSCHFELD, AL, and SAROYAN, WILLIAM. *Harlem as Seen By Hirschfeld.* New York: The Hyperion Press, 1941. NcD, NcU.
A collection of twenty-four original lithographs with commentary by Saroyan.

LOCKE, ALAIN. *Negro Art: Past and Present.* Washington: Associates in Negro Folk Education, 1936. Pp. 122. NcD, NcU, NcC.
The story of how the Negro's art heritage was lost and how it is being regained.

LOCKE, ALAIN, ed. *The Negro in Art: A Pictorial Record of the Negro Artist and of the Negro Theme in Art.* Washington: Associates in Negro Folk Education, 1940. Pp. 224. NcD, NcU, NcC.
An illustrated sequel to the editor's *Negro Art: Past and Present.*

THE Negro Artist Comes of Age: A National Survey of Contemporary American Artists. Introduction, "Up Till Now," by Alain Locke. Albany, New York: Albany Institute of History and Art, 1945. Pp. vii, 77. NcD, NcC.
"The aim is to lift the Negro artist from the patronizing sphere of a group set off by itself and regarded as Negro artists rather than as artists who happen to be Negroes." "A representative over-view of the work of contemporary artists."

NEGRO ARTISTS: An Illustrated Review of Their Achievements. New York: Harmon Foundation, 1935. Pp. 59. NcU.
Increasing public interest and steady growth in activity have marked the development of art by Negroes.

"THE Negro in Art From Africa to America." *The Negro History Bulletin, II* (March, 1939), 49 ff. NcD, NcC.
  A short summary.

PORTER, JAMES A. "Versatile Interests of Early Negro Artists: A Neglected Chapter of American Art History," *Art in America and Elsewhere*, XXIV (January, 1936), 16-27. NcD, NcU.
  Research on the Negro artist in American art history is urged in this article.

PORTER, JAMES A. *Modern Negro Art*. New York: The Dryden Press, 1943. Pp. viii, 272. NcD, NcU, NcC.
  A comprehensive record of Negro art from colonial days to the present.

RODMAN, SELDEN. *Horace Pippin: A Negro Painter in America*. New York: The Quadrangle Press, 1947. Pp. 88. NcD.
  A beautiful portfolio listing and reproducing Pippin's works.

SWEENEY, JAMES JOHNSON, ed. *African Negro Art*. New York: The Museum of Modern Art, 1935. Pp. 58. NcD, NcU, NcC.
  "The art of Negro Africa is a sculptor's art. As a sculptural tradition in the last century it has had no rival. It is as sculpture we should approach it."

XXVIII. Negro Personality
and Social Types

ATWOOD, J. HOWELL, WYATT, DONALD W., DAVIS, VINCENT J., and
WALKER, IRA D. *Thus Be Their Destiny.* Washington: American Council on Education, prepared for the American Youth Commission, 1941.
Pp. xi, 96. NcD, NcU, NcC.
Community structure and the part it plays in racial reactions is studied in connection with the personality development of Negro youth in three communities.

DAI, BINGHAM. "Negro Personality and the Learning Process," *Harvard Educational Review,* XVI (Summer, 1946), 173-93. NcD, NcU.
Negroes do not stop being Negroes and subject, therefore, to all the personality problems of a caste order just because they have come to college.

DANIEL, ROBERT P. "Personality Differences between Delinquent and Non-delinquent Negro Boys," *Journal of Negro Education,* I (October, 1932), 381-87. NcD, NcU, NcC.
In this study of Negro boys in Virginia the author questions the applicability of white norms to Negro subjects.

DAVIS, ALLISON. "Racial Status and Personality Development," *Scientific Monthly,* LVII (October, 1943), 354-63. NcD, NcU, NcC.
"The myth of racial types of personality is even more deeply rooted in our folklore than is the myth of racial types of culture."

DAVIS, ALLISON, and DOLLARD, JOHN. *Children of Bondage. The Personality Development of Negro Youth in the Urban South.* Washington: American Council on Education, 1940. Pp. xxviii, 299. NcD, NcU, NcC.
A description of the method of personality analysis used; a report on the principal social controls operative in New Orleans and in Natchez; and the data and analysis of eight representative cases.

EDDY, G. NORMAN. *The Human Face: A Study in Culture and Social Interaction.* Ph.D. dissertation, Duke University, 1943. Pp. v, 304. NcD.
Fresh and interesting material on race and face.

FRAZIER, E. FRANKLIN. *Negro Youth at the Crossways: Their Personality Development in the Middle States.* Washington, D. C.: American Council on Education, 1940. Pp. xxiii, 301. NcD, NcU, NcC.
The general purpose of this work is "to determine what kind of a person a Negro youth is or is in the process of becoming as a result of the limitations which are placed upon his or her participation in the life of the communities in the border states."

GIBSON, CHARLES F. "Concerning Color," *The Psychoanalytic Review,* XVIII (October, 1931), 413-25. NcD, NcU.
A discussion of the attitudes and personalities of black, brown, and light Negroes.

JOHNSON, CHARLES S. *Growing Up in the Black Belt. Negro Youth in the Rural South.* Washington: American Youth Commission, 1941. Pp. xxiii, 360. NcD, NcU, NcC.
This study of six rural counties in the South gives a picture of a restive, changing, and bewildered younger generation of Negroes.

JOHNSON, GUY B. "The Stereotype of the American Negro," in Otto Klineberg, ed., *Characteristics of the American Negro.* New York: Harper and
Brothers, 1944. NcD, NcU, NcC.
The author illustrates the many mental pictures of Negroes held by both
white and Negro Americans.

MYRDAL, GUNNAR. *An American Dilemma.* 2 vols. (Vol. II, Chap. 36). New
York: Harper and Brothers, 1944. NcD, NcU, NcC.
The protest motive and Negro personality.

PARK, ROBERT E. "Behind our Masks," *Survey,* LVI (May, 1926), 135-39.
NcD, NcU.
A consideration of the role of "face" in race relations.

PARRISH, CHARLES H. "Color Names and Color Notions," *Journal of Negro
Education,* XV (Winter, 1946), 13-20. NcD, NcU, NcC.
In Negro society unfavorable attitudes are more likely to be directed toward
the color extremes, that is, toward the very light and the very dark.

POSTON, TED. "The Revolt of the Evil Fairies," *The New Republic,* CVI
(April 16, 1942), 458-59. NcD, NcU, NcC.
In one of the annual dramatic offerings of the Booker T. Washington Colored
Grammar School the perennial chief of the black Evil Fairies turns unexpectedly
but understandably on the light Prince Charming.

REID, IRA DE A. *Negro Youth, Their Social and Economic Backgrounds: A
Selected Bibliography of Unpublished Studies, 1900-1938.* Washington, D. C.:
The American Youth Commission of the American Council on Education,
1939. Pp. 71. NcD, NcU.
"A bibliography of unpublished manuscripts available at the various colleges
and universities throughout the country."

REID, IRA DE A. *In a Minor Key: Negro Youth in Story and Fact.* Washington: American Youth Commission, 1940. Pp. 134. NcD, NcU, NcC.
Basic and general information about Negro youth in the United States.

SOCIAL Worlds of Negro Youth. Social Science Source Documents No. 5. Nashville: Social Science Institute, Fisk University, 1946. Pp. 293. NcD, NcC.
Interviews with Southern Negro young people on personal, social, and racial
adjustment experiences. Mimeographed.

STEWARD, GUSTAVUS ADOLPHUS. "The Black Girl Passes," *Social Forces,*
VI (September, 1927), 99-103. NcD, NcU, NcC.
"A scarcely noted result of the interaction between whites and blacks in this
country is the gradual and steady elimination of the black girl from all participation in community life."

STRONG, SAMUEL M. "Social Types in a Minority Group. Formulation of
a Method," *American Journal of Sociology,* XLVIII (March, 1943), 563-73.
NcD, NcU, NcC.
Negro social types in Chicago include the "mammy," the "white man's nigger,"
the "bad nigger," the "dicky," the "striver," the "peola," and many others.

STRONG, SAMUEL M. "Negro-White Relations as Reflected in Social Types,"
American Journal of Sociology, LII (July, 1946), 23-30. NcD, NcU, NcC.
Social types that reflect the nature of race relations are more common among
lower class Negroes. Those reflecting race pride are more common among upper
class Negroes.

SUTHERLAND, ROBERT L. *Color, Class and Personality.* Washington:
American Council on Education, 1942. Pp. xxiii, 135. NcD, NcU, NcC.

Final volume of the American Youth Commission series summarizing the findings of the field studies and stating their implications for educational and social planning.

THOMPSON, ERA BELL. *American Daughter*. Chicago: The University of Chicago Press, 1946. Pp. x, 300. NcD, NcU, NcC.

The significant thing about this naïvely written autobiography of a Negro girl from North Dakota is that there is practically nothing racial about it.

WARNER, W. LLOYD, JUNKER, BUFORD H., and ADAMS, WALTER A. *Color and Human Nature: Negro Personality Development in a Northern City*. Washington: American Youth Commission, 1941. Pp. xv, 301. NcD, NcU, NcC.

Color is the major symbol of the social subordination of the Negro. It is the badge of racial separateness and the basis of position in the Negro social hierarchy.

WRIGHT, RICHARD. *Black Boy*. New York: Harper and Brothers, 1945 Pp. 228. NcD, NcU, NcC.

This autobiography tells how it feels to be a Negro growing up in the South

XXIX. Leadership in Negro Affairs

ANDREWS, ROBERT M. *John Merrick: A Biographical Sketch.* Durham, N. C.: Seeman Printery, 1920. Pp. 220. NcD, NcU, NcC.
A biography of the founder of the North Carolina Mutual Life Insurance Company in Durham, N. C.

BAKER, HENRY E. "Benjamin Banneker, the Negro Mathematician and Astronomer," *Journal of Negro History,* III (April, 1918), 99-118. NcD, NcU, NcC.
Banneker was appointed by President Washington to serve on the original commission which surveyed and defined the District of Columbia.

BOND, HORACE M. "Negro Leadership Since Washington," *South Atlantic Quarterly,* XXIV (April, 1925), 115-30. NcD, NcU.
Booker T. Washington has no real successor among Negroes today. Migration and urbanization have caused a shift to the more aggressive political policies of DuBois and his followers. Yet Tuskegee and Hampton institutes laid down the foundations for both leaderships.

BRAWLEY, BENJAMIN G. *Women of Achievement.* Chicago: Woman's American Baptist Home Mission Society, 1919. Pp. 92. NcD.
Short sketches of Harriet Tubman, Nora Gordon, Meta Warrick Fuller, Mary McLeod Bethune, and Mary Church Terrell.

BRAWLEY, BENJAMIN G. *Paul Lawrence Dunbar, Poet of His People.* Chapel Hill: The University of North Carolina Press, 1936. Pp. xi, 159. NcD, NcU, NcC.
An uninspired biography of the poet.

BRAWLEY, BENJAMIN G. *Negro Builders and Heroes.* Chapel Hill: The University of North Carolina Press, 1937. Pp. xi, 315. NcD, NcU, NcC.
The careers of certain Negroes written for readers on the high-school level constitute the subject matter of this book. In race-conscious literature such as this it is perhaps inevitable that trivial achievements frequently are exaggerated and some ordinary characters are elevated to the rank of genius.

BRAWLEY, BENJAMIN G. *The Negro Genius.* New York: Dodd, Mead and Co., 1937. Pp. xiii. 366. NcD, NcU, NcC.
A more comprehensive treatment of the author's *The Negro in Literature and Art in the United States.*

BROWN, HALLIE Q., comp. *Homespun Heroines and Other Women of Distinction.* Xenia, Ohio: Aldine Publishing Co., 1926. Pp. viii, 248. NcD, NcC.
Biographies of noted American Negro women from the eighteenth century to 1926.

BULLOCK, RALPH W. *In Spite of Handicaps.* New York: Association Press, 1927. Pp. 140. NcD, NcU.
Portrays the "character, personality and achievements of others" through biography, with the hope that it will serve to inspire "youth to the worthwhile achievements of life and at the same time help to develop attitudes of interracial good will."

CALDWELL, ARTHUR B., ed. *History of the American Negro and His Institutions.* 7 vols. Atlanta: A. B. Caldwell Publishing Co., 1917. NcU.

This is not a history of the American Negro but a collection of short biographies of race leaders in various Southern states. It is, however, a unique and interesting book.

CHILD, LYDIA MARIA. *The Freedmen's Book.* Boston: Ticknor and Fields, 1865. Pp. vi, 277. NcD, NcU.
A word of hope for the Negro given in 1865 by means of a compilation of the accomplishments of colored men and women.

COOK, MERCER. *Five French Negro Authors.* Washington: Associated Publishers, 1943. Pp. xiv, 164. NcD, NcU, NcC.
Sketches of Julien Raimond, Charles Bissette, Alexander Dumas, Auguste Lacaussade, and René Maran.

CROSS, SAMUEL HAZZARD, and SIMMONS, ERNEST J. *Alexander Pushkin, 1799-1837: His Life and Literary Heritage.* New York: American Russian Institute, 1937. Pp. 79. NcD.
The great Russian poet "liked to think of his great grandfather as a Negro."

CUTHBERT, MARION. *Juliette Derricotte.* New York: The Woman's Press, 1933. Pp. 56. NcD, NcU.
A sketch of one of America's outstanding Negro women.

DABNEY, WENDELL P. *Cincinnati's Colored Citizens.* Cincinnati, Ohio: The Dabney Publishing Co., 1926. Pp. 440. NcD, NcU, NcC.
"More spice and flavor than generally appears in biographies of Negroes."

DANIEL, SADIE IOLA. *Woman Builders.* Washington, D. C.: Associated Publishers, 1931. Pp. xviii, 187. NcD, NcU, NcC.
Biographical sketches of seven Negro women.

DOUGLASS, FREDERICK. *Narrative of the Life of Frederick Douglass, An American Slave.* Boston: Anti-Slavery Office, 1845. Pp. xvi, 125. NcD, NcU.
Best known of all the writings of former slaves. Douglass made his story effective by the use of some proportion and some constraint.

DOUGLASS, FREDERICK. *Life and Times of Frederick Douglass.* New York: Pathway Press, 1941. Pp. 752. NcD, NcU, NcC.
In this book, first published in 1882, a famous Negro tells the story of his days in slavery, of his escape and work for abolition, and of his honors from the Federal Government.

DOWNS, KARL E. *Meet the Negro.* Pasadena, California: Login Press, 1943. Pp. xvi, 179. NcD.
Short sketches of about sixty Negro leaders.

DUBOIS, W. E. B. "The Talented Tenth," in Booker T. Washington et al, *The Negro Problem.* New York: James Pott and Company, 1903. NcD.
The author argues that the Negro masses can hope to improve their status only by first advancing the more talented members of the race.

DUBOIS, W. E. B. *Dusk of Dawn: An Essay Toward the Autobiography of a Race Concept.* New York: Harcourt, Brace and Co., 1940. Pp. viii, 334. NcD, NcU, NcC.
The autobiography of a Negro intellectual.

EMBREE, EDWIN R. *Thirteen Against the Odds.* New York: The Viking Press, 1944. Pp. 261. NcD, NcU, NcC.
Life stories of Mary McLeod Bethune, Richard Wright, Charles S. Johnson, Walter White, George Washington Carver, Langston Hughes, Mordecai Johnson, A. Philip Randolph, Joe Louis, Marian Anderson, William Grant Still, Paul Robeson, and W. E. B. DuBois.

FAUSET, ARTHUR HUFF. *For Freedom.* Philadelphia: Franklin Publishing
Co., 1928. Pp. 200. NcU, NcC.
A biographical story of the American Negro.

FAUSET, ARTHUR HUFF. *Sojourner Truth, God's Faithful Pilgrim.* Chapel
Hill: The University of North Carolina Press, 1938. Pp. viii, 187. NcD,
NcU, NcC.
A biography of a fearless leader of her people during the anti-slavery period.

FISHER, MILES MARK. *The Master's Slave, Elijah John Fisher.* Philadelphia: The Judson Press, 1922. Pp. 195. NcD, NcU.
An exceptionally important biography of a Negro Baptist preacher written by
his son, now a minister in Durham, N. C.

FLEISCHER, NAT. *Black Dynamite.* 4 vols. New York: The author, Madison
Square Garden, 1938-39. NcD, NcU, NcC.
Vol. I tells the story of the Negro in the prize ring from 1782 to 1938; Vol. II
(Jolting Joe and Homicide Hank) deals with Joe Louis and Henry Armstrong;
Vol. III *(Three Colored Aces)* gives sketches of George Dixon, Joe Gans, and
Joe Walcott; Vol. IV *(Fighting Furies)* is an account of Jack Johnson, Sam
Langford, and some of their contemporaries.

FLEMING, WALTER L. " 'Pap' Singleton, the Moses of the Colored Exodus,"
American Journal of Sociology, XV (July, 1909), 61-82. NcD, NcU.
In 1879-80 Benjamin Singleton, ex-slave, led thousands of his people to settle
in Kansas, the state of "Old John Brown."

FRAZIER, E. FRANKLIN. "Garvey: A Mass Leader," *Nation,* CXXIII
(August 18, 1926), 147-48. NcD, NcU.
Garvey has the distinction of initiating the first real mass movement among
American Negroes.

FRAZIER, E. FRANKLIN. "American Negro's New Leaders," *Current History,*
XXVIII (April, 1928), 56-59. NcD. NcU.
Leadership in terms of the growth of literacy, the urbanization, and the in-
crease of wealth of Negroes.

GOLLOCK, GEORGINA ANNE. *Lives of Eminent Africans.* New York:
Longsmans, Green and Co., 1928. Pp. viii, 152. NcD.
A supplementary reader for use in upper grades and in teacher training col-
leges in Africa.

GRAHAM, SHIRLEY, and LIPSCOMB, GEORGE D. *Dr. George Washington Carver, Scientist.* New York: J. Messner, Inc., 1944. Pp. viii, 248. NcD,
NcC.
The story of Dr. Carver's interesting and unusual life told especially for young
people.

HANDY, W. C. *Father of the Blues.* New York: The Macmillan Co., 1941.
Pp. xiv, 317. NcD, NcU, NcC.
"Much of the musical superiority and force of jazz," says Alain Locke, "comes
from the fact that the men who play it create it." This is the autobiography of
a man who created much of it.

HANDY, W. C., ed. *Unsung Americans Sung.* New York: Handy Brothers
Music Co., 1944. Pp. 236. NcD, NcU, NcC.
Tributes to twenty Negro figures of American history by Negro writers and
composers.

HARE, MAUD CUNEY. *Norris Wright Cuney: A Tribune of the Black People.*
New York: The Crisis Publishing Co., 1913. Pp. 230. NcD.
A biography of an important Texas Negro politician written by his daughter.

HARRISON, JUANITA. *My Great Wide Beautiful World.* New York: The
Macmillan Co., 1936. Pp. xii, 318. NcD, NcU, NcC.
The author is an American Negro woman who, in eight years, lived and
traveled in twenty-two different countries with her employer. This naïve account
of her travels suggests that new experience is as humdrum as routine unless one
assimilates it. Miss Harrison experienced much but realized little.

HELM, MACKINLEY. *Angel Mo' and Her Son, Roland Hayes.* Boston: Little,
Brown & Co., 1942. Pp. viii, 289. NcD, NcU, NcC.
A biography of the great singer written as an autobiography. "I, Roland Hayes,
a Negro, had first to measure my racial heritage and then to put it to use. It
remained for me to learn, humbly at first, and then with mounting confidence,
that my way to artistry was a Negro way."

HENDERSON, EDWIN BANCROFT. *The Negro in Sports.* Washington: The
Associated Publishers, Inc., 1939. Pp. 371. NcD, NcU, NcC.
This volume gives a broad picture of the Negro in sports and the social
significance of his contributions to athletics.

HOLT, RACKHAM. *George Washington Carver.* Garden City, N. Y.: Doubleday, Doran & Co., 1943. Pp. viii, 342. NcD, NcU, NcC.
An engaging biography of a famous Negro.

HUGHES, LANGSTON. *The Big Sea.* New York: A. A. Knopf Co., 1940. Pp.
335. NcD, NcU, NcC.
The autobiography of the famous Negro poet, author, and playwright.

HURSTON, ZORA NEALE. *Dust Tracts on a Road.* Philadelphia: J. B. Lippincott Company, 1942. Pp. 148. NcD, NcU, NcC.
The autobiography of a Negro girl who became an anthropologist.

JACKSON, WALTER CLINTON. *A Boy's Life of Booker T. Washington.* New
York: The Macmillan Co., 1922. Pp. xi, 147. NcD, NcU, NcC.
Boyhood days of Booker T. Washington during slavery, his desire for an educa-
tion, and the obstacles he overcame.

JACQUES-GARVEY, AMY, comp. *The Philosophy and Opinions of Marcus
Garvey.* New York: Universal Publishing House, 1925. Pp. 102. NcU.
A compilation by his wife of the Negro crusader's articles and speeches.

JENNESS, MARY. *Twelve Negro Americans.* New York: The Friendship Press,
1936. Pp. x, 180. NcD, NcU, NcC.
Biographies of Negroes, including a few contemporaries.

JOHNSON, JAMES WELDON. *Along This Way.* New York: The Viking Press,
1933. Pp. 418. NcD, NcU, NcC.
A famous Negro tells the story of his life as poet, critic, musician, and
diplomat.

JOHNSTON, ALEXANDER. *Ten and Out! The Complete Story of the Prize
Ring in America.* Rev. ed. New York: Ives Washburn, 1943. Pp. 347. NcD,
NcU.
Includes the story of Molyneaux the Moor, ex-slave, said to have been the
first heavy-weight champion of American fistiana.

KORNGOLD, RALPH. *Citizen Toussaint.* Boston: Little, Brown and Co., 1944.
Pp. xvii, 358. NcU.
The story of Toussaint L'Ouverture, founder of the Haitian Republic.

LAWSON, VICTOR. *Dunbar Critically Examined.* Washington, D. C.: Associated Publishers, Inc., 1941. Pp. xvi, 151. NcD, NcU, NcC.
An evaluation of the poetry and prose of Dunbar in an effort to find his place
in American letters.

LOTZ, PHILIP HENRY, ed. *Rising Above Color.* Washington: Association
Press, 1944. Pp. viii, 112. NcD, NcU, NcC.
Biographical sketches of thirteen American Negroes.

McKAY, CLAUDE. *A Long Way From Home.* New York: Lee Furman, Inc.,
1937. Pp. 354. NcD, NcU, NcC.
The autobiography of a Negro writer and poet giving meaningful impressions
of Negro life in America and in Europe.

MALONEY, ARNOLD H. *Amber Gold.* New York: Wendell Malliet and Co.,
1943. Pp. 448. NcD, NcC.
The autobiography of a pioneering Negro pharmacologist and a document
showing the possibilities of Negro success in the field of scientific research.

MERRITT, RALEIGH H. *From Captivity to Fame, or the Life of George
Washington Carver.* Boston: Meador Publishing Co., 1929. Pp. 196. NcD,
NcU, NcC.
A very inadequate and uncritical biography.

MILLER, MARGERY. *Joe Louis: American.* New York: Current Books, 1945.
Pp. x, 181. NcD, NcU, NcC.
The champ is more than a great fighter; he is a representative of g d will
for the Negro race.

MOTON, ROBERT R. *Finding a Way Out: An Autobiography.* Garden City,
N. Y.: Doubleday, Page and Co., 1920. Pp. 295. NcD, NcU.
The successor of Booker T. Washington at Tuskegee Institute tells the story
of his own life and work.

MYRDAL, GUNNAR. *An American Dilemma.* 2 vols. (Vol. II, Chaps. 33, 34,
37, and Appendix 9). New York: Harper and Brothers, 1944. NcD, NcU,
NcC.
The American pattern of individual leadership and mass passivity has been
assimilated by American Negroes.

THE National Cyclopedia of the Colored Race. Montgomery, Alabama:
National Publishing Co., 1919. Pp. 630. NcU.
Brief biographies of prominent Negroes.

NEWBOLD, N. C., ed. *Five North Carolina Negro Educators.* Chapel Hill: The
University of North Carolina Press, 1939. Pp. xii, 142. NcD, NcU, NcC.
Biographical sketches prepared by five joint committees of white and Negro
college students.

PERKINS, A. E., ed. *Who's Who in Colored Louisiana, 1930.* Baton Rouge,
La.: Douglas Loan Co., Inc., 1930. Pp. 153. NcD.
"A record of the achievements of outstanding colored men and women of
present Louisiana, together with brief outlines and sketches of the earlier history,
traditions and progress of the race."

PORTER, GEORGE F., ed. "Isaiah T. Montgomery," *Journal of Negro History,*
VIII (January, 1923), 87-92. NcD, NcU, NcC.
Why has no one yet written a biography of "Uncle" Isaiah Montgomery, one-
time slave and body-guard of Jefferson Davis and later founder of Mound
Bayou?

POWELL, ADAM CLAYTON. *Against the Tide: An Autobiography.* New
York: Richard R. Smith, 1938. Pp. x, 327. NcD, NcU, NcC.
The autobiography of a Negro pastor in New York City.

PROCTOR, HENRY HUGH. *Between Black and White.* Boston: The Pilgrim
Press, 1925. Pp. ix, 189. NcD, NcU, NcC.
Autobiographical sketches of a Negro minister.

QUARLES, BENJAMIN. *Frederick Douglass.* Washington, D. C.: The Associated Publishers, Inc., 1948. Pp. xi, 378. NcD.
A competent biography of the great Negro leader.

ROBESON, ESLANDA GOODE. *Paul Robeson, Negro.* New York: Harper and Brothers, 1930. Pp. 178. NcD, NcU, NcC.
A biography of the great singer written by his wife.

ROGERS, JOEL A. *World's Greatest Men and Women of African Descent.* New York: The author, 1935. Pp. 71. NcU.
Brief sketches, with numerous illustrations.

ROWLAND, MABEL. *Bert Williams, Son of Laughter.* New York: The English Crafters, 1923. Pp. 218. NcU.
A symposium of tributes to the great Negro comedian.

SAVAGE, W. SHERMAN. "The Influence of John Chavis and Lunsford Lane on the History of North Carolina," *Journal of Negro History,* XXV (January, 1940), 14-24. NcD, NcU, NcC.
An account of John Chavis, Negro educator, who numbered among his students several eminent white North Carolinians, and of Lunsford Lane, a slave who won freedom for himself and his family.

SHAW, GEORGE CLAYTON. *John Chavis, 1763-1838. A Remarkable Negro Who Conducted a School in North Carolina for White Boys and Girls.* Binghamton, New York: Vail-Ballou Press, Inc., 1931. Pp. xv, 60. NcD, NcU, NcC.
"About 1820 John Chavis, a full-blooded Negro, taught a preparatory school in North Carolina and had for his pupils the sons of leading families. He prepared for the University Willie P. Mangum, and his brother Priestly, and the two sons of Chief Justice Henderson. The grandfather of a brilliant Episcopal bishop not only went to school to this Negro teacher but boarded in his family."
—John Spencer Bassett.

SIMMONS, ERNEST J. *Pushkin.* Washington: Howard University Press, 1937. Pp. 485. NcD, NcU, NcC.
A study of the life of the great Russian Negro poet.

SMITH, EDWIN W. *Aggrey of Africa: A Study in Black and White.* London: Student Christian Movement, 1929. Pp. xii, 292. NcD, NcU, NcC.
The life of Dr. James Aggrey, African Negro leader, who worked to improve race relations.

STOKES, ANSON PHELPS. *A Brief Biography of Booker Washington.* Hampton, Virginia: Hampton Institute Press, 1936. Pp. x, 42. NcD, NcU, NcC.
In the preface to this brief biography the author asks why no scholarly and adequate "life" of Booker Washington has ever been published. A definitive biography of Washington written with imagination and insight would be, at the same time, an important contribution to our knowledge of the American Negro, of education, and of race relations in the United States.

TERRELL, MARY CHURCH. *A Colored Woman in a White World.* Washington, D. C.: Ransdell, Inc., 1940. Pp. 436. NcD, NcU, NcC.
The autobiography of a distinguished Negro woman who reached a unique place of leadership in American life.

ULANOV, BARRY. *Duke Ellington.* New York: Creative Age, 1946. Pp. x, 322. NcD, NcU, NcC.
A biography of the Negro jazz band leader.

VAN DEUSEN, JOHN G. *"Brown Bomber": The Story of Joe Louis.* Philadelphia: Dorrance and Co., 1940. Pp. 163. NcD, NcU, NcC.
A biography of Joe Louis.

VEHANEN, KOSTI. *Marian Anderson.* New York: Whittlesey House, McGraw-Hill Book Co., Inc., 1941. Pp. 270. NcD, NcU, NcC.
A portrait of a great singer who has become symbolic of the cause of her people is given by her accompanist.

WASHINGTON, BOOKER T. *Up from Slavery.* New York: Doubleday, Doran and Co., 1937. Pp. vii, 330. NcD, NcU, NcC.
The autobiography of a famous Negro American.

WERNER, M. R. *Julius Rosenwald.* New York: Harper and Brothers, 1939. Pp. xiv, 381. NcD, NcU, NcC.
A biography of "one of the largest contributors to efforts for the advancement of the Negro."

WESLEY, CHARLES H. *Richard Allen, Apostle of Freedom.* Washington, D. C.: Associated Publishers, Inc., 1935. Pp. xi, 300. NcD, NcU, NcC.
A biography of the founder of the A. M. E. Church.

WHO'S Who in Colored America. A Biographical Dictionary of Notable Living Persons of Negro Descent in America, 1927-1944. New York: Who's Who in Colored America Corporation. NcD, NcU, NcC.
Biographical data on American Negroes whose position or record of achievement makes them of general interest.

WILLIAMS, J. GRENFELL, and MAY, HENRY JOHN. *I Am Black: The Story of Shambala.* London: Cassell, 1936. Pp. 239. NcD.
". . . a uniquely accurate and sympathetic account of the experiences of a young Zulu who leaves his tribe and comes to seek work in the towns of the White Man."

WILSON, ROBERT FORREST. *Crusader in Crinoline: The Life of Harriet Beecher Stowe.* Philadelphia: J. B. Lippincott Co., 1941. Pp. 706. NcD, NcU, NcC.
A "full-length portrait" of the author of *Uncle Tom's Cabin.*

WOODSON, CARTER G. *African Heroes and Heroines.* Washington: Associated Publishers, 1939. Pp. 249. NcD, NcU, NcC.
An account of black men who have risen to prominence "in the complicated history of tribal movement in Africa."

XXX. The Negro in Wartime

"The American Negro in World Wars I and II," *Journal of Negro Education*, XII, No. 3 (Spring, 1943). NcD, NcU, NcC.
The twelfth Yearbook of the Journal.

APTHEKER, HERBERT. *The Negro in the Civil War*. New York: International Publishers, 1938. Pp. 48. NcD, NcU.
A left-wing view of the Negro's efforts in behalf of his own freedom.

BEECHER, JOHN. *All Brave Sailors*. New York: L. B. Fischer Publishing Co., 1945. Pp. 208. NcD, NcU.
The story of the *S. S. Booker T. Washington*, first liberty ship named for a Negro and first skippered by a Negro.

CLARK, KENNETH B. "Morale Among Negroes," in Goodwin Watson, ed., *Civilian Morale*. New York: Houghton Mifflin Co., 1942. Pp. 228-48. NcD, NcU.
"The basic factor of Negro morale . . . is frustration, complicated by deep seated bitterness and resentment at the mockery of democracy of which so much of their lives is a constant reminder."

FRAZIER, E. FRANKLIN. "Ethnic and Minority Groups in War-Time," *American Journal of Sociology*, XLVIII (November, 1942), 369-77. NcD, NcU, NcC.
"Unlike his reactions to the first World War, the American Negro has exhibited considerable militancy in regard to discrimination."

JOHNSON, GUION G. "The Impact of War Upon the Negro," *Journal of Negro Education*, X (July, 1941), 596-611. NcD, NcU, NcC.
Like the American Revolution, the Civil War, and the First World War, the present war will bring something of hope and advance to the Negro.

"THE Negro's War," *Fortune*, XXV (June, 1942), 77-80, 157-64. NcD, NcU, NcC.
". . . the American Negro community is at home here in the United States, beyond any temptation from abroad, inextricably rooted into this country's soil."

NELL, WILLIAM COOPER. *The Colored Patriots of the American Revolution*. Boston: R. F. Wallcut, 1855. Pp. 396. NcD.
The theme of this book, narrating the Negro's share in the effort to free the colonies, is that the Negro himself was worthy of freedom.

SCHOENFELD, SEYMOUR J. *The Negro in the Armed Forces: His Value and Status, Past, Present, and Potential*. Washington: Associated Publishers, 1945. Pp. x, 84. NcD, NcU, NcC.
Facts on the Negro in the armed services and proof of his capability as a serviceman.

SCOTT, EMMETT JAY. *Scott's Official History of the American Negro in the World War*. Chicago: Homewood Press, 1919. Pp. 511. NcU.
A popular narration of the Negro in World War I.

SHALLOO, JEREMIAH P., and YOUNG, DONALD, eds. *Minority Peoples in a Nation at War*, Annals of the American Academy of Political and Social Science, CCIII (September, 1942). Pp. viii, 276. NcD, NcU, NcC.
". . . intended to increase the understanding of American minority peoples in relation to the war so that their special problems may be appreciated and their integration into the national body may be advanced by constructive, positive

measures rather than by the repressive devices likely to be engendered by war spirit."

WEAVER, ROBERT C. "The Negro Veteran," *Annals of the American Academy of Political and Social Science,* CCXXXVIII (March, 1945), 127-32. NcD, NcU, NcC.

At least 750,000 Negro veterans will return to a greatly changed civilian life.

WELLIVER, WARMAN. "Report on the Negro Soldier," *Harper's Magazine,* CXCII (April, 1946), 333-39. NcD, NcU, NcC.

An experienced white army officer says ". . . colored soldiers can be used as effective combat infantrymen in large numbers only in mixed units of white and colored troops."

WHITE, WALTER F. *A Rising Wind.* New York: Doubleday, Doran and Co., Inc., 1945. Pp. 155. NcD, NcU, NcC.

The executive secretary of the NAACP reports on the status of Negro troops overseas and points out that the Negro problem is no longer an exclusively American problem.

WILLIAMS, CHARLES H. *Sidelights on Negro Soldiers.* Boston: B. J. Brimmer Co., 1923. Pp. 248. NcD, NcU, NcC.

Not a history, but some "sidelights" on the Negro soldier in World War I.

WILLIAMS, GEORGE WASHINGTON. *A History of the Negro Troops in the War of the Rebellion, 1861-1865.* New York: Harper and Brothers, 1885. Pp. xvi, 353. NcD, NcU, NcC.

An exhaustive report on the activities of Negro soldiers in the Civil War.

WILSON, JOSEPH THOMAS. *The Black Phalanx: A History of the Negro Soldiers of the United States in the Wars of 1775-1812, 1861-1865.* Hartford, Conn.: American Publishing Co., 1888. Pp. 528. NcD, NcU.

The American Negro as a soldier in three wars.

WILSON, RUTH DANNENHOWER. *Jim Crow Joins Up: A Study of Negroes in the Armed Forces of the United States.* New York: William J. Clark, 1944. Pp. ix, 129. NcD, NcU, NcC.

How the peacetime pattern of segregation and discrimination followed the Negro into the armed forces.

XXXI. "The Negro Problem"

APTHEKER, HERBERT. *The Negro People in America.* New York: International Publishers, 1946. Pp. 80. NcD, NcU.
A critique of Myrdal's *An American Dilemma.*

BAKER, PAUL E. *Negro-White Adjustment: An Investigation and Analysis of Methods in the Interracial Movement in the United States.* New York: Association Press, 1934. Pp. 267. NcD, NcU, NcC.
The history, philosophy, program, and techniques of ten national interracial agencies. Methods discovered through a study of cases, situations, and projects in race relations.

BAKER, RAY STANNARD. "The Tragedy of the Negro in the North," editorial announcement of a new series, *American Magazine*, LXV (December, 1907), 193. The series: "The Color Line in the North," LXV (February, 1908), 345-57; "The Negro's Struggle for Survival in the North," LXV (March, 1908), 473-85; "The Tragedy of the Mulatto," LXV (April, 1908), 582-98; "An Ostracized Race in Ferment," LXVI (May, 1908), 60-70; "The Negro in Politics," LXVI (June, 1908), 169-80: "The Black Man's Silent Power," LXVI (July, 1908), 288-300; "The New Southern Statesmanship," LXVI (August, 1908), 381-91; "What to do About the Negro," LXVI (September, 1908), 463-70. NcD, NcU.
This series of articles was never published in book form as were the author's articles which became *Following the Color Line.* But they are equally as interesting if not as important.

BECKER, CARL L. *Freedom and Responsibility in the American Way of Life.* New York: A. A. Knopf, 1945. Pp. xlii, 124. NcD, NcU.
The survival of democracy in America is finally a matter of individual responsibility.

BOND, HORACE M. "Self-Respect as a Factor in Social Advancement," *Annals of the American Academy of Political and Social Science*, CXL (November, 1928), 21-26. NcD, NcU, NcC.
Self-respect is the name we give to the various devices by means of which sufficient stability of personality is achieved to compete successfully.

BREARLEY, H. C. "Culture Change and Race Relations," *Social Forces*, XX (December, 1941), 260-63. NcD, NcU, NcC.
Abrupt social change is noted as a disturbing factor in harmonious racial relationships. Not only the *nature* of the change, but also the *time* of the change, affects racial cooperation and harmony.

BROWN, WILLIAM O. "Interracial Cooperation: Some of the Problems," *Opportunity*, XI (September, 1933), 272 ff. NcU.
Interracial cooperation "is a movement of the elite of both races . . . not a movement of the masses of both races." There is a tendency to mistake programs for achievements.

BUCK, PEARL S. *What America Means to Me.* New York: The John Day Co., 1943. Pp. x, 212. NcD, NcU, NcC.
"The freedom for which we fight will have to be won, not race by race, or nation by nation, but as a human essence."

[175]

BUNCHE, RALPH J. "The Programs of Organizations Devoted to the Improve-
ment of the Status of the American Negro," *Journal of Negro Education*,
VIII (July, 1939), 539-50. NcD, NcU, NcC.
An account of some of the numerous post-Emancipation organizations, black,
white, and mixed, that have sought and are seeking to improve the lot of the
Negro.

CHATTO, CLARENCE I., and HALLIGAN, ALICE L. *The Story of the Spring-
field Plan*. New York: Barnes and Noble, Inc., 1945. Pp. xviii, 201. NcD,
NcU.
Boys and girls of all races learn from childhood to live together and like it.

COLOR: Unfinished Business of Democracy, *Survey Graphic*, No. 11 (November,
1942). NcD, NcU, NcC.
A corps of writers look at the lot of the Negro in the United States and elsewhere in the world. The editor, Alain Locke, introduces the symposium with a
discussion of the race problem as "the unfinished business of democracy."

Directory of Agencies in Race Relations: National, State and Local. Chicago:
Julius Rosenwald Fund, 1945. Pp. 124. NcD, NcU.
A listing of over two hundred agencies operating to improve relations between
the races with brief descriptions of their purposes and activities.

DOWNS, MARY ISABELLE. *Brothers All*. Nashville, Tennessee: Board of
Missions, Methodist Episcopal Church, South, 1930. Pp. 56. NcD.
The work of the Board of Missions of the Methodist Episcopal Church, South,
among Mexicans, Italians, Cubans, Orientals, and other foreign-born groups in
the South.

DOYLE, BERTRAM W. "Some Observations on Progress in Race Relations
Prior to and Since 1868," *Journal of Negro History*, XVIII (January, 1933),
12-32. NcD, NcU, NcC.
An attempt to evaluate change in race relations especially during the past
three generations.

DUBOIS, W. E. B. *Darkwater: Voices From Within the Veil*. New York: Harcourt, Brace and Howe, 1920. Pp. viii, 276. NcD, NcU, NcC.
The indignant protest of the Negro against an unsympathetic and hostile
environment.

DUBOIS, W. E. B. *The Souls of Black Folk: Essays and Sketches*. Chicago:
A. C. McClurg and Co., 1931. Pp. viii, 264. NcD, NcU, NcC.
"I have sought here to sketch, in vague, uncertain outline, the spiritual world
in which ten thousand thousand Americans live and strive." Really has to do
with the souls of black folk in the North.

DUBOIS, W. E. B. *Color and Democracy: Colonies and Peace*. New York:
Harcourt, Brace and Co., 1945. Pp. 143. NcD, NcU, NcC.
A small book which is bound to leave the ordinary reader decidedly disturbed.

*THE Durham Statement, October 20, 1942; the Atlanta Statement, April 8, 1943;
the Richmond Statement, June 16, 1943*. Pamphlet. Atlanta: Commission on
Interracial Cooperation, Inc., 1943. NcD.
The Durham statement was formulated by Southern Negroes, the Atlanta
statement by Southern whites, and the Richmond statement by a group composed
of both Negroes and whites.

FLEMING, WALTER L. "Deportation and Colonization: An Attempted Solution of the Race Problem." Chap. I in *Studies in Southern History and
Politics*. New York: Columbia University Press, 1914. NcD, NcU.

Deportation and colonization of the Negroes as a solution of the race problem in the United States is as old as the feeling against slavery and the prejudice against the Negro race.

GALLAGHER, BUELL G. "What Would Constitute Progress?" *Journal of Negro Education*, VIII (July, 1939), 571-82. NcD, NcU, NcC.

Progress of the Negro in the American social order is discussed in two areas: (1) *intra-group* changes, and (2) *inter-group* changes. These latter are of primary importance as indices of progress.

GALLAGHER, BUELL G. *Color and Conscience: The Irrepressible Conflict.* New York: Harper and Co., 1946. Pp. ix, 244. NcD, NcC.

An indictment of the Christian church in America.

HALSEY, MARGARET. *Color Blind: A White Woman Looks at the Negro.* New York: Simon and Schuster, 1946. Pp. 164. NcD, NcU, NcC.

The author has discovered that cooperative effort across the color line reduces racial feeling faster than discussion.

HARRIS, ABRAM L., and SPERO, STERLING D. "Negro Problem," *Encyclopaedia of the Social Sciences*, XI, 335-56. NcD, NcU.

The evolution of the Negro problem from the fifteenth century, when it appeared as a "by product" of the expansion of Europe, to the present day. An excellent summary article.

JOHNSON, CHARLES S. *A Preface to Racial Understanding.* New York: Friendship Press, 1936. Pp. ix, 206. NcD, NcU, NcC.

Written to aid the great majority of *white* Americans in taking a more liberal attitude toward the Negro and race problems.

JOHNSON, CHARLES S. "Race Relations and Social Change." Chap. X in Edgar T. Thompson, ed., *Race Relations and the Race Problem.* Durham: Duke University Press, 1939. NcD, NcU, NcC.

The so-called Negro problem in the United States is a phenomenon of freedom and of change. The essence of the problem is change itself.

JOHNSON, CHARLES S., McCULLOCH, MARGARET C., et al. *Into the Main Stream: A Survey of Best Practices in Race Relations in the South.* Chapel Hill: The University of North Carolina Press, 1946. Pp. xiv, 355. NcD, NcU, NcC.

Reports of efforts to improve race relations in the South in the fields of citizenship, health, education, politics, employment, recreation, housing, and general public relations.

JOHNSON, GUY B. "Does the South Owe the Negro a New Deal?" *Social Forces*, XIII (October, 1934), 100-3. NcD, NcU, NcC.

The answer is yes. "Self-interest, simple justice, and common sense demand that the South give the Negro a new deal."

JOHNSON, GUY B. "Some Methods of Reducing Race Prejudice in the South," *Southern Workman*, LXIV (September, 1935), 272-78. NcD, NcU, NcC.

There are no short cuts to interracial peace, says Dr. Johnson, but there are several things to be done and to keep on doing.

JOHNSON, JAMES WELDON. *Negro Americans, What Now?* New York: The Viking Press, 1934. Pp. viii, 103. NcD, NcU, NcC.

An appraisal of the Negro's present and potential place in American life. Johnson advocates the more complete integration of Negroes into American life.

LaFARGE, JOHN. *The Race Question and the Negro: A Study of the Catholic Doctrine on Interracial Justice.* New York: Longmans, Green and Co., 1943. Pp. xiv, 315. NcD, NcU.

A Catholic priest looks at the race problem in the United States and advances a solution.

LOGAN, RAYFORD W., ed. *What the Negro Wants*. Chapel Hill: The University of North Carolina Press, 1944., Pp. xxiii, 352. NcD, NcU, NcC.

Fifteen Negro leaders tell what they think Negroes want. It seems they want just about what other Americans want.

LOGAN, RAYFORD W. *The Negro and the Post-War World—A Primer*. Washington: The Minorities Publishers, 1945. Pp. viii, 95. NcD, NcU.

". . . a brief interpretation and analysis of the plight of the Negro in all parts of the world today."

LOGAN, SPENCER. *A Negro's Faith in America*. New York: The Macmillan Co., 1946. Pp. vi, 88. NcD, NcU, NcC.

"I am a Negro American—all my life I have wanted to be an American."

LOHMAN, JOSEPH D., et al. *The Police and Minority Groups: A Manual Prepared for Use in the Chicago Park District Police Training School*. Chicago: Chicago Park District, 1947. Pp. xiii, 133. NcD.

A pioneer effort contributing significantly to the development of a more professional attitude toward minority peoples on the part of the police.

McCORMICK, THOMAS C. "The Negro," in T. C. McCormick, ed., *Problems of the Postwar World*. New York: McGraw-Hill Book Company, 1945. NcD, NcU.

An excellent summary of the more important facts.

MacIVER, R. M. *The More Perfect Union: A Program for the Control of Inter-group Discrimination in the United States*. New York: The Macmillan Co., 1948. Pp. 311. NcD.

It is not sufficient merely to prevent violence. The author proposes a plan of action designed to remove or to reduce the prejudice which leads to violence.

MacIVER, R. M., ed. *Unity and Difference in American Life*. New York: Harper and Brothers, 1947. Pp. 168. NcD.

The addresses and discussions of twelve scholars before the Institute for Religious and Social Studies.

MARKHAM, R. H. "Case of the Negro Wacs: An Analysis of the Facts and the Implications," *Christian Science Monitor* (May 5, 1945). NcD, NcU.

In this news analysis of the mutiny and trial of four Negro Wacs the nature of the race problem as a problem of communication is strikingly evident.

MASUOKA, JITSUICHI. "Can Progress in Race Relations Be Measured?" *Social Forces*, XXV (December, 1946), 211-17. NcD, NcU, NcC.

An attempt to interpret progress in terms of the race relations cycle.

MEKEEL, SCUDDER. "Cultural Aids to Constructive Race Relations," *Mental Hygiene*, XXIX (April, 1945), 177-89. NcD, NcU, NcC.

"The whole problem of reconstituting cultures—reconstituting the whole basis upon which we live—makes the particular problem of race prejudice seem small indeed."

MILLER, KELLY. *Race Adjustment: Essays on the Negro in America*. 2nd ed. New York: The Neale Publishing Co., 1909. Pp. 306. NcD, NcU.

A challenge to the Negro race to progress and adjust to the higher living standards and civilization of which they are capable.

MOTON, ROBERT R. *What the Negro Thinks*. Garden City, N. Y.: Doubleday, Doran and Co., 1929. Pp. vii, 267. NcD, NcU, NcC.

The Negro doing the thinking here is the late president of Tuskegee Institute and if what he writes is actually what the Negro is thinking then it does not differ significantly from what the members of any underprivileged, disfranchised, or humiliated group think. For "the thinking Negro wants for himself and his children the same things the white man wants for himself and his children."

MURPHY, EDGAR GARDNER. *Problems of the Present South: A Discussion of Certain of the Educational, Industrial ·and Political Issues in the Southern States.* New York: Longmans, Green and Company, 1909. Pp. xi, 335. NcD, NcU.

A collection of essays on "the industrial, educational, and political problems of the South as phases of the essential movement toward a genuinely democratic order" that are as significant today as when they were written.

MURPHY, EDGAR GARDNER. *The Basis of Ascendency: A Discussion of Certain Principles of Public Policy Involved in the Development of the Southern States.* New York: Longmans, Green and Company, 1910. Pp. xxiv, 250. NcD, NcU, NcC.

A white Southerner writes with deep insight into the race problem.

MYRDAL, GUNNAR. *An American Dilemma.* 2 vols. New York: Harper and Brothers, 1944. Pp. 1843. NcD, NcU, NcC.

The American dilemma is the glaring discrepancy between creed and deed. The creed holds high the ideal of equality of opportunity; the deed is written in terms of discrimination and insecurity for Negroes and other minority peoples. The Introduction and Chaps. 1-3 in Vol. I and Chap. 45 in Vol. II are especially important in elaborating the theme. Chaps. 35 and 39 in Vol. II discuss what Negroes are trying to do about the problem and Appendix 5 calls attention to the parallel position of, and feeling toward, women and Negroes in our culture. A condensed edition of this work prepared by Arnold Rose, one of the co-authors, and entitled *The Negro in America,* was published by Harper and Brothers in 1948. NcD, NcU.

OLDHAM, JOSEPH H. *Christianity and the Race Problem.* New York: George H. Doran Co., 1924. Pp. xx, 280. NcD, NcC.

A consideration of the contribution which the Christian church can make to the solution of the problems involved in the contact of the various races.

PAGE, THOMAS NELSON. *The Negro: The Southerner's Problem.* New York: Charles Scribner's Sons, 1904. Pp. xii, 316. NcD, NcU, NcC.

A Southerner of the old school believes that the problem is solved when Negroes and whites each know their traditional place and stay in it.

REUTER, EDWARD B. "Why the Presence of the Negro Constitutes a Problem in the American Social Order," *Journal of Negro Education,* VIII (July, 1939), 291-98. NcD, NcU, NcC.

The race problem is a phenomenon of freedom. "The Negro is a problem in the American social order because his aspirations and his behavior are oriented toward a goal that a dominant majority does not want realized."

SEABROOK, J. W. "The North Carolina Negro Views His Home State," *Southern Workman,* LXIII (May, 1934), 148-55. NcD, NcU, NcC.

A Negro speaks, not as a Negro, but as a citizen of his state.

SELIGMANN, HERBERT J. *The Negro Faces America.* New York: Harper and Brothers, 1920. Pp. 318. NcD, NcU.

A general survey of the Negro in America with the thesis that race problems are fundamentally economic and political problems.

SMITH, RUTH. *White Man's Burden: A Personal Testament.* New York: The Vanguard Press, 1946. Pp. 222. NcD, NcU.

The white woman who wrote this book is race conscious, that is, Negro race conscious.

SOPER, EDMUND D. *Racism: A World Issue.* New York: Abingdon-Cokes-bury Press, 1947. Pp. 304. NcD.

Race and culture contacts in Nazi Germany, Russia, India, the Far East, Africa, Brazil, Spanish America, and the United States considered from the point of view of a Christian world-order.

SPEER, ROBERT ELLIOTT. *Race and Race Relations: A Christian View of Human Contacts.* Chicago: Fleming H. Revell Company, 1924. Pp. 434. NcD.

"The effort has been made to supply in this volume a source book of material on the race question as well as a consistent and constructive statement of the Christian view."

SPERRY, W. L., ed. *Religion and Our Racial Tensions.* Cambridge: Harvard University Press, 1945. Pp. ix, 106. NcD, NcU.

Five chapters by Clyde Kluckholm, Everett Clinchy, Edwin Embree, Margaret Mead, and Robert Abernethy.

TANNENBAUM, FRANK. *Darker Phases of the South.* New York: G. P. Putnam's Sons, 1924. Pp. vii, 203. NcD, NcU, NcC.

Mr. Tannenbaum, apparently, would solve the race problem "by making the South afraid of other things as well as the Negro . . . by giving it a greater variety of hate, a greater opportunity for a diversification of emotional exaspera-tion." There is now too great an emotional fixation on the Negro.

WILLIAMS, ROBIN M. *The Reduction of Intergroup Tensions: A Survey of Research on Problems of Ethnic, Racial, and Religious Group Relations.* Social Science Research Council Bulletin 57. New York: Social Science Re-search Council, 1947. Pp. 134. NcD.

An appraisal of techniques and procedures in use by action agencies.

WIRTH, LOUIS. "Race and Public Policy," *Scientific Monthly,* LVIII (April, 1944), 302-12. NcD, NcU, NcC.

We have far to go but we are making strenuous efforts toward a more en-lightened policy with respect to our minority groups.

WIRTH, LOUIS. "The Problem of Minority Groups," in Ralph Linton, ed., *The Science of Man in the World Crisis.* New York: Columbia University Press, 1945. NcD, NcU.

"The influence which the United States will exert in the solution of these prob-lems abroad is contingent upon the national conscience and policy toward minorities at home."

WISE, JAMES WATERMAN, and ALLAND, ALEXANDER. *The Springfield Plan.* New York: The Viking Press, 1945. Pp. 136. NcD, NcU, NcC.

A pictorial presentation of the work of the Springfield, Mass., schools in the improvement of good will among the various racial and national groups of the city.

WOOFTER, THOMAS J., JR. *The Basis of Racial Adjustment.* Boston: Ginn and Co., 1925. Pp. viii, 258. NcD, NcU, NcC.

A balanced and sane survey of the American race problem. Informative and constructive.

WRIGHT, RICHARD. *12 Million Black Voices.* New York: The Viking Press, 1941. Pp. 152. NcD, NcU, NcC.

"The differences between black folk and white folk are not blood or color," says the Negro author, "and the ties that bind us are deeper than those that separate us. The common road of hope which we all have traveled has brought us into a stronger kinship than any words, laws, or legal claims.

"Look at us and know us and you will know yourselves, for *we* are you, look-ing back at you from the dark mirrors of our lives!

"What do we black folk want?"

XXXII. Bibliographies, Fact Books, and Study Outlines

BROWN, STERLING A. *Outline for the Study of the Poetry of American Negroes.* New York: Harcourt, Brace and Co., 1931. Pp. 52. NcD.
Questions and assignments prepared for use with James Weldon Johnson's *The Book of American Negro Poetry.*

DEBARDELEBEN, MARY. *A Course for Adults on the Negro in America.* New York: Council of Women for Home Missions and Missionary Education Movement, 1935(?). Pp. 48. NcD.
This study guide is based upon Charles S. Johnson's *A Preface to Racial Understanding.*

DUBOIS, W. E. B., and JOHNSON, GUY B. *Encyclopedia of the Negro.* New ed. New York: The Phelps-Stokes Fund, 1947. Pp. 207. NcD, NcU, NcC.
A volume preparatory to the proposed four-volume encyclopedia of the Negro.

EMBREE, EDWIN R. *American Negroes: A Handbook.* New York: The John Day Company, 1942. Pp. 79. NcD, NcU, NcC.
A brief statement, designed for study groups, dealing with the situation of the Negroes, their background, heritage, handicaps, progress, and special talents.

FOREMAN, PAUL B., and HILL, MOZELLE. *The Negro in the United States: A Bibliography.* Bulletin of the Oklahoma A. and M. College. Vol. 44, No. 5 (February, 1947). Pp. 24. NcD, NcU.
1941. Pp. 152. NcD, NcU, NcC.
A select reference and minimum college library resources list.

The Inquiry. *And Who Is My Neighbor? An Outline for the Study of Race Relations in America.* 2nd ed., rev. New York: Association Press, 1928. Pp. x, 250. NcD, NcU.
A guide for the study of the neighbor problem, particularly in America where many races and peoples daily rub elbows.

The Inquiry. *All Colors: A Study Outline on Woman's Part in Race Relations.* New York: The Woman's Press and Association Press, 1926. Pp. 153. NcD, NcU.
A study outline addressed "more particularly to those who recognize a special concern for woman in the existing American problems of race relations."

JENNESS, MARY. *A Course for Intermediates on the Negro in America.* New York: Council of Women for Home Missions and Missionary Education Movement, 1936 (?). Pp. 58. NcD.
Based primarily on the author's *Twelve Negro Americans.*

LOCKE, ALAIN. *The Negro in America.* Reading with a Purpose Series. Chicago: American Library Association, 1933. Pp. 64. NcD, NcU, NcC.
Contains a bibliography and full discussion of eight recommended books on the Negro. Especially adapted for individual or group study of the Negro in the United States.

MURRAY, FLORENCE, ed. *The Negro Handbook.* New York: Wendell Malliet and Co., 1942, 1944, 1946. NcD, NcU, NcC.
A handbook of current facts, statistics, and general information on the American Negro. Published biennially.

PARKS, MARTHA. *The Negro: A Selected List For School Libraries of Books By or About the Negro in Africa and America.* Rev. ed. Nashville, Tennessee: State Department of Education, 1941. Pp. 48. NcD.
Prepared especially for teachers in colored schools.

WORK, MONROE N., comp. *The Negro Yearbook. Annual Encyclopedia of the Negro.* Tuskegee, Alabama: Negro Yearbook Publishing Co., ten editions published between 1912 and 1947. NcD, NcU, NcC.
A very important compendium of information on the Negro. The 1947 Yearbook was edited by Jessie Parkhurst Guzman.

WORK, MONROE N. *A Bibliography of the Negro in Africa and America.* New York: The H. W. Wilson Co., 1928. Pp. xxi, 698. NcD, NcU, NcC.
This standard bibliography was twenty years in preparation and lists over 17,000 items including not only books but a large number of pamphlets and fugitive papers. There is a typed supplement to this bibliography prepared by Monroe Work listing books published through 1935. NcD.

Author Index

www.ingramcontent.com/pod-product-compliance
Lightning Source LLC
Chambersburg PA
CBHW020352270326
41926CB00007B/402